THE FINANCING OF SMALL BUSINESS

STUDIES OF THE MODERN CORPORATION
Columbia University Graduate School of Business

Francis Joseph Aguilar, *Scanning the Business Environment*
Herman W. Bevis, *Corporate Financial Reporting in a Competitive Economy*
Richard Eells, *The Corporation and the Arts*
Jay W. Lorsch, *Product Innovation and Organization*
Irving Pfeffer, *The Financing of Small Business*
George A. Steiner and Warren M. Cannon, *Multinational Corporate Planning*
George A. Steiner and William G. Ryan, *Industrial Project Management*
Gus Tyler, *The Political Imperative*

IRVING PFEFFER

EDITOR

The Financing of Small Business:
A Current Assessment

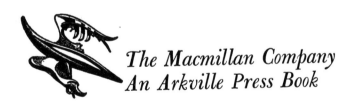

The Macmillan Company
An Arkville Press Book

THE MACMILLAN COMPANY, *New York*
COLLIER-MACMILLAN LIMITED, *London*

TO

Diana G. Pfeffer

STUDIES OF THE MODERN CORPORATION

Columbia University Graduate School of Business

The Program for Studies of the Modern Corporation is devoted to the advancement and dissemination of knowledge about the corporation. Its publications are designed to stimulate inquiry, research, criticism, and reflection. They fall into four categories: works by outstanding businessmen, scholars, and professional men from a variety of backgrounds and academic disciplines; prize-winning doctoral dissertations relating to the corporation; annotated and edited selections of business literature; and business classics that merit republication. The studies are supported by outside grants from private business, professional, and philanthropic institutions interested in the program's objectives.

Richard Eells
EDITOR

CONTRIBUTORS

Irving Pfeffer is Professor of Insurance in the Graduate School of Business Administration at UCLA. An economist, he has served as a financial consultant to small businesses.

Neil H. Jacoby is Dean of the Graduate School of Business Administration at UCLA. A former member of the Council of Economic Advisors under President Eisenhower, he is a leading economist and author.

Theodore A. Andersen is a Professor of Finance in the Graduate School of Business Administration at UCLA. He was the first Commissioner of the California State Economic Development Agency.

Neil R. Bersch is a partner in the national accounting firm of Touche, Ross, Bailey and Smart.

Bernard L. Boutin is Administrator of the Small Business Administration. He has served in important positions in the administrations of Presidents Kennedy and Johnson.

Eugene F. Brigham is a Professor of Finance in the Graduate School of Business Administration at UCLA. He is a co-author of a leading text on managerial finance.

O. D. Dickerson is Professor of Insurance in the Graduate School of Business at Florida State University. He is a consulting actuary and is an active member of several professional and technical insurance organizations.

Royce Diener is an international investment banker and serves on the board of directors of several corporations.

James N. Holtz is a Professor of Finance in the Graduate School of Business Administration at UCLA and a consultant to the Rand Corporation. He is an authority on technology transfers between the government and private sectors of the economy.

Greene F. Johnson is Vice President of Investments at the Metropolitan Life Insurance Company. He has played a leading role in the field of direct placements by financial institutions.

Benjamin Z. Katz is a management consultant specializing in financial aspects of business planning. He has played an important role in many small business mergers and acquisitions.

Michael Kawaja is a Professor of Finance and Business Economics in the Graduate School of Business Administration at UCLA. He is a financial consultant and an authority on consumer credit.

Bertram K. Massing is a member of the California Bar and is associated with the firm of Ervin, Cohen and Jessup.

Dale S. May is President of the George S. May International Company, one of the largest and oldest management consulting firms in the world.

R. Bruce Ricks is a Professor of Finance in the Graduate School of Business Administration at UCLA. He is an authority on computerization of financial planning.

George A. Steiner is a Professor of Management and Director of the Division of Research in the Graduate School of Business Administration at UCLA. He is a prominent scholar in the field of long-range planning.

J. Fred Weston is Professor of Finance in the Graduate School of Business Administration at UCLA. He is a past president of the American Finance Association and is the author of many books and articles in the fields of finance and economics.

Donald H. Woods is a Professor of Finance in the Graduate School of Business Administration at UCLA. He has studied the small business investment company industry in depth.

FOREWORD

Financing small business is a perennial problem of the American economy. It has recurrently engaged the attention of businessmen, lawmakers, and economists in the past and will doubtless continue to do so in the future. The problem endures because it is never completely resolved. Owners and managers of new and small firms continue to believe that they confront undue difficulties in obtaining the funds to carry out their plans. They suspect that the banking and financial machinery of the American economy is designed and operated to meet the capital and credit needs of large, established firms but throws up high barriers against the founders of new firms and the operators of small enterprises. Because new and small businesses usually carry high risks, investors who supply them with capital and credit expect above-average returns. They seek to limit their risks by imposing constraints upon management.

No one will doubt that both a steady infusion of new firms and the growth of small firms is essential to the health of our competitive market economy. Only if new enterprises, involving new men and fresh ideas, are able to be born, and only if small firms are able to grow and to challenge the positions of their larger rivals, will the national economy continue to be vigorous. The nation's taxation and other economic policies, as well as its financial machinery, must be such as to ensure adequate business birth and growth rates.

Congress has long shown solicitude for the financing problems of small business by authorizing public programs for their assistance. The business loan program of the Reconstruction Finance Corporation—primarily for small firms—was initiated in 1934. The Federal Reserve Banks were authorized to make direct loans to medium and small businesses under Section 13b of the Federal Reserve Act in the same year. In 1958, the Small Business Administration was established as a permanent Federal agency to offer technical, managerial, and financial assistance to small firms. All of these programs have reflected a concern that the "legitimate" needs of small enterprises for credit should not suffer from any structural gaps in the private machinery of business finance.

Despite recurrent attention to the problem, a good many years have passed since a comprehensive assessment has been made of the economic condition of small business in the economy, of its financial requirements, and of the respective roles of private financial institutions and government agencies in meeting them. These were the assigned missions of a research seminar held by the Graduate School of Business Administration at the University of California, Los Angeles, during November 1966.

The authors of this book do not claim to have written the last word on small business financing. They have brought up to date the relevant facts, have applied contemporary theories of finance, and have presented an assessment of the functioning of small business financing markets at the present time. Thus, they hope to have pushed the analysis of this important problem a few steps forward. It is hoped that the product of this seminar, set forth in this book, will be of material value to financiers, lawmakers, economists and—not least— to the owners and operators of small enterprises.

Neil H. Jacoby

Preface

The small business sector of the American economy has been the subject of increasing attention by economists and other persons concerned with problems of economic growth and opportuntiy. Congressional committees have devoted a great deal of effort to explorations and analyses of the problems of small business and, under the auspices of the Small Business Administration, there has been a massive outpouring of scholarly and descriptive work. The small businessman and his advisors have been overwhelmed with specialized literature covering many critical areas of business development and management. What is needed today is a re-examination of the status and prospects of small business. This book is designed to help fill a major gap by providing a current assessment of the financing of small business.

This volume is the end-product of a Research Seminar on Financial Aspects of Profit Planning for Small Business conducted by the Division of Research in the Graduate School of Business Administration at the University of California, Los Angeles, late in 1966. The Seminar, which was attended by representatives of government, small business, investment banking, universities, and the professions of law and accounting, was supported by a generous grant from the George S. May International Foundation.

The Financing of Small Business deals with the subject from six different perspectives. Part I examines the economic condition of small business in historical and contemporary terms; Part II relates capital management theory to the decision areas of small firms; Part III offers a variety of approaches to financial planning for small businesses; Part IV explores the requirements of the capital markets and of specific institutional types of lender for the financing of small businesses; Part V treats the legal and tax accounting aspects; and Part VI evaluates and defines the scope and limitations of the government's role in small business finance.

In Part I, there are four empirical chapters that provide a factual basis for a discussion of the financial problems of small business. Dale May provides one of the few historical accounts of the small businessman in American history that have ever appeared in the literature. He traces the evolution of the small entrepreneur in terms of the nature and scope of his activity from colonial times to the present day. J. Fred Weston attacks the problem of the small businessman in terms of comparative advantage. His contribution is a closely reasoned analytical treatment of the small business sector in the economy, industry by industry, including a wealth of statistical material as a basis for further study. He concludes that the small businessman is most likely to succeed by operating in those industries in which he has the greatest comparative advantage. Professor Weston identifies the industries characterized by the greatest opportunities for the small firm. Theodore A. Andersen's treatment of the available materials on the relationship of size to rates of return in manufacturing provides confirmation for Weston's thesis and offers valuable insights on the comparative rates of return by industry over different phases of the business cycle. Dickerson and Kawaja review the literature on survival probabilities of small companies and conclude that survival is a function of factors largely within the control of entrepreneurs. They provide a statistical picture of failure rates which builds upon the Dun and Bradstreet studies.

The second part of the book comprises theoretical discussions by Eugene Brigham and James Holtz. Brigham attempts to relate the concepts of cost of capital, which are usually applied to large publicly held firms, to the small business field. He shows that the concepts are applicable and how they may be used to conceptualize small business investment decisions. Holtz treats the cash budgeting problem in terms of the transformation of assets into cash flows over time.

Part III is concerned with strategic planning. George Steiner develops a number of eminently practical approaches to long-range planning for small business, proceeding from the simplest to relatively sophisticated techniques. Benjamin Katz describes three case histories that exemplify the fruits of failure to adhere to the principles of formal planning. The human element in strategic decision-making for the firm is illustrated in each of his examples.

The fourth part of the volume, comprising three chapters, deals with current conditions in the practice of small business financing. Bruce Ricks describes the capital markets from the viewpoint of sources of funds. Royce Diener discusses the techniques of investment bankers who make analyses of the financing potentials of businesses. Greene Johnson describes, in some detail, the procedures employed by large life insurance companies in preparing for long-term senior financing for small businesses through the direct placement route.

Part V contains two chapters dealing with the legal and tax ramifications of small business financing. Bertram Massing describes many of the pitfalls involved in the blue-sky law area of securities legislation and suggests ways and means of achieving the expansionary ends of the firm at minimum cost. Neil Bersch recommends a variety of decision rules relating to choice of fiscal year, accounting basis, legal form of organization, and tax planning which suggest that one major technique for increasing after-tax income is to minimize tax exposure. He suggests numerous strategies for reducing the burden of taxation for the small firm.

Part VI concerns the role of government in small business finance. Donald Woods provides an economic analysis of the Small Business Investment Act which suggests the need for more rational policies in providing incentives for efficient and growing firms. He demonstrates the economic inconsistency in present leverage limitations in the law. Bernard Boutin, Administrator of the Small Business Administration, provides an overview of small business loans from government sources in terms of recent history, current developments, and the stated missions of the SBA. Mr. Boutin's statement of policy makes clear the intent of the federal authorities to help create a more favorable environment for the small businessman.

This book will be useful for the economist who seeks a point of departure for further analytical work in the field of small business. It will prove valuable for the small businessman who seeks additional answers to his financing problems. It will be helpful to government officials and legislators who seek an objective perspective on the condition of small business. It will provide guidelines for those who counsel the small businessman. For the entrepreneur who wants to see a map of the problem areas in the financing of small business, this work offers many insights.

The editor is grateful to Richard Eells, who provided encouragement and assistance at every stage of the project, and to George Steiner and the Division of Research of the Graduate School of Business Administration at UCLA for material assistance. To the many persons and organizations who kindly permitted reproduction of their materials, as acknowledged in the text, and to the participants in the Research Seminar, the editor owes a debt of thanks. Mary McMurray, Betsy Christmas, and Patsy Parsons cheerfully bore the burdens of arranging for and typing the various drafts of the manuscript.

Partly because of the wealth of "how-to-do-it" literature, serious scholars have been reluctant to engage in research in the field of small business. Hopefully, the work represented in this book will help overcome their reluctance.

Irving Pfeffer

University of California, Los Angeles

Contents

Foreword by Neil H. Jacoby   ix

Preface by Irving Pfeffer   xi

Part I. THE ECONOMIC CONDITION OF SMALL BUSINESS

1. The Small Businessman in American History   3
   DALE S. MAY
2. The Position of Small Business in the American Economy   34
   J. FRED WESTON
3. The Effect of Size on Profits in Manufacturing Industries   67
   THEODORE A. ANDERSEN
4. The Failure Rates of Business   82
   O. D. DICKERSON and MICHAEL KAWAJA

Part II. CAPITAL MANAGEMENT THEORY FOR SMALL BUSINESS

5. The Cost of Capital to the Small Firm   97
   EUGENE F. BRIGHAM
6. Cash Budgeting in Small Business   126
   JAMES N. HOLTZ

Part III. APPROACHES TO FINANCIAL PLANNING FOR SMALL BUSINESS

7. Approaches to Long-Range Planning for Small Business   147
   GEORGE A. STEINER

8. Strategic Decision-Making: Three Case Histories   177
     BENJAMIN Z. KATZ

Part IV. LENDER REQUIREMENTS FOR SMALL BUSINESS FINANCING

9. The Capital Markets for Small Business   197
     R. BRUCE RICKS
10. Analyzing the Financing Potential of a Business   211
     ROYCE DIENER
11. Long-Term Senior Financing for Small Business   229
     GREENE F. JOHNSON

Part V. LEGAL AND TAX ASPECTS OF SMALL BUSINESS FINANCING

12. Legal Aspects of Small Business Finance   253
     BERTRAM K. MASSING
13. Tax Incentives for Small Business   275
     NEIL R. BERSCH

Part VI. THE GOVERNMENT ROLE IN SMALL BUSINESS FINANCE

14. The Economic Role of SBICs   303
     DONALD H. WOODS
15. Small Business Loans from Government Sources   314
     BERNARD L. BOUTIN

     Notes   337
     Index   349

THE FINANCING OF SMALL BUSINESS

Part 1

THE ECONOMIC CONDITION
OF SMALL BUSINESS

1

The Small Businessman
in American History

Dale S. May

President Lyndon B. Johnson observed that, "Our nearly five million small businesses supply more than a third of the nation's goods and services, and are a fertile source of new ideas and new products to enrich the lives of our citizens and stimulate the growth of our economy." Continuing in this same optimistic vein, the President said: "The small, privately owned concern has played a fundamental role in the development of the American way of life, and continues to represent the door of opportunity for millions of enterprising citizens."[1]

In view of the conspicuous role that the small businessman has occupied in the history of the American nation, one would expect to find a good deal written about him. Unfortunately this has not been the case. For reasons that are difficult to fathom, he has been ignored by the historian. One of the reasons is perhaps that only within recent years has business history come into its own as a field of scholarly investigation. More significantly perhaps, the small businessman has remained an inarticulate individual who only recently has grasped the need for organizing to protect and advance his interests.

The Colonial Period

Business is a word that came into prominence during the latter half of the nineteenth and the early part of the twentieth centuries. At first the words *merchant* or *commerce* were used commonly. In late colonial times expressions such as "going into business" or "going into merchandising" came into greater use, but the word *businessman* rarely was employed.[2] Traditionally, the citadels of small business have been commerce or trade; services such as inns, hotels, restaurants, barbers, cleaners, and the like; construction; manufacturing; mining and quarrying; and transportation.[3]

In colonial times business was conducted in a most rudimentary fashion. Except for the fortunate few who financed the building of larger ships, engaged in foreign commerce, and supplied the colonies with their needs, the overwhelming majority of businessmen were small. A small businessman could have been a master craftsman, household manufacturer, carpenter, blacksmith, tobacconist, barbershop proprietor, shoemaker, peddler, storekeeper, or a member of a number of other callings. Normally he had a product or service to sell, and he furnished this on a relatively small scale. Regardless of the nature of the product and service offered, small businessmen had several things in common. They catered chiefly to the local or neighboring market; they lacked capital; they often produced the commodities or services they sold; they depended on England and her merchants for many of the luxuries they dispensed; they relied heavily on the members of their family for the labor they needed; and they encountered more competition than is generally believed.

The master craftsman was the small businessman par excellence who had to pass through several stages before reaching his position. He could have started as an itinerant worker, settled down to become a "custom order" worker, and finally hired others who made goods which he sold from his retail shop. If he was successful as a merchant-employer, he also sold his products to retail merchants. He usually built his business around his family. As head of the household and master craftsman, he made the goods he sold, and if he combined this with keeping a shop, his wife and children tended to the retail store. The older boys in the family performed the more menial tasks in the shop and usually became apprentices.[4] Elevating himself and his family up the social and economic ladder of success was often one of the prime goals of the small craftsman's life. As a rule, he and his family led a quiet life consisting of long hours of hard work. Generally, he was a serious and steady individual of temperate habits who attended church regularly.

Differences between the master craftsmen of the city and country village were few. The master craftsmen of the village, who often farmed on the side, owned their establishments instead of renting them and usually had more warehouse space than the city craftsmen. The latter had smaller houses—usually two stories, with the shop occupying the first floor. Whereas most village craftsmen made products on demand and seldom had a surplus for sale, the city craftsmen kept a large supply of goods on display for shoppers. Because money, especially small change, was scarce even in the northern colonies, goods and services were usually exchanged in lieu of money payments, or in some instances credit was extended.

The artisan's shop was predominant until the end of the seventeenth century, when the country storekeeper and the "petty traders" became more prevalent. The craftsman turned businessman was common during this period.

Manufacturing of all kinds was done on a small scale as late as the end of the seventeenth century. This was true of "the paper mills—such as the one early founded at Germantown—the grist mills, glass works, brickkilns, nail making, shoe making, the production of leather goods and coarse clothes, the tanning of leather, making of candles, brewing of beer and a long list of other manufactures."[5] Each undertaking represented a moderate investment and was carried on either in small plants or the household.

We have little information on the amount of capital needed to launch a small business in the Colonial Era. According to one source, "Of the hundreds of occupations practiced at London in 1747 it was estimated that eight required 5 pounds 'to set up a master'; ten needed 10 pounds; twenty-five needed 20 pounds; ninety needed 50 pounds; and seventy-five required 100 pounds. In present day values this means that $150 to $2,500 would be sufficient capital for a man to enter a trade, purchase tools and stock, and maintain himself until he completed his work for sale. The amounts would have been the same in the colonies."[6]

The traveling shoemaker was among the numerous small business-men who did not wait for trade to come to their shops. He journeyed from household to household, applying his art to the leather tanned by the family of the householder. He had a simple tool kit that could be carried easily from one job to another. Every home probably had someone who was "a fair hand at shaping or repairing footware," but work on the farm and around the household was so pressing that the services of a specialist were highly welcome.

Another small businessman was the tinker, a jack-of-all trades, who traveled from house to house. The tinker followed a flexible itinerary, if any at all, and repaired any utensil made of metal. "With his stove, solder, soldering irons, metal scraps and all sorts of odds and ends he put in order many articles that had come to be the despair of the housewife." He ate and slept with the family he served. While at work or while relaxing, he passed on to his listeners the gossip or news he had picked up in his wanderings.[7]

Because colonial farmers lived great distances from stores and one another, the peddler had a real service to offer. He usually bought his wares from sedentary artisans and then traveled to the country to dispose of them. He attended markets and fairs, and on court days he competed with the local storekeeper. "The Connecticut Yankee, bare-boned and shrewd, was the first colonial pedlar. On his own back, afoot or on horseback, or atop cleverly designed wagons full of in-genious compartments, he carried his wares into the remotest regions. With his stock of tinware, brassware, watches, clocks, pins, wooden-ware, brooms, buckets, 'ribbons and laces to set off the faces of pretty young sweethearts and wives,' it is no wonder that the pedlar's visits were occasions of excitement, long awaited and never forgotten. Novelties from the city, necessities, and news arrived at the homestead door together."[8]

The extent to which peddlers plied their wares may be gauged by the numerous laws passed to regulate them in the colonies. The colo-nial governments disliked itinerant peddlers. Those who could prove that they were rendering a real service to the community could keep their place, but this was difficult to do because they dealt largely with luxuries. Influential shopkeepers sought legislation that placed the peddlers at a great disadvantage. The local merchants, who resented the competition, complained that the peddler paid no taxes to the community. To protect themselves against abuses by peddlers, communities passed laws compelling peddlers to pay large fees for licenses and restricting them to the handling of domestic products. In periods of epidemics they were prohibited from entering a community. As a rule, however, the legislation against peddlers was stricter in the North than the South, where there were fewer stores and the services of the peddlers were highly prized.[9]

Regulatory curbs pervaded many, if not most, phases of colonial economic life. Most of these curbs were based on the English experience. "Inns, mills and ferries were subject to control. Charges were limited by law, and the obligations of such institutions were legislatively defined. From the control of quasi-public businesses, it was no far cry to regulation of general commercial practices. Efforts were made to determine fair prices, fair wages and reasonable profits. The quality of goods offered for sale was frequently the object of legislation."[10]

Another inhibiting factor was the attitude toward profits and wealth-seeking. Religion took precedence over all forms of activity, especially during the early seventeenth century. Business was, at best, a secondary consideration. Control of wealth-getting was central to seventeenth century colonial thought. "There was little or no confidence in the liberal doctrine that spontaneous self-seeking would provide a self-adjusting mechanism for the increase in wealth. Government was charged with the duty of overseeing and sanctioning various types of economic pursuits. . . . Wealth-getting, according to colonial opinion, must be harmonized with social and religious ideals. Government must lay down economic policies consistent with these ideals."[11]

Even though the small businessman was most representative of the colonial businessmen, "the first type of big business" was the traveling merchant. He was a specialist who became more conspicuous when the town economy began replacing the village economy. He sold to other merchants, artisans, and storekeepers in town, instead of to consumers and peddlers. He had more capital and often owned a ship and a cargo. The activities of the artisans and mechanics who pursued their trades with industry, and of the shopkeepers who supplied the

city people and the country folk with goods, were controlled to a
degree by a few wealthy merchants who tried to extend their influence
over the trade of their respective towns.[12]

As the Colonial Period came to an end, the small businessmen
greatly outnumbered the larger businessmen, who rose to a more influential role after the Revolution. Agriculture, rather than commerce
and industry, was the dominant calling. The market was local and the
capital scarce. Government regulations were enforced with varying
degrees of effectiveness. Competition was keen; the omnipresent small
businessman of the village and town, ever-lacking in power and influence, remained a voiceless cog in an economy that was trying to shake
off the mercantilist restraints of Great Britain.

The Post-Revolutionary War Period

We have only fragmentary information concerning the effects of
the American Revolution on small business. The presumption is that
many, perhaps most, small businessmen suffered from the lack of supplies, excessive paper money issues, and high prices. Some probably
reaped handsome profits by trafficking in scarce items. Except in a few
of the larger cities, the most ordinary business facilities were lacking,
transportation was in a primitive state, and the United States was
without a single bank until the Bank of North America was chartered
by Congress in December 1781. The maritime industries, on the other
hand, benefitted from the activities of privateers, the lifting of restrictions that had been imposed on the thirteen colonies by the British,
and the opening of many parts of the world to American shipping.[13]

By the end of the War of 1812 some important changes had taken
place. In 1780 some 76,000 persons lived in five cities with more than
8,000 inhabitants each; and by 1810 eleven cities had a combined
population of 356,000. The colonies had no bank in 1775; in 1815 they
had 208. Only seven business corporations had been formed before
1775; by 1815 several hundred had been chartered for the purpose of
building bridges, turnpikes, aqueducts, and canals, insuring property,
providing banking facilities, and operating factories. Nothing comparable to a stock market existed in 1775; however, in 1815, brokers
in Philadelphia and New York were dealing primarily with securities
of the United States Government.

Despite the growth of cities, population, and establishments of various kinds, most aspects of business remained essentially unaltered from what they had been in colonial times. The group of small businessmen was made up of master craftsmen, small merchants, storekeepers, and commercial farmers. Most were owners of the businesses they managed, and as individual proprietors they assumed the risks and were liable for the debts. Next in importance was the unincorporated partnership, which usually involved two or more persons who pooled their capital, discharged the responsibilities of management, assumed individual liability for all debts of partnerships, and shared the profits. This arrangement was used especially by shipowners and merchants engaged in foreign trade, and to a much lesser extent by the owners of furnaces, forges, mines, and mills. A third form of business enterprise was the unincorporated company of shareholders, which rested on written articles of agreement. Such an arrangement resembled a partnership in that all members were individuals liable for all debts.[14]

The financial policies of Alexander Hamilton—asking for the funding of the national debt at par, the creation of a Bank of the United States, the assumption of state debts by the newly formed federal government, and the establishment of a sinking fund to facilitate the payment of the national debt and stabilize the price of government securities—were viewed by many as being more of a direct aid to the big businessmen than to the smaller ones. The degree to which Hamilton's program helped the small businessman is debatable, but the presumption is that it must have been more of a help than a hindrance. Assisting the economy in this fashion must have been beneficial to all business—big and small.[15]

In the North after 1800, new opportunities appeared for the small businessman which reflected the economic changes that were taking place. The village storekeeper was still an important part of the local economy. The storekeeper—besides catering to the needs of the nearby city or distant port, the farms in the outlying districts, and the villagers themselves—facilitated the growth of manufacturing. During the first third of the nineteenth century, this occurred in most of the New England states and wherever New England life was transplanted, and in many communities in the eastern half of the Ohio Valley-Great Lakes region.

The storekeeper found himself in a strategic position to assume such a role once a market emerged outside his community; in fact he was in the best position to develop this outside market. If established in a maritime town he came in contact with foreign merchants; if in an inland town he probably knew those in the larger coast towns. In the village the storekeeper bartered with the "English and West India goods" that once constituted his chief stock in trade. In the outlying districts he had farmer customers who came to town—perhaps once or twice a year—to buy iron, salt, glass, powder and shot, and maybe a few imported articles. This was more of a barter trade than the one with the village folk, because he had to accept such products of the farm and fireside as the farmers had to offer in exchange.

One of the arch competitors of the village storekeeper was the ubiquitous peddler, who had figured prominently in the lives of many of the colonists. Hundreds of these itinerant merchants probably traveled the roads of New England at the start of the nineteenth century. The peddler, although held in disrepute in many quarters, made his contributions to the fledgling American economy by opening up new channels of trade and introducing new goods, some of which were to become staples. In Connecticut, for instance, he helped the growth of the brass, clock, silver plate, and hardware industries. Most of his wares lay wholly within the province of the housewife.

Another competitor of the storekeeper was the craftsman who manufactured and marketed his own goods. The craftsman more likely followed the lead of the merchant, entering the market after the storekeeper had demonstrated the possibilities of profit. This was to be expected because of the valuable business contacts of the storekeeper within and without the community. Often the craftsman-turned-manufacturer established a store through which he paid his employees and marketed his products. In effect, to succeed in manufacturing he became a merchant.

In a number of instances, then, the storekeeper and the craftsman gave way to the "merchant-capitalist" and the more highly capitalistic factory system.[16] This evolving phase of small business—the merchant-manufacturer stage—was rooted in most of the southern New England communities after the Revolutionary War and the War of 1812. Although it was significant in the development of the New England economy and affected the future course of small business, by 1860 the merchant-manufacturer stage had almost disappeared except in the boot and shoe industry, where it was declining, and in the ready-made garment industry.

In the merchant-manufacturer stage, the merchant was the actual entrepreneur who had a three-fold function: He put out materials to be manufactured by workmen and their families in their homes or tiny shops; he designated the type of work to be done, which was determined by the availability of materials; and he collected and sold the finished and partly finished goods from the workers. Only if he could raise sufficient capital for the necessary buildings and machinery could he hope to begin a factory.

Shoemaking was one of the industries in which the merchants assumed an early prominence. Except for textiles, this was the leading manufacture of New England during most of the nineteenth century. Of course, it was also possible for craftsmen and others in allied trades, such as tanners, curriers, booksellers, and village storekeepers, to become manufacturers of boots and shoes. In and around Boston a large percentage of the shoe manufacturers were former custom shoemakers. Outside the Boston area, storekeepers were more likely to begin manufacturing for market.

A merchant could also become a hat-manufacturer. The profits in this field, as in shoemaking, attracted those who had a few technical skills. This industry was in full swing in Danbury, Conn., within less than a decade after 1800. A noncraftsman entrepreneur, for instance, sometimes made a craftsman his partner. Many farmers became interested in hat-manufacturing. Those who entered the business probably sold farm and dairy products in New York City to obtain the small amount of capital they needed to erect a hat shop and acquire crude equipment.[17]

The carriage business was still another trade that had appeal. Merchants in Concord, N.H., for example, who were located between the inland back country to the north and west and the seaboard towns, including Boston, benefitted from the mounting trade and formed the nucleus of the carriage business in the area. The craftsman also was in a position to become a merchant-manufacturer of carriages.

The first manufacturers of furniture were city craftsmen who combined the selling of ready-made furniture with their custom business. A craftsman turned entrepreneur had to concentrate more on the supervision of his hired help and the development of his business than on the making of furniture. Thus he was becoming more of a merchant. The store of the merchant, combined with furniture-making in the basement, attic, or some small building nearby, constituted his factory down to the 1830's. By this time men who had never been craftsmen also were entering the field as manufacturers of furniture.

A craftsman of the old order who wanted to become a manufacturer had to satisfy certain requisites. He had to have at least enough capital to function on a small basis; if the capital requirements were large, he was eliminated. He had to acquire the market contacts and the bargaining experience of the village storekeeper and the city merchant or else he faced a great disadvantage. The craftsmen may have lacked the inclination to bargain, which was the mark of the successful merchants, yet many became entrepreneurs, some independently and some as partners of merchants. Those making the transition from craftsmen to merchants had some sales ability and were able to anticipate or create styles; they were also skillful in determining the qualities to be produced and the credits needed.

As the merchant-manufacturer stage developed in New England, specialization became the rule. Men from various walks of life entered the manufacturing business as capitalists and entrepreneurs. Markets expanded rapidly. As competition became keen, it became necessary to curb production costs in every possible way. The average storekeeper unable to meet the manufacturing needs of the inland village had two alternatives: he could give up manufacturing and return to storekeeping as his primary business, or he could occupy an intermediary position, remaining partly a general storekeeper and becoming partly a local distributing agent for some large manufacturer in a larger town.

The South did not undergo the same changes as the New England States. The "Old South" of ante-bellum days remained primarily a region of yeoman farmers and small traders. With few exceptions, the small business unit and attitude was prevalent in the commercial areas of the South. A successful crossroads storekeeper moved on to a town and ultimately to a seaboard city, if his capital accumulations or business experience justified the step. Failure was equally important in causing him to find a new location, and this is what happened to many as a result of the Panic of 1837. We have fragmentary information on how storekeepers resolved their financial problems in periods of economic stress.

The itinerant merchants plied their trade in the South after the War of 1812 as they did during the Colonial days. They still had to pay fees to carry on their business, and the tax laws of the various states reflected the value of their services. In Virginia, for instance, peddlers who operated west of the mountains paid smaller fees than those working the older parts of the state. County tax rates likewise varied, depending on the value of the services.[18]

Unfortunately, the peddler acquired a shady reputation. This unfavorable image of him reflects in part the smallness of his business and the fact that he left few records. If he had records, the migratory character of his trade and the lack of storage facilities eventually forced him to discard them. Hence what we know about the peddler we have learned from rival merchants with whom he had dealings, hostile newspaper accounts, impressions recorded by customers, and legislative regulations governing his trade.

Peddlers often were young people in search of adventure, experience, and capital for larger undertakings. During the 1820's and 1830's Georgia required the listing of peddlers holding state licenses. Of the 46 listed in the Milledgeville paper in 1831, one was nineteen years old, 35 were in their twenties, and only one had reached his fortieth birthday. Peddling was an occupation for the healthy, those who were able to be on the road constantly and away from their families and were capable of enduring the hardships imposed by limited funds. A peddler also faced danger and the prospects of a violent death. Flatboats manned by upcountry farmer-traders or their agents were proof that the itinerant merchants were capable of making adjustments to the peculiarities and changes in the markets they served. With well-arranged stocks of goods and capable clerks, they sold produce along the Mississippi and its tributaries.

Peddling probably would have acquired a higher degree of respectability if it had attracted only adventurers and ambitious young men. Unhappily it likewise appealed to failures in other occupations and those anxious to flee from their communities because of brushes with the law. Southern merchants complained about peddlers who absconded with goods that had been advanced to them on credit; customers resented their sharp practices; and planters accused them of inciting the slaves. Peddling also served as an attraction to "the crippled and the disabled," who depended on the sympathy of the prospective purchasers.

Table 1-1—Manufactures in the United States During the Year Ending June 1, 1860

	Number of Establishments	Capital Invested ($)	Cost of Raw Materials ($)	Number of Employees		Cost of Labor ($)	Annual Value of Product ($)
Woolen Goods	1,260	30,862,654	36,586,887	Male	24,841	9,808,254	61,895,217
				Fem.	16,519		
					41,360		
Boots & Shoes	12,487	23,358,527	42,729,649	Male	94,515	30,938,920	91,891,498
				Fem.	28,514		
					123,029		
Men's Clothing	3,793	24,939,193	39,976,845	Male	41,172	18,942,888	73,219,765
				Fem.	57,730		
					98,903		
Hats & Caps	622	4,126,572	8,333,454	Male	7,338	3,638,596	16,665,475
				Fem.	3,503		
					10,841		
Hardware	443	6,707,000	4,402,758	Male	9,458	3,443,664	10,903,106
				Fem.	1,263		
					10,721		
Iron Castings	1,412	24,249,966	15,181,410	Male	26,008	9,968,346	36,132,033
				Fem.	21		
					26,029		
Bar, Short & Rr. Iron	256	19,924,473	19,242,743	Male	19,227	6,514,258	31,888,705
				Fem.	35		
					19,262		
Coal (Mined)	622	29,428,670	2,752,972	Male	21,357	9,650,264	20,243,637
				Fem.	11		
					21,368		
Printing	1,666	19,622,318	12,844,288	Male	1,786	7,588,096	31,063,898
				Fem.	2,333		
					4,119		

Source: U.S. Bureau of the Census, Manufactures of the United States in 1860; Eighth Census (Washington, D.C., 1865).

The census reports, incomplete as they are, show that the South had fewer peddlers than the North. In 1850, for instance, New York listed 3,883 peddlers and Pennsylvania, 1,317. Louisiana claimed only 292, whereas the majority of the Southern states reported less than 100 each. In 1860, Louisiana again led with 317 peddlers and most states in the South again listed less than 100; New York reported over 6,000; Ohio, 1,588; and Pennsylvania, 1,315.

Some of the itinerant traders settled in a community as soon as they could be assured of a steady clientele. Ultimately, many traveling tailors became proprietors of clothing stores, traveling silversmiths became jewelers, and other traveling artisans underwent similar developments. Some added manufactured goods to their stocks and gradually became general retailers.

The census reports of 1840 show that a substantial amount of money was invested in the merchant stores of mid-America. Illinois, which had less than $5,000,000 invested in retail stores, ranked second to Missouri, whose investments exceeded $8,000,000. This was small compared with the $42,000,000 invested in New York and the $35,000-000 in Pennsylvania. However, if one considers the average amount of capital per store, mid-America compares favorably with the East. In Arkansas the amount was $6,003 per store and in Missouri, $7,370. These sums exceeded those for stores in Pennsylvania, where the average was $5,485, and those of New York and Massachusetts, which had average investments of about $3,500. The relatively large investment per store in the West may be explained by the wider area of customers served and the absence of specialized stores that required less capital. Except for a few towns such as St. Louis, specialized stores were uncommon in the West.

Few of the western merchants seem to have inherited their capital. Forty-six per cent of a small group of merchants whose backgrounds were studied began as clerks in the stores of other men; 15 per cent entered merchandising directly from farming; another 5 per cent taught school to get their start; and others came from the ranks of the skilled artisans, hotel keepers, and to a lesser extent, day laborers. Only one per cent inherited money enough to be of any appreciable help in opening a store. Generally, the merchant of mid-America was a person who had to accumulate his own capital.[19]

Table 1-1, extracted from the United States Census of 1860, leaves little doubt that manufacturing, for the most part, was conducted on a relatively small scale. In terms of the number of establishments and the annual value of the product, the manufacturers of boots and shoes were clearly in the lead, followed by the makers of men's clothing.

Impact of the Civil War

The Civil War ruined many small businessmen. Once the fighting began, Southerners repudiated Northern debts, thus destroying many drygoods merchants, clothiers, boot and shoe dealers, and jewelers. During the first year of fighting thousands of Northern "commercial houses" collapsed. The war also broke down barriers such as tolls on bridges, ferries, roads, and tonnage taxes on railroads, which had kept outsiders from encroaching on the monopoly enjoyed by the local merchants. Not until the greenbacks appeared in April 1862 did business seem to regain its former equilibrium.[20]

The small businessman remained a conspicuous part of post-Civil War America. Many small manufacturers, wholesalers, distributors, and shopkeepers had prospered from the fighting by expanding their operations or moving into some new or related sphere of influence. The most significant development of the postwar decades, however, was the emergence of larger and more powerful units in industry, transportation, commerce, and finance, which the smaller businessmen viewed with alarm.

Despite this, the small manufacturing plant remained a conspicuous part of the American economy. This can best be illustrated by contrasting the size of the average establishments, the number of employees, and the capital invested in 1850 and in 1910. In 1850 the average manufacturing establishment had a capital investment of $4,300, seven wage-earners, and products valued at $8,200. By 1910 the average manufacturing establishment had a capital investment of $64,800, 25 wage-earners, and products valued at $76,900. In short, before 1900 the average unit of production ceased to be a single family or a small group of persons working on small quantities of material with a few cheap, simple tools. Instead, it employed a labor force consisting of hundreds of individuals using large quantities of expensive and intricate machinery.[21]

In 1910 the census reported that of a total of more than 268,000 manufacturing establishments, slightly more than 3,000, or 1.1 per cent of the total, made products valued at $1,000,000 or more. The medium-large establishments that produced goods valued from $100,000 to $1,000,000 constituted about 10 per cent of the total, and those that produced $5,000 worth or less comprised one-third of the total. The large establishments, those representing 1.1 per cent of the total, employed 30 per cent of the labor force in manufacturing and accounted for more than 35 per cent of the value of manufactures. Manufacturing was thus being concentrated in very large firms.

Far more menacing, in the opinion of many, was the wave of consolidations and combinations that occurred during the 1890's and the early 1900's. At various stages they were aided by the formation of pools, trusts, mergers, and holding companies; and by the enactment of special legislation in the states of New Jersey, Delaware, and West Virginia. Among the largest companies incorporated in New Jersey were the American Tobacco Company (1890), the American Sugar Refining Company (1891), the International Paper Company (1898), the National Biscuit Company (1898), the United States Shoe Machine Corporation (1899), the United States Steel Corporation (1901), the International Harvester Company (1902), and E. I. Dupont de Nemours Powder Company (1903).[22]

Meanwhile, a strong public reaction set in against these combinations. This assumed various forms. A series of state antitrust laws enacted between 1889 and 1893 indicated that the public interest had shifted from railroad regulation to that of industrial monopoly.[23] Those fearing the loss of their businesses and profits became resentful, as were those frozen out of the market. Cotton growers selling cottonseed to manufacturers, grain producers selling to whiskey manufacturers, and oil producers selling to refiners—all of whom were deprived of buyer competition and had to sell for less—became aroused. Representatives of these groups protested in their respective state capitals and Washington, but they themselves were ineffective in creating a strong antimonopoly movement. They needed the support of an alerted general public that government officials and policy makers could not afford to ignore. Before long the producers of the primary commodities had behind them the support of the small businessmen frightened by secret corporate interests, consumers haunted by the rise of living costs, and antimonopoly writers such as Henry George, Henry Demarest Lloyd, and others who wrote with considerable force.

Small businessmen, especially employers, had to contend with the rise in labor costs as well as the fear of being driven out of business by their larger and more powerful competitors. This certainly was true of the small businessman in the post-Civil War years when union activities and demands for higher wages spread among the employees. As a result a rash of employers' associations was formed to resist the demands of the unions, combat strikes, and insure a steady supply of labor. The earlier employers' associations were loosely knit and comprised of employers who were not much beyond the master craftsman stage. But with the growth of the larger corporations the leadership in the employers' associations was assumed by the employers of a larger number of workers. However, many a small employer joined forces with the larger ones on the theory that both were menaced by the rising cost of labor.[24]

Competition from larger business rivals naturally threatened the smaller businessman. The rise of the giant packers in the period from 1865 to 1878 forced many of the local butchers in the East out of business.[25] Severe competition in the boot and shoe industry and the silk trade in the late nineteenth century made close figuring by the small man necessary to realize a profit. Department stores made life more difficult for the small dry goods merchants. The department stores required relatively fewer clerks; paid proportionately less for rent, bookkeeping, and superintendence; and obtained discounts on their purchases because they were able to make cash payments. This situation prevailed in many other industrial, commercial, and financial areas. The small businessman lived in constant fear of his future.[26]

Commercial failures were quite common among small businessmen in the period from 1861 to 1915. The reasons for these failures have not been clearly established, but poor management, competition, overoptimism, the lack of capital, and technological innovations apparently took their toll. Table 1-2 bears out that over this period there was a steady increase in the number of commercial failures and a decrease in the average liabilities.

Studies bear out that from 1844 to 1873 the larger relative mortality in infant years was due to an unwarranted expansion following the rapid growth of the community.[27] Similarly, 26 per cent of the retail failures from 1890 to 1931 were due to incompetence or inexperience, according to the estimate of Dun and Bradstreet.[28] In the final analysis, the small businessman of late nineteenth century America conducted his business on a trial-and-error basis. Apparently he asked himself what location would give him the best business advantage, what his minimum capital needs were or were going to be, and what was the danger point of debt.

Table 1-2—Commercial Failures, 1861–1915

Year	Number of Failures	Aggregate Liabilities ($ Thousands)	Average Liabilities ($)
1861	6,993	207,210	29,631
1865	530	17,625	33,255
1870	3,546	88,242	24,885
1875	7,740	201,060	25,977
1880	4,740	95,352	13,886
1885	10,637	134,220	11,678
1890	10,907	189,857	17,406
1895	13,197	173,196	13,124
1900	10,774	138,496	12,854
1905	11,520	102,676	8,913
1910	12,652	201,757	15,947
1915	22,156	302,286	13,644

Source: U.S. Department of Commerce, Statistical Abstract of the United States, 1931 (Washington, D.C., 1931), 329.

Statistics indicate that the greatest number of failures occurred shortly after a war was declared or during the course of a major depression. The outbreak of the Civil War in 1861 helped bring about what was then a record number of failures—6,993. From then until the end of the war there was a decline in failures. A record was established from 1873 to 1878, when a total of 47,185 concerns went under. Another, much longer wave of failures began in 1883 and lasted through 1917, the year the United States entered World War I. The lowest point in this period was 1883, when 9,184 concerns closed their doors, and the highest was in 1915, when 22,156 failed. America's entry into World War I brought a decline in failures that ended a couple of years after peace was restored.[29]

The farm, without a doubt, was one of the strongholds of the individual-entrepreneur system. In the number of people involved and the value of the product, the farm was the chief industrial unit before the European war broke out in 1914. The business side of the farm often was overlooked by the farmer himself, but it was there. The size of the farm was limited by the value of the land, the entrepreneurial ability of the farmer, the character of the crop and soil, and the amount of labor and capital available. Small-scale farming was best representative of the single entrepreneur organization in which the entrepreneurial function was combined with other factors, the labor factor being the most significant.

The census shows that the number of farms increased simultaneously with the growth of industry and the rise of the city. Industrialization and urbanization, at least, did not retard the spread of commercialized agriculture and the idea of the family-sized farm during the last half of the nineteenth century. Table 1-3 points out that from 1850 to 1900 the number of farms increased and the average size of the farm decreased.

Table 1-3—Farm Units: Number and Average Size, 1850–1900

Year	Number of Farms	Average Number of Acres per Farm
1850	1,449,073	202.6
1860	2,044,077	199.2
1870	2,659,985	153.2
1880	4,008,907	133.7
1890	4,564,641	136.5
1900	5,737,372	146.2

Source: U.S. Department of Commerce, *Statistical Abstract of the United States, 1904* (Washington, D.C., 1904), 509.

Commercial agriculture required something more than farming for food and fuel and the adding of a cash crop as a means of raising the farmer's standard of living. It compelled the small farmer to take cognizance of the condition of the market, the tariff, transportation rates, labor costs, machinery and fertilizer prices, land values, foreign competition, the weather, and various other elements that influenced his profits and losses.

The financial rewards of farming were relatively small. This was as true during the first half of the nineteenth century as it was during the latter half. Later studies indicate that "the real per capita incomes of farm people fell badly from 1870 to about 1895." In 1901 the United States Industrial Commission reported that the capital employed in farming yielded a lower rate of return than it had thirty years earlier.[30]

But the farmers, unlike the small businessmen of the cities and towns, began to organize on a sectional or regional, if not a national, basis. From 1867 through 1902 one organization after another emerged to better the lot of the farmers: the Patrons of Husbandry or Grange;

the Agricultural Wheel; the Farmers Mutual Benefit Association; the Farmers Alliance and its political offshoot, the Populist Party; the Farmers Union; and the American Society of Equity.

During the 1870's the Grange focused attention on the need of the farmers for lower and cheaper railroad rates, fair treatment from public carriers, the curbing of middlemen profits and malpractices, cheaper credit facilities, taxation and tariff reform, and a more practical education for the students attending land-grant agricultural colleges. Beginning about the mid-1870's some of the emphasis was shifted from the railroad issue to campaigns for the establishment of cooperative stores and marketing associations. The cooperative stores enjoyed limited success. Shortlived cooperative grain elevators, livestock shipping associations, and cheese factories helped bring the farmers lower marketing costs and greater returns. Perhaps more permanent and prosperous were the farmers mutual life insurance companies, which enjoyed remarkable success from the start. Granger efforts to manufacture farm machinery and implements, sewing machines, wagons, and other needs ended in failure.

The one major difference between the commercial farmers and the small businessmen of the towns and cities is that they and their leaders had a keener appreciation of the need for organization. This is ironical in view of the greater difficulties faced in organizing the farmers and the fact that they were more numerous. At first the farmers appealed to the state and federal governments to regulate those industrial, commercial, and manufacturing groups that they believed oppressed them through their antisocial behavior. Later they buttressed these actions by approaching the federal government with specific proposals to liberalize credit facilities, encourage cooperative marketing, and adopt other measures designed to bring higher prices to the farmers and lighten their debt burdens.

Woodrow Wilson, as governor of New Jersey, sponsored stringent antitrust laws that ended, temporarily at least, the welcome that his state had extended to big corporations. As a Presidential candidate in 1912 he made much of his "New Freedom." Wilson said that, "American industry is not free, as once it was free. American enterprise is not free; the man with only a little capital is finding it harder to get into the field, more and more impossible to compete with the big fellow. Why? Because the laws of this country do not prevent the strong from crushing the weak."[31]

The purpose of the Wilson administration was to restore some of the older opportunities and competition. The two pieces of legislation seeking to help fulfill this objective were the Federal Trade Commission and Clayton Anti-Trust acts of 1914. Both measures were based on the premise that, because the Sherman Anti-Trust Act had failed to protect the small from the big, additional legislation was necessary to prevent monopoly. Despite these actions, the legislation failed to check the drift toward monopolistic practices. The laws, as enacted, were designed to maintain or restore competitive conditions of an economic order that was rapidly changing. Administrative enforcement of the laws, if adequate, was very difficult because of the lack of funds, staff, and executive leadership. Ignorance on the part of government officials also was a hindrance. Thus what was intended to aid the small entrepreneur ended either as a complete failure or a realization of a limited degree of success.

World War I and Its Aftermath

The impact that World War I had on small business is difficult to assess, although in the earlier stages of the war small business apparently fared little better than big business. Our entry into the war was accompanied by a relaxation of the effort to enforce the anti-trust laws and the desire of the government to obtain the full cooperation of industry in the defense of the nation. Well before the United States became involved militarily, American business—small business in particular—suffered heavily. In 1914 a total of 18,280 industrial and commercial failures was reported, with an average liability of $19,579. This was the highest number of failures since the panic of 1893. The following year the number of failures climbed to 22,156 with an average liability of $13,644. From then on there was a steady decline, the low point in failures being 6,451 in 1919.

One of the disturbing features of the 1920's and early 1930's was the growing number of failures, as Table 1-4 brings out.

Also significant was the decline in the number of new business formations beginning in 1926. This may have been brought about by the availability of alternative forms of investment. The relatively high rate of returns on securities may have enticed a number of potential entrepreneurs. However, the failure of new businesses to increase in significant numbers after the business revival starting in 1933 may be attributed to the lack of confidence in a business future, the absence of capital owing to financial reverses in 1932 and 1933, and the rise in business taxes.[32]

Table 1-4—Commercial Failures, 1921–1933

Year	Number of Failures	Current Liabilities ($ Thousands)	Average Liabilities ($)
1921	19,652	627,401	31,926
1922	23,676	626,895	26,351
1923	18,718	539,387	28,816
1924	20,615	543,226	26,351
1925	21,214	443,744	20,918
1926	21,773	409,233	18,795
1927	23,146	520,105	22,471
1928	23,842	489,559	20,533
1929	22,909	483,252	21,094
1930	26,355	668,282	25,357
1931	28,285	736,310	26,032
1932	31,822	928,313	29,172
1933	20,307	502,830	24,761

Source: U.S. Department of Commerce, *Statistical Abstract of the United States, 1948* (Washington, D.C., 1948), 471.

Meanwhile, the trade association, whose antecedents may be traced back into the nineteenth century, became more prominent in business circles. However, its objectives changed. After the Civil War one of its principal functions had been to regulate prices among members, limit production, and divide up the market. During the 1890's one of its aims was cooperation for the betterment of conditions in the industry. Annual meetings were held; inspection and grading of products was undertaken; credit-rating bureaus were established; and cooperative advertising was encouraged. In 1912 Arthur J. Eddy, a Chicago lawyer, published *The New Competition,* which advanced the idea of open-price agreements for business. He claimed that if information about prices and volume of production was made available, and the market made free and open, prices would become stabilized.

Trade associations grew rapidly under such an atmosphere. During World War I their growth was encouraged by the government, which wanted to make an effective use of raw materials of the nation and control prices. These associations published information about the capacity, output, location of factories, and the names of the owners, which was of great aid in planning for war production.

After World War I the activities of the trade associations increased considerably. Again this was due in part to the encouragement of the government and its agencies. The Department of Commerce, headed by Herbert C. Hoover, became especially interested in the statistical work of these associations. Beginning in 1921 the Department of Commerce published a series of business statistics intended to aid small businessmen who did not belong to trade associations. Much of this, however, had been compiled originally by the associations.[33]

Despite this headway, the traditional skepticism of business associations for self-help reasserted itself. Many of the activities of the associations were socially desirable and served the trade without being a disservice to the customers. Encouraging cooperative industrial research, market surveys, mutual insurance, the publication of trade journals, and joint advertising was consistent with the preservation of competition among members. But other activities of the trade association involved the imposition of restraints. These included the establishment of uniform cost accounting methods; the dissemination of statistics on capacity, output, orders, and shipments; the use of price-reporting plans; and the standardization of products and the terms of sale. Such practices often helped members of the associations, but on other occasions they were employed to restrain trade. Court decisions handed down displayed an unmistakably hostile attitude "to the efforts of the small, independent businesses to achieve through association the security already won by big business." This rankled many small businessmen and gave encouragement to a movement for amendment, if not outright abolition of the antitrust laws.[34]

The Great Depression

The Great Depression of the 1930's ruined many businesses, but it proved more perilous to the small businessman than to the large, who had reserves to carry him through. No matter how well managed a business was, it was difficult for a small man to foresee probable developments in the markets for his products. During the depression many small businesses were placed in the precarious position of depending on one customer or a specialized product. This made the small producer inflexible and incapable of readjusting his productive facilities to depressed conditions.[35]

Small businessmen who were unhappy with the policies of President Herbert Hoover contributed to the election of Franklin Delano Roosevelt in 1932. But the National Recovery Act (NRA), which many small businessmen had hoped would aid them, instead bore heavily on them. Administration spokesmen had nothing but a broad set of principles to guide them. These were not enough to prevent the representatives of big business, who had more experience and greater knowledge of the intricacies of the industry they represented, from coming into control of the code authorities. Big business, finding itself thus in a position to benefit from the suspension of the antitrust laws that the NRA permitted and from price-fixing, entrenched itself in its already secure position. The undistributed-profits tax hit both the big and the little fellow, but the big fellow could bear it for he had an umbrella of reserves to protect him and the small one had none. Other phases of the New Deal, notably the SEC, likewise were intended to help the small businessman and investor. If the New Deal represented the interests and philosophy of any one group of the population, that group was the middle class, of which the small businessman, the investor, and the professional were the principal constituents.[36]

The belief quickly developed that the federal government had extended most of its consideration to big business and the laboring class, whereas small business was being massacred. The proof of this was the unionization of labor and the enactment of minimum wage laws, which put the small firm at a disadvantage in competing with big business. Another piece of evidence was the Social Security Act, which aimed to provide old age pensions for all workers outside agriculture and domestic workers but made no provision for the small shopkeeper, who was compelled to pay a substantial percentage of the cost of making old age safe for his employees.

If the small businessman was reluctant about organizing in the past, the New Deal cured him of his lethargy. He began to agitate and demand legislation in his behalf. Of the 390 small-business bills introduced in Congress from 1933 to 1942, only 26 became law, including amendments to the Federal Reserve Act and the Reconstruction Finance Corporation Act. Later, Congress passed the Robinson-Patman Act, the Miller-Tydings amendment to the Sherman Act, and an act which created the Temporary National Economic Committee.[37]

Besides seeking to overcome the effects of the depression, the small shopkeepers had to deal with formidable foes in the chain stores. A number of the small retailers came together and formed special associations to defend themselves from their powerful rivals. The small grocers banded together in the National Association of Retail Grocers (NARG) and the druggists in the National Association of Retail Druggists (NARD). They, and representatives of other retail groups, then began pressing for fair-trade and antiprice-discrimination laws.

Another kind of association was comprised of independent businessmen scattered throughout the business community. Such an association usually had "small" or "independent" in its title. It differed from the special trade association, composed of small businessmen of the same trade, in that it believed that the small size of the firm, regardless of the trade, was sufficient to produce shared attitudes capable of sustaining united action over a period of time. Representative of this was the National Federation of Independent Business (NFIB); it claimed in its publications that "no longer must one particular vocation fight its battles alone." The assumption of the NFIB was that acting strictly as druggists, bakers, or grocers was insufficient to deal effectively with the problems of the small businessman. Comparable sentiments were expressed by other such groups. The National Small Business Men's Association (NSBMA) argued that "there is little question that small business needs strong representation when we consider the strength of organizations representing other groups."[38]

The first small business associations transcending trade lines appeared in 1937, although the initial activity occurred earlier. These associations began largely as a result of the activities of single individuals or small groups of individuals who wanted to capitalize on the symbolic value of small business that had been generated by the trade associations. This was facilitated by the Small Business Conference of 1938. On January 26, 1938, Secretary of Commerce Daniel Roper announced that President Franklin D. Roosevelt and other administration officials would confer with small businessmen on February 2. Roper sent invitations to 500 persons who had written the President suggesting that a cross section of all industry meet with administration officials to formulate a recovery program. At the time any business having a total annual gross sales of less than $1,000,000 was considered a small business.[39]

Out of the diverse interests of the small businessmen assembling in Washington came a curious assortment of "cure-alls." One was that there should be more human labor in the product, obviously the position of an antimachine businessman. A small-scale button-hole manufacturer, who, in competing with mass-producers of button holes, got more out of his employees by giving them better tools and new machinery, proposed lower wage rates for the employees of "little business." A used-car dealer suggested that the federal government remove a major menace from the highways of the nation by buying up all used cars.[40] Among the 23 recommendations submitted to the President by this conference was one advocating the establishment of a permanent advisory council for small business interests. Other recommendations included the repeal of the undivided profits tax, modification of the capital gains tax and the regulations of the Securities and Exchange Commission, curtailment of government expenditures, and loans to business.[41]

These antiadministration resolutions were proposed by a group of small businesses caught between monopoly pressure on the one side and government controls on the other. They were reacting against higher tax burdens and higher wage rates. The administration, however, recognized the seriousness of the small businessman's problem and promised to take additional measures to remedy his economic position through easing credit and strengthening his position in relation to monopolies.

One result of the conference was the introduction of a bill by Senator Carter Glass making it easier for the little businessman to get funds from the Reconstruction Finance Corporation. Another result was the attempt to perpetuate the Conference through the formation of permanent organizations. Some fifty such organizations sprang into existence within a year. Perhaps the most immediate aim of each of these newly-formed groups was to create the impression that it had government approval to serve as a liaison agent between the small businessman and the administration. In response to a suggestion by Secretary of Commerce, Daniel Roper, the Nation's Smaller Business Conference was organized. After undergoing a series of reorganizations and changes in name, the National Advisory Council of Independent Small Business came into being. One of its roles was "to advise the Department of Commerce of the needs and desires of small business" and it demanded representation in that Department. However, the Department was unconvinced that the Council was representative of the small business community and began an active campaign of opposition to the small business movement.[42] By 1941 only the National Small Business Men's Association remained in existence.

Meanwhile, the administration also launched an antitrust campaign as a means of allaying the fears of monopoly. In 1937 Attorney General Robert Jackson attacked the Supreme Court for its leniency in antitrust cases. This was followed up by recommendations from the President to strengthen the antitrust proceedings and revive the patent laws. Assistant Attorney General Thurman Arnold was assigned the task of enforcing the laws against monopolies and he did this with success.

The President then sought to strengthen the hand of the government through the appointment of the Temporary National Economic Committee (TNEC) to investigate the problem of monopoly. The TNEC was created in 1938 after Congress heard the President make the following statement:[43]

> Unhappy events abroad have retaught us two simple truths about the liberty of a democratic people.
>
> The first truth is that the liberty of a democracy is not safe if the people tolerate the growth in private power to a point where it becomes stronger than their democratic state itself. That, in essence, is fascism—ownership of government by an individual, by a group, or by any other controlling private power.
>
> The second truth is that liberty of a democracy is not safe if its business system does not provide employment and produce and distribute goods in such a way as to sustain an acceptable standard of living.
>
> Among us today a concentration of private power without equal in history is growing.
>
> This concentration is seriously impairing the economic effectiveness of private enterprise as a way of providing employment for labor and capital and as a way of assuring a more equitable distribution of income and earnings among the people of the nation as a whole.

The TNEC, during the thirty months of its existence, conducted 193 days of hearings, heard 552 witnesses, and published 31 volumes of testimony and 43 monograph studies. It recommended that, "The fullest use of technology should be encouraged, and the competitive system should be so operated as to insure the passing on of all technological gains," and that "serious attention . . . should be given to the proper location of strategic industries, to avert, among other things, the dangers of great size and undue concentration of plants and facilities. Ghost towns and unhealthy slums both all too frequently occur without economic or social justification."[44] However, most of the TNEC's proposals were sidetracked because of the growing need of the government for full cooperation from big business in defense and war production.

The Impact of World War II

During the 1940's three major developments pushed the small businessman toward the center of the political stage. The need for developing new subcontracting firms brought the small concerns to the public view in a somewhat new light. The shrinkage in the total number of concerns—especially new ones, which between 1941 and 1943, during the earlier stages of the war, amounted to about half a million or roughly 14 per cent of the total—raised new fears of a concentration of economic power. Finally, "the emergence of the full employment problem" emphasized the need of maintaining a satisfactory volume of production after the war.[45]

Jesse Jones, Secretary of Commerce at the time, echoed the sentiments of the administration and small business thus:[46]

> It would certainly be more healthy for the national economy to save even a portion of distressed small business through transmitting information and advice than to let those who can be saved perish for the lack of it. Extending this sort of help to the small businessman directly would be to give him no greater an advantage than that which the government has for years been offering to the farmer.

Congress, as part of its efforts to promote fuller participation in the war by the smaller concerns, passed a law creating the Small War Plants Corporation (SWPC). This corporation was authorized to purchase and lease equipment to smaller industrial concerns and make direct loans to them for expansion or operating purposes. The SWPC, during its existence, authorized a total of $504,000,000 in such leases and loans. The corporation also was empowered to collect and disseminate scientific and technical information to small concerns that would have had scant access to data necessary for efficient operation as a part of the war production system.

World War II, besides bringing about sharp dislocations in small business in the early years, contributed to the dominance of big business. According to the *Census of Manufactures and Business* in 1939, 92.5 per cent of all business fell within the Department of Commerce's definition of small business. The volume of small business increased considerably during the fighting and it operated very profitably. But big business also grew and increased its share of the total production, which meant that the relative position of the small business had grown weaker. Big business, by improving its methods of production and making great strides in scientific research, came out of the war stronger financially and acquired a large share of the technical plants built during the war. Big business was bigger, whereas a larger number of small businesses were scrambling for a dwindling share of the total market.[47]

Except for aid to veterans seeking to open small businesses, federal legislation after the war aimed at meeting the problems of some 24,000 manufacturers who hired from 50 to 500 workers. In other words the small-sized business units, which made up about 90 per cent of all business firms, were not the ones taken into account. Instead, those who appeared before the Federal Trade Commission or Small Business Committee of Congress to plead the case of the small man, and who usually represented firms within the top 10 per cent of the business enterprises, were the ones for whom provisions were made.[48]

After the war, the Office of Small Business in the Department of Commerce limited its efforts to the publication of data on procurement opportunities. The Small Business Committee of the Senate, on the other hand, was opposed to having the Office of Small Business remain in the Department of Commerce, which was viewed as an adjunct of big business. Given its way, the Small Business Committee would have created a Department of Small Business with cabinet rank. However, groups such as the Conference of American Small Business Organizations (CASBO) and the National Small Business Men's Association (NSBMA) opposed the Small Business Committee of the House and Senate. CASBO actively sided with the Department of Commerce in its battle against the Small Business Committees. Legislation to set aside percentages of the contracts for small businesses was resisted by the procuring agencies after World War II.[49]

Origins of the Small Business Administration

With the coming of the Korean War, the House and Senate committees on small business began another campaign to give the Office of Small Business an independent status. Negotiations with other groups, such as trade associations, resulted in the calling of the Small Business Anti-Monopoly Conference, which urged the passage of the Small Defense Plant Administration Bill. The Small Defense Plants Administration (SDPA), which became a reality in 1951, is important because it served as a forerunner of the Small Business Administration. Before the first year of the SDPA's existence, plans were made to expand it into the Small Business Administration and to aid all small business, regardless of utility to the war effort.

The politics behind the creation of the Small Business Administration in 1953 has a lengthy and involved history of its own. The SBA was unique in that it was given responsibility for the entire community. Until 1953 government-sponsored small business agencies confined their activities to meeting defense production or essential civilian needs in a mobilized economy. Now the SBA was to represent a broader set of interests but with a reduced responsibility.

The task of defining a small business was left to the administrator of the SBA. He was subjected to pressure from various directions. The Small Business Committees of Congress wanted a definition that would help "the little fellows" whose business would increase competition within a particular industry, regardless of the actual size of the business. Smallness, in its opinion, was a relative matter. Opposition to such a definition came from the Department of Commerce, the Department of Defense, and the very small businesses. However, the most intense resistance came from the Department of Defense, which during World War II considered all firms employing more than 500 as large firms, regardless of the industry. It wanted this definition perpetuated. This 500 limit would restrict the areas in which the SBA could review contracts, for a large proportion of the defense contracts were placed in industries employing more than 500 people.[50]

Despite these and other pressures, the SBA succeeded in obtaining a split definition of small business. In 1964 a business qualified as "small" for SBA lending purposes on the basis of these criteria:[51]

1. Wholesale—annual sales of not more than $5 million.

2. Retail or Service—annual sales or receipts of not more than $1 million.

3. Manufacturing—small if it has no more than 250 employees, large if it has more than 1,000; within these breaking-points are specific size standards for specific industries.

Conclusion

As a group, the small businessman has been with us since colonial times and, if the past is any criterion, he is likely to be with us for many years to come. He had his problems in the colonial period when society was much simpler than it is today. He lacked capital then as he does today; he faced ruinous competition, rising labor costs and taxes, and had to learn how to make adjustments to social changes. But unlike the small family-sized farmer who has been slowly disappearing, the small businessman has not been eliminated from the scene. Each year thousands of new small businesses are born and thousands more fail, discontinue their operations or merge with former competitors.

The birth and mortality rates of small business have been well-described within recent years by Professor John H. Bunzel:[52]

[O]nly one of every five small businesses will survive a decade and . . . the great majority . . . but seven years. In a normal year over 300,000 go out of business and approximately 400,000 more are sold or transferred to someone else. In the shadow of these statistics is still another: 400,000 pin their hopes each year to the American Dream and take a flyer at being small and independent. Most of these self-styled businessmen have no business going into business, since they not only have insufficient capital but are lacking in training and experience. They do not know very much about the market into which they are entering, frequently cannot be bothered to keep records, and would not recognize a constructive management plan if one were handed to them. Taxes are high and profits are low, which means the local banks, taking a dim view of the small businessman's chances for survival, are reluctant to stake him to his dubious venture. When the conventional sources of credit dry up, the Small Business Administration is called upon annually to disperse hundreds of thousands of dollars to stem the tide of small business failures, but these business and disaster loans have met with little permanent success.

Studies on business mortality are incomplete and the rates vary from industry to industry, but available data suggests that there is a relationship between the net worth and the life span of a business. Newcomers have been confined to businesses where the profits frequently are small and the failure rates high—where entrance was easy, competition keen, and the chances of survival poor. Profits have tended to be highest in fields where the capital needs have been high and expensive facilities needed.[53]

Technological changes have destroyed the handicraft industries and numerous other small enterprises, but they also have resulted in a series of small businesses. "[T]he development of electricity has produced the electrician and the electrical appliance store; radio created the radio shop, the repair shop, and the trucking business; the rapid expansion of the cosmetics industry has produced a large number of beauty parlors. . . . This is a typical process which will insure the continued existence of large numbers of small retail and service enterprises."[54]

Small enterprises have also held their own in certain areas of manufacturing. The small manufacturer enjoyed the advantage in businesses that were "dependent on personal taste, individual needs, and rapid changes in fashion, such as the clothing industry, or the manufacturing of novelties, high-grade furniture, and many other items." This was true especially in industries that catered to local markets and those that depended heavily on skilled labor.

If, as the small businessman often feels, technological changes and the concentration of a larger percentage of business in the large corporation has made the tradition of American individualism a thing of the past, it behooves him to learn from big business. After all, it is big, not little, business that has displayed the greater foresight, imagination, and creativity in coping with the technological, social, and political issues of the day; small businessmen have too often resisted to the bitter end political measures that held out the promise of achieving for them the major hope for their salvation—high-level employment and a high national income. Coming to a recognition of the need for such increased learning in all phases of business management, the present-day small businessman can make the most of the opportunity that history discloses is his rightful heritage.

2

The Position of
Small Business in the
American Economy

J. Fred Weston

This chapter seeks to assess the economic advantages and disadvantages of small business in the functioning of the United States economy. Both the factors that favor small business and those that limit its role will be identified to provide the background necessary for a better understanding of the appropriate role of small business in a competitive economy.

Two broad topics will be excluded from treatment in this study. The far-reaching issues of public policy toward small business will not be evaluated. The issues are much too complex for adequate treatment in a discussion limited to some fundamental economic considerations related to those issues. Nor will the present study review the many propositions that have been set forth on the comparative economic roles of small firms and large firms in a competitive economy.

The economic consequences of concentrated versus less concentrated industries is another broad subject with many fundamental propositions that would require extended analysis. The present study will, however, provide some fundamental background for understanding these problems.

The present paper will cover seven main topics: the characteristics of the business population; the economics of the large firm; the impact of general economic factors on small firms; economic factors favoring small firms; identification of industries in which small firms predominate; the influence of technological, social, and economic trends on small business; and forecasts of future developments in the position of small business in the economy. The coverage of each topic will not be in equal depth and detail. Emphasis will be placed on those economic aspects of small business operations neglected in previous studies and discussions of the role of small business.

General Characteristics of the Business Population

The first set of data, which presents an overview of the composition of national output, provides a picture of the relative importance and growth rates of the segments of the American economy. This information is valuable background for the study of the position of small business in the United States economy because, as will be demonstrated later, the characteristics of some industry segments are particularly favorable to small business and others are not.

Table 2-1 presents the composition of national income by broad industry segments between the years 1959 and 1965. The manufacturing segment of the national economy now accounts for less than one-third of national income generated. The next largest segment—wholesale and retail trade—accounts for about 15 per cent, or one-half the amount for manufacturing. The categories of government, services, and finance follow closely behind.

The distribution of national economic activity when measured by the number of persons engaged in production differs importantly from the distribution when measured by national income generated (Table 2-2). Manufacturing continues to be the largest individual segment but accounts for only about one-fourth of total employment; wholesale and retail trade accounts for nearly one-fifth; and services and government each represent about 17 per cent.

Table 2-1—National Income by Industry (1959–1965) ($ Billions)

Industry	1959		1965		Per Cent Change in Share of Market (1959– 1965)	Growth Rate (1959– 1965)
	Amount	Per Cent	Amount	Per Cent		
All industries, total	400.0	100.0	559.0	100.0	—	5.7
Agriculture, forestry, and fisheries	16.0	4.0	21.0	3.7	(7)	4.6
Mining	5.5	1.4	6.4	1.1	(21)	2.6
Contract construction	20.5	5.1	28.3	5.1	0	5.5
Manufacturing	124.0	31.0	170.4	30.5	(2)	5.4
Transportation	17.9	4.5	22.9	4.1	(9)	4.2
Communication	7.7	1.9	11.2	2.0	5	6.4
Electric, gas, and sanitary service	8.1	2.0	11.6	2.1	5	6.1
Wholesale and retail trade	63.3	15.8	83.6	14.9	(6)	4.7
Finance, insurance and real estate	43.8	11.0	61.0	10.9	(1)	5.7
Services	41.7	10.4	63.0	11.3	9	7.1
Government and government enterprises	49.3	12.3	75.3	13.5	10	7.3
Rest of world	2.2	0.6	4.3	0.8	33	11.8

Source: U.S. Department of Commerce, Survey of Current Business (Washington, D.C.: U.S. Government Printing Office), XLV (August 1965), p. 45, and XLVI (July 1966), p. 15.

The two tables present data on the changes in the share of the total economy for each of the industry segments as well as growth rates over the six-year period 1959–1965. Manufacturing has lost some of its share of national income generated in the economy, but has increased its share of employment during the past six years. Agriculture, mining, contract construction, transportation, and trade have all been declining segments when measured both by national income generated and by number of persons engaged in production.

Two areas in which substantial declines have taken place, contract construction and trade, are industry segments characterized by the prevalence of small business. However, a segment in which considerable expansion has taken place—the service industries—is an area in which small business predominates. The impact of these broad eco-

Table 2-2—Number of Persons Engaged in Production by Industry (1959–1965) (millions)

Industry	1959		1965		Per Cent Change in Share of Market (1959–1965)	Growth Rate (1959–1965)
	Amount	Per Cent	Amount	Per Cent		
All industries, total	66.4	100.0	71.2	100.0	—	1.1
Agriculture, forestry, and fisheries	5.2	7.8	4.0	5.6	(0.28)	(4.3)
Mining	0.7	1.1	0.7	1.0	(9.0)	(0.1)
Contract construction	4.3	6.5	4.0	5.6	(13.8)	(1.2)
Manufacturing	16.4	24.7	18.4	25.8	4.5	1.9
Transportation	2.6	3.9	2.5	3.5	(10.3)	(0.7)
Communication	0.8	1.2	0.9	1.3	8.3	2.0
Electric, gas, and sanitary services	0.6	0.9	0.6	0.8	(11.1)	(0.1)
Wholesale and retail trade	13.3	20.0	13.1	18.4	(8.0)	(0.25)
Finance, insurance and real estate	2.9	4.4	3.1	4.4	0	1.7
Services	9.5	14.3	11.8	16.6	16.1	3.7
Government and government enterprises	10.1	15.2	12.1	17.0	11.8	3.3
Rest of world	Nil	Nil				

Source: U.S. Department of Commerce, *Survey of Current Business*, (Washington, D.C., U.S. Government Printing Office), XLVI (July 1966), Table 6.6, p. 31, and XLIII, Table 55, p. 34.

nomic changes will be explored in greater detail after additional analytical background has been developed.

Some statistical presentations of the business population place the total number of firms in the United States at over eleven million; other statistics place the number at about five million. This wide disparity in the measurement in the size of the business population results from differences in the definition of firms in operation. The larger number is based on the number of firms reported by the Internal Revenue Service. It includes firms in agriculture, forestry, fishing, and the professional services. In addition, a self-employed person is regarded as a firm if he files a partnership or corporation income tax return. This series also includes all firms in operation at any time during a given year. In contrast, the business population series developed by the Office of Business Economics of the Department of Commerce excluded agriculture and professionals. A self-employed person was regarded as a firm only if he had either one or more employees or an established place of business. Additionally, the business population series was measured at a given point in time. Thus it missed firms discontinuing operation as well as many firms, especially in finance, formed to execute only one short-lived transaction.[1] The data in the following tables on the distribution of the business population in the United States will be variously based on the population from the Internal Revenue Service records and from the Business Population Series from the Department of Commerce, whichever was available.

Table 2-3—Legal Form of U.S. Business Enterprise Distribution by Number, 1962

Legal Form	Number (Thousands)	Per Cent of Total
Sole proprietorships	9,183	80.7
Partnerships	932	8.2
Corporations	1,268	11.1
Totals	11,383	100.0

Source: *Statistical Abstract of the U.S., 1965* (Washington, D.C.: U.S. Government Printing Office, 1965), p. 490.

Table 2-3 presents the distribution of firms by legal form of organization. Over 80 per cent of the firms in the United States are organized as sole proprietorships. The remaining 20 per cent are almost equally divided between partnerships and corporations.

When the distribution of business firms is broken down on a basis of receipts or total income, the percentages are almost reversed, as shown in Table 2-4. Almost 80 per cent of total receipts of business

Table 2-4—Legal Form of U.S. Business Enterprise Distribution by Receipts, 1962

Legal Form	Receipts* ($ Millions)	Per Cent of Total
Sole proprietorships	178,420	15.6
Partnerships	72,304	6.3
Corporations	895,120	78.1
Totals	1,145,844	100.0

Source: *Statistical Abstract of the U.S., 1965* (Washington, D.C.: U.S. Government Printing Office, 1965), p. 490.

* Receipts—From sales and services less returns and allowances: a) for sole proprietorships, excludes capital gains or losses and investment income not associated with taxpayers business; b) for partnerships and corporations engaged in finance, insurance and real estate, excludes a sizeable part of income because reporting instructions prescribe separate entries for investment income.

enterprises are received by corporations. Something over 15 per cent are received by sole proprietorships. This has significance for the position of small business. Sole proprietorships and partnerships are predominantly small business firms. Thus, these statistics suggest that about 90 per cent of the firms by number are small but account for some 20 per cent of total receipts. This is a rough relationship that will be refined with further analysis.

Table 2-5 distributes business enterprise on the basis of the size of receipts rather than by legal form. Almost 85 per cent of the firms

Table 2-5—Distribution of U.S. Business Enterprises By Receipts, 1962

Receipts	Number of Enterprises (Thousands)	Per Cent of Total Enterprises
Under $50,000	9,584	84.2
$50,000 to $100,000	774	6.8
$100,000 or more	1,024	9.0
Totals	11,382	100.0

Source: *Statistical Abstract of the U.S., 1965* (Washington, D.C.: U.S. Government Printing Office, 1965), p. 489.

have total receipts of less than $50,000 per annum. Table 2-6 presents a size distribution organized by number of employees. Some 58 per cent of reporting firms have three or less employees. Over 90 per cent

Table 2-6—Distribution of U.S. Business Enterprises By Employee Size Class, 1962

Employee Size Class	Number of Reporting Units*	Per Cent of Total Reporting Units
1–3	1,935,754	57.8
4–7	628,338	18.8
8–19	462,598	13.8
20–49	198,979	5.9
50–99	64,780	1.9
100 or more	57,198	1.7
Totals	3,347,647	99.9**

Source: *Statistical Abstract of the U.S., 1965* (Washington, D.C.: U.S. Government Printing Office, 1965), p. 492.

* Based on reports of employers under the Federal Insurance Contribution Act. A reporting unit is, generally, a single establishment; however, for nonmanufacturing industries, a group of similar establishments of an employer located in the same county are also considered one reporting unit. Data for the following types of employment covered by the Social Security Program in whole or in part are excluded: farm workers, domestic workers, self-employed persons, members of the uniformed services of the United States, federal civilian employees, employees of state and local governments. Also excludes railroad employment subject to the Railroad Retirement Act and employment on oceanborne vessels.

** Does not add to 100 owing to rounding.

of the reporting firms have less than 20 employees. Again, the predominance of small firms by numbers is emphasized.

The number of new businesses established represents a 9 per cent
increase per year. The disappearances represent about 8 per cent a
year. So the business population is characterized by a very high birth
rate and a very high mortality rate. The mortality rate represents
predominantly an infant mortality rate since the median age of firms
that disappear is from 1–3 years. Thus, the net new additions to the
business population each year average about one per cent per year.
Interestingly, therefore, the net business population growth rate is less
than the human population growth rate, since in the United States the
human population growth rate has been 1.5 per cent per year or more.

Some detail on these trends is provided in Table 2-7. The number
of net new corporations has been growing at about the same rate as
Gross National Product—about 6 per cent a year. The growth in sole

Table 2-7—Legal Form of U.S. Business Enterprise Growth Rates by Number, 1957–1962

Legal Form	Number–1957 (Thousands)	Number–1962 (Thousands)	Ratio	Growth Rate (Compounded)
Sole proprietorships	8,738	9,183	1.050	1.0
Partnerships	971	932	0.959	(0.8)
Corporations	940	1,268	1.348	6.1
Totals	10,649	11,383	1.068	1.3

Source: *Statistical Abstract of the U.S., 1965* (Washington, D.C.: U.S. Government Printing Office, 1965), p. 490.

proprietorships has been only about one per cent a year. But because
the sole proprietorships represent the chief form of the business population when measured by numbers, it dominates the over-all growth
rate for all forms of business enterprises. Table 2-7 shows this figure
to be 1.3 per cent per annum for the period 1957–1962.

Table 2-8 measures the growth patterns when the relative position
of the legal form of business enterprise is expressed in terms of receipts
rather than in number of firms. Because corporations dominate, when
the relative position of legal forms is measured by receipts, the over-all
growth rate of firms rises to 4.3 per cent.

Table 2-9 analyzes the growth rates of business enterprises by size,
based on receipts. The table shows that for the three-year period
1960–1962, relative growth rates were positively correlated with the

size categories provided. For this shorter and later time period, the growth in the over-all number of firms is slightly less than one per cent per annum. When the size breakdown is developed in greater detail in Table 2-10, the employee size class of 50–99 was the smallest,

Table 2-8—Legal Form of U.S. Business Enterprises
Growth Rates by Receipts, 1957–1962

Legal Form	Receipts–1957 ($ Millions)	Receipts–1962 ($ Millions)	Ratio	Growth Rate (Compounded) ($ Millions)
Sole proprietorships	162,687	178,420	1.096	1.9
Partnerships	83,430	72,304	0.866	(2.8)
Corporations	684,883	895,120	1.306	5.5
Totals	930,991	1,145,844	1.230	4.3

Source: *Statistical Abstract of the U.S.* (Washington, D.C.: U.S. Government Printing Office, 1965), p. 490.

with a growth rate of 0.8 per cent; the size class with 3 or less employees is the second lowest, with a compound growth rate of 1.7 per cent per annum.

Table 2-9—Growth Rates of U.S. Business Enterprises
By Size Based on Receipts, 1960–1962

Receipts	Number of Enterprises 1960 (Thousands)	Number of Enterprises 1962 (Thousands)	Ratio	Growth Rate (Compounded)
Under $50,000	9,495	9,548	1.005	0.3
$50,000 to $100,000	741	774	1.044	2.2
$100,000 or More	935	1,024	1.095	4.6
Totals	11,171	11,382	1.018	0.9

Source: *Statistical Abstract of the U.S.* (Washington, D.C.: U.S. Government Printing Office), 1965, p. 489; 1963, p. 489.

These statistics provide a picture of industry composition in the United States and the main characteristics of the business population measured by legal form, number of firms, size of total receipts and number of employees. The broad patterns suggested are the following: by numbers, the United States economy is dominated by small firms and sole proprietorships; when measured by total receipts, the American economy is dominated by corporations and larger firms; the growth rate of the total number of firms has been at about two-thirds the rate of the human population.

With this factual background, an analysis of the relative economic advantages of large and small firms can be undertaken. The relative position of small firms, upon which this study focuses, will be better understood by reference to the characteristics of large firms.

Table 2-10—Growth Rates of U.S. Business Enterprises
By Size Based on Employee Size Class, 1960–1962
(Based on Reports of Employers Under F.I.C.A.)

Employees Size Class	NUMBER OF REPORTING UNITS* 1956	1959	Ratio	Growth Rate (Compounded)
0–3	1,830,070	1,923,051	1.050	1.7
4–7	589,370	625,460	1.061	2.0
8–19	422,129	463,365	1.097	3.1
20–49	175,584	187,666	1.068	2.2
50–99	60,270	61,830	1.025	0.8
100 or more	51,725	54,770	1.058	1.9
Totals	3,129,148	3,316,142	1.059	1.9

Source: *Statistical Abstract of the U.S.* (Washington, D.C.: U.S. Government Printing Office), 1963, p. 491; 1960, p. 487.

* Based on reports of employers under old-age and survivors insurance provisions of the Social Security Act. A reporting unit is, generally, a single establishment or group of similar establishments of an employer. Excludes self-employed and railroads.

Economic Factors That Result in
Large-Scale Operations

Ten factors that have resulted in large-scale operations are as follows:

1. Economies of production scale.
2. Large-scale sales promotion.
3. Advertising.
4. Economies of research.
5. Patents.
6. Control over sources of supply.
7. Product differentiation.
8. Large initial investment.
9. Effective use of management staff.
10. Interconnections—organizations built up through time.

Economies of production scale are achieved when a firm is able to spread fixed costs over a large number of units. An example in the automobile industry is the reduction of the heavy costs of dies, jigs, and tools by spreading them over a large number of models and by a large production run for each model.

Large-scale sales promotion is necessary when the volume is large enough to warrant a large and effective sales distribution system. For some lines of products, the necessity of using a manufacturer's or sales representative results in higher sales distribution expenses than those of a well-organized sales organization.

The ability to spread advertising costs over a large number of units may represent a substantial advantage for the large organization, particularly with the growth of national advertising media such as radio and television. Partially offsetting this trend has been the increased use of regional sections in national magazines. Thus the issues of a national magazine distributed in the West Coast may have advertising content that is regionally oriented.

In the area of research, some studies have concluded that large firms have an advantage; others, that the entrepreneurial initiative of the individual provides an advantage. A balanced conclusion would recognize the relative contributions of each. For some kinds of research very heavy capital investments are required. On the other hand, many important inventions in the last 40 years have come from individual inventors. A notable example of this is the development of the jet engine. Related to research activity is the availability of patents and the ability to control further product developments.

Control over sources of supply provides an obvious basis for having a limited number of firms in a given activity and thus contributes to largeness. The aluminum industry is the standard example. One way that a firm may achieve control over supply is through product differentiation. However, product differentiation can also result in competitive innovation and can represent an important competitive force.

For many kinds of products, however, to engage in the competitive struggle for innovation and product differentiation may require large initial sums of investment. This necessity may represent a very important barrier, so that a relatively small number of large firms will be found in a given industry.

Another important aspect of the effective development of the large-scale organization is efficient use of management staff. The small firm may not have sufficient resources to support specialists and expert staff, or staff services purchased may not be effectively utilized. Thus in the area of organization efficiency, an advantage may be found in large-scale operations.

Finally, there is a factor that must be recognized as interconnected with some of the preceding factors. An organization that has been built up over a long period of time may not be easily duplicated by another firm starting from the beginning. The most dramatic example of this was the attempt of new entrants into the automobile industry in the early 1950's. The manufacturing plants of the automobile companies could have been duplicated well within the capital investment capabilities of the new entrants. However, the dealer and service organizations could be developed only over a period of time and required the existence of a successful product marketed in large volume. The interdependence of these various segments of an integrated total business operation militated against the successful entry of other large firms that otherwise had the financial resources to become an effective rival to existing large firms.

The foregoing discussion of factors resulting in large scale operations has not distinguished between absolute versus relative size. This is an important distinction. A firm may be large in itself yet small in relation to the rest of the industry. American Motors, for example, has total sales of over $1 billion, yet its share of the market is only about 3 per cent. On the other hand, a firm in a narrow product segment, such as cured fish, which is a small industry to start with, may have a high percentage of the market and yet represent a firm of small absolute size.

The Small Business Administration on September 14, 1966, announced regulations that reflect this distinction. The SBA stated that effective 30 days after September 14, 1966, for both the automobile industry and the tire industry, small business would be defined as those companies that produce less than 5 per cent of the dollar total of industry shipments of their product a year. By this definition, American Motors Corporation qualified as a small business firm because its share of the automobile market was approximately 3 per cent. A number of tire companies qualified as small businesses under this ruling. However, some tire companies that would qualify under this ruling would fail to meet a second SBA requirement that it may have no larger than a 10 per cent share of the market in its other product lines.

The existence of these fundamental economic factors that result in large-scale operations in either an absolute or relative sense is likely to result in a diminished role for small business. Having carved out some general economic factors that limit the role of small business, we next turn to those factors that invite its development.

Economic Factors That Result in Small-Scale Operations

Small business is likely to perform a more important role if, other things being equal, the following four general economic conditions exist:

1. The rate of growth in GNP is cyclically high.
2. The pace of technological change is rapid.
3. A new industry is established and is in the early stages of its life cycle.
4. Industries in which economic circumstances favor small firms are growing fast relative to other industries or to the economy as a whole.

The first two influences relate to sales-capacity relationships. If GNP is growing rapidly, or if a new industry is in its early stages and sales press beyond its capacity, this favors the establishment of small firms to fill a need; unfortunately, however, this need may be relatively temporary. Rapidity of technological change is often the basis for providing new and very specialized services, which may lead to the need for new companies, and may thus create new industries. These new industries may be in the early, small state of their life cycle. Finally, in periods of rapid economic growth the industries in which small business operates are probably also growing rapidly. In general, the service industries are dominated by small firms, which provide a personalized service not possible in larger operations. Thus, a high income economy in which services are purchased outside the household favors small business operations.

In addition to these broad factors there are more specific types of economic influences that favor the small business firm.

Characteristics of Industries in Which Small Firms Dominate

When the conditions that lead to the existence of large firms prevail, these usually militate against small firms having an important share in such industries. However, even in industries dominated by large organizations, small firms may perform an important role. Manufacturing of automobiles, for example, is dominated by three large corporations, yet it is an industry characterized by literally thousands of small firms of a number of types. The automobile dealership is characteristically a small firm. Service stations, garages, small repair shops are also a part of the automobile industry. The aftermarket for automobile parts includes thousands of small retail outlets. Many firms continue to supply original parts to the manufacturers, although backward integration has reduced the relative importance of the independent automobile-parts manufacturer. Thus an industry dominated by large firms in some of its aspects may also provide abundant opportunities for small business.

But the industries or segments of industries in which small business predominates exhibit certain general attributes. These include the following:

1. Technological requirements minimal.
2. Managerial experience requirements perceived as unimportant.
3. Capital requirements are low.
4. Localized nature of the market.

In the characteristic small business, knowledge of complex technologies is not required. This is not to argue, however, that all small business is bereft of technological capabilities. Particularly in technologically fertile industries, such as electronics and chemicals, an individual with training and experience in one area of the industry may leave the employment of a larger firm to establish his own independent operation. However, in a wide range of wholesale and retail trade establishments, little technological background is required.

Managerial experience requirements are regarded as unimportant by many organizers of small business. It is not implied that this is the conclusion of a considered assessment of the critical capability for success, but rather that the managerial requirements for the successful conduct of a business often are not considered. Even in the small firm that represents the technological offshoot from a complex technology, or where the owner has previously been a successful executive in a larger firm, neither he himself nor his firm is likely to possess a full range of managerial competences.

For the establishment of many small firms, the initial capital requirements are characteristically low. This makes entry into the activity easy. Low initial capital requirements may also be reinforced by the availability of trade credit. In many areas of wholesale and retail trade, credit from suppliers of goods is abundant, even for the firm with a previous record of losses. As such firms expand, financing needs will grow. Often, however, what are regarded as financial needs in actuality represent needs for managerial skills. The growing small firm may have inadequate accounting records and lack financial control systems. Profit margins suffer, and because any new growing firm is heavily dependent on internal financing, low profits aggravate the problem of limited availability of funds from external sources.

The localized nature of the market may protect the small firm from competition from the large because of geographic segmentation and dispersion of markets. When transportation costs are high in relation to the value of the product, when sources of supply are local, and particularly when the economies resulting from the use of large-capital equipment are small, the localized nature of the market may provide comparative advantages for the small firm.

Conditions under which small firms proliferate create substantial problems. The fundamental problem is that under conditions where entry conditions into lines of activity are easy, a tendency for excess capacity in the industry develops. Unfavorable sales-to-capacity relationships are aggravated by a number of influences. In the early stages of the life cycle of an industry or during a business upswing, the number of new firms is increased in response to economic forces whose strength is only temporary. The general ease of entry, associated with lack of well-rounded managerial skills, throws the small business firm into an environment that is overcrowded and that places a premium on managerial skills where the possession of such skills is likely to be highly uneven.

These fundamental economic characteristics explain in considerable measure the statistics on the establishment and discontinuance of business covered in the first section of this chapter. Over 90 per cent of businesses established are small businesses organized in response to easy entry conditions. But changing economic environments, overcrowding of industries in geographic areas, lack of requisite managerial breadth, all combine to produce a high attrition rate among newly established firms in the early years of their existence. As was described above, the high birth rate of 9 per cent a year is associated with a high mortality rate of 8 per cent a year, so that net new businesses that continue in existence represent only one per cent a year. But these figures now take on much more meaning. The 9 per cent growth in new establishments is accompanied by a veritable flood of optimistic expectations and happy confidence in the benevolent opportunities provided by an enterprise system. When these are followed by the disappointments of limited sales and small profits or persistent losses, the disillusionment and disappointments are widespread. It is these unhappy experiences that give rise to vociferous lamentations and demands that "something be done for small business."

The fundamental economic position of small business is not, however, so bleak as the foregoing would imply. Another perspective on small business operations reflects more specific comparative advantages of small business.

Characteristics Peculiar to Small Businesses

There are certain characteristics found almost exclusively in small operations that give them a distinct advantage over large organizations. These attributes include the following:

1. Flexibility.
2. Speed of adaptability.
3. Personalized service.
4. Desire by the consumer for specialized or custom service or product.

Where products or production are subject to frequent changes in design or specification, the large firm is at a handicap with its heavy fixed commitments. The small firm has a greater investment in the experience and person of its owners. With a relatively small investment in fixed equipment, the owners are in a position to shift from one type of product or service to another. If heavy fixed outlays make for economies of scale, they also make for inflexibility.

Thus, for every strength of the large firm, economic circumstances can be envisaged in which such advantage becomes a weakness. One of the fundamental propositions and strong emphases of this study is that almost any accounting of the strengths and weaknesses of large and small business represent in many ways opposite sides of the same coin. A set of economic circumstances can be specified in which the attributes of large business will have a substantial advantage. On the other hand, an opposite set of economic circumstances provides a significant advantage for small business. It is, therefore, the fundamental characteristics of the economic environment that determine what the relative positions of small business and large business will be in the economy. The devil theory of the pernicious encroachment of the octopus-like tentacles of large firms squeezing out of existence the small enterprise is a fantasy that fails to look at the realities characteristic of the economic environment.

When the nature of the industry is such that management at the local levels involves complexity and rapidly changing conditions, a premium is placed on speed of adaptability. This is achieved most effectively by individual initiative. Also, where product changes are rapid, where specific product differentiation for the few is required, there is likely to be an important fundamental advantage for small business.

Inevitably in the large organization, uniformity of treatment of customers and employees requires policies to guide and control actions. This makes for a certain degree of standardized treatment and a depersonalization of activities. Personalized treatment of employees and customers will always be comparative advantages for the small firm. Thus, in basic human psychology, a bulwark is provided for the economic position of small business.

Another fundamental economic trend favors small business. In the relatively high-income, high-leisure society, increasing portions of the population desire a specialized or custom service or product. In a world in which so many products are made on a mass production basis, the desire for distinction and for products that meet the individual needs of consumers increases. The ability to purchase such desired products also increases in the high-income economy. Thus offsetting the advantages of low price that results from large-scale operations may well be the increasing competitive position of the customized product that results from the individualized approach of the small firm.

These factors that are peculiar to the favorable position of small business do not carry with them the aggravating pathologies that the more general factors described above involve. These favorable factors demonstrate basic and unique economic roles for small business.

The Position of Small Business in Individual Industries

At least three distinct classes of small business may be identified. One is the new firm in new industries. The second class is the older, relatively long-established small firm in trade with easy entry. A third is the small firm in specialized segments of technologically complex industries or where other bases for product differentiation exist. The first type may represent attractive growth opportunities. The second is subject to periodic overcapacity and expansion and contraction in the number of firms with the business cycle fluctuations. The third represents a more stable activity whose growth is likely to parallel the industry of which it is a part. Clearly, the economic position and opportunity for each of these three types of small business are substantially different.

Whether these segments of the economy in which small business is entrenched and will not be dislodged will be growing or dwindling segments depends on such economic factors as the comparative growth of industries and on the economic, social, technological, and political trends that will shape the world economy in the decades ahead.

Earlier in this study, Tables 2-1 and 2-2 provided data on the twelve broad industry classifications into which the national economy is grouped by the Department of Commerce in organizing national income statistics. Manufacturing, only one of the twelve broad industry groups, accounts for 30 per cent of national income generated and 26 per cent of employment. Within the manufacturing industries eight of the largest firms have accounted for a high percentage of output, whereas in other industries the large firms account for a very small percentage of output.

There are a total of 443 industries in manufacturing. In 121 of these, or about 27 per cent, eight firms account for more than 65 per cent of shipments. These industries are listed in Table 2-11. A review of these industries indicates that they fall in two main types of group.

One group represents those industries in which the list of factors favoring large firms operate in the industry to a considerable degree. Some of these industries (and the source of large-scale advantages) are as follows: cigarettes (advertising); petroleum products (economies of large-scale and integrated operations); tires and inner tubes (economies of scale); steel mills (economies of scale); computing and related machines (economies of scale); aircraft (large investments required); locomotives (economies of scale, integrated production).

Table 2-11—List of Products for Which the Largest Eight Firms Account for More Than 65 Per Cent of Shipments, 1963

INDUSTRY CODE	INDUSTRY	PER CENT OF LARGEST EIGHT COMPANIES
	Group 20: Food and Kindred Products	
2032	Canned specialties	83
2043	Cereal preparation	96
2044	Rice milling	66
2045	Blended and prepared flour	82
2046	Wet corn milling	93
2052	Biscuit, crackers, and cookies	68
2062	Cane sugar refining	83
2063	Beet sugar	97
2072	Chocolate and cocoa products	87
2073	Chewing gum	97
2085	Distilled liquor, except brandy	74
2087	Flavorings	70
2092	Soybean oil mills	70
2093	Vegetable oil mills, n.e.c.	83
2095	Roasted coffee	68
	Group 21: Tobacco Manufacturers	
2111	Cigarettes	100
2121	Cigars	81
2131	Chewing and smoking tobacco	83
2141	Tobacco stemming and redrying	92
	Group 22: Textile Mill Products	
2271	Woven carpets and rugs	88
2284	Thread mills	85
2291	Felt goods, n.e·c.	75
2296	Tire cord and fabric	96
2297	Scouring and combing plants	79

INDUSTRY CODE	INDUSTRY	PER CENT OF LARGEST EIGHT COMPANIES
	Group 24: Lumber and Wood Products	
2445	Cooperage	71
	Group 26: Paper and Allied Products	
2611	Pulp mills	72
2646	Pressed and molded pulp goods	88
2647	Sanitary paper products	76
2654	Sanitary food containers	74
2655	Fiber cans, tubes, drums, etc.	72
2661	Building paper and board mills	68
	Group 27: Printing and Publishing	
2771	Greeting card manufacturing	71
	Group 28: Chemicals and Allied Products	
2812	Alkalies and chlorine	88
2813	Industrial gases	86
2814	Cyclic (coal tar) crudes	100
2815	Intermediate coal tar products	70
2816	Inorganic pigments	84
2822	Synthetic rubber	80
2823	Cellulosic man-made fibers	100
2824	Organic fibers, noncellulosic	99
2833	Medicinals and botanicals	79
2841	Soap and other detergents	80
2861	Gum and wood chemicals	71
2892	Explosives	86
2895	Carbon black	100
	Group 39: Petroleum and Coal Products	
2952	Asphalt felts and coatings	66
2999	Petroleum and coal products, n.e.c.	84
	Group 30: Rubber and Plastics Products, n.e.c.	
3011	Tires and inner tubes	89
3021	Rubber footwear	77
3031	Reclaimed rubber	100
	Group 31: Leather and Leather Products	
3121	Industrial leather belting	77
	Group 32: Stone, Clay, and Glass Products	
3211	Flat glass	99+
3221	Glass containers	72
3229	Pressed and blown glass, n.e.c.	81
3253	Ceramic wall and floor tile	69
3261	Vitreous plumbing fixtures	78
3262	Vitreous china food utensils	88
3263	Fine earthenware food utensils	83
3264	Porcelain electrical supplies	67
3275	Gypsum products	97
3291	Abrasive products	67
3292	Asbestos products	76
3296	Mineral wool	83
3297	Nonclay refactories	66

INDUSTRY CODE	INDUSTRY	PER CENT OF LARGEST EIGHT COMPANIES
	Group 33: Primary Metal Industries	
3312	Blast furnaces and steel mills	69
3313	Electrometallurgical products	95
3331	Primary copper	98
3332	Primary lead	100
3333	Primary zinc	90
3334	Primary aluminum	100
3339	Primary nonferrous metals	78
3351	Copper rolling and drawing	67
3352	Aluminum rolling and drawing	79
3356	Rolling and drawing, n.e.c.	66
3392	Nonferrous forgings	91
	Group 34: Fabricated Metal Products	
3411	Metal cans	85
3421	Cutlery	76
3425	Hand saws and saw blades	66
3431	Metal plumbing fixtures	68
*3492	Safes and vaults	95
3496	Collapsible tubes	92
3497	Metal foil and leaf	78
	Group 35: Machinery	
3511	Steam engines and turbines	98
3534	Elevators and moving stairways	73
3562	Ball and roller bearings	76
3571	Computing and related machines	80
3572	Typewriters	99
3576	Scales and balances	69
3579	Office machines, n.e.c.	71
3581	Automatic vending machines	72
3586	Measuring and dispensing pumps	80
	Group 36: Electrical Machinery	
3612	Transformers	79
3622	Industrial controls	69
3624	Carbon and graphic products	92
3631	Household cooking equipment	68
3632	Household refrigerators	91
3633	Household laundry equipment	95
3635	Household vacuum cleaners	96
3636	Sewing machines	93
3641	Electric lamps	96
3652	Phonograph records	75
3661	Telephone; telegraph apparatus	96
3671	Electron tubes, receiving type	99
3672	Cathode ray picture tubes	95
3673	Electron tubes, transmitting	77
3691	Storage batteries	78
3692	Primary batteries, dry and wet	98
3693	X-ray apparatus and tubes	79
3694	Engine electrical equipment	79

INDUSTRY CODE	INDUSTRY	PER CENT OF LARGEST EIGHT COMPANIES
	Group 37: Transportation Equipment	
3715	Truck trailers	69
3717	Motor vehicles and parts	83
3721	Aircraft	83
3722	Aircraft engines and parts	77
*3723	Aircraft propellers and parts	99
3741	Locomotives and parts	99
3742	Railroad and street cars	73
3751	Motorcycles, bicycles, and parts	77
	Group 38: Instruments and Related Products	
3822	Automatic temperature controls	75
3861	Photographic equipment	76
3872	Watches	72
	Group 39: Miscellaneous Manufacturing	
3914	Silverware and plated ware	66
3943	Children's vehicles	67
3982	Hard surface floor coverings	98
3983	Matches	92

Source: U.S. Bureau of the Census, *Concentration Ratios in Manufacturing Industry, 1963,* Report Prepared for the Subcommittee on Antitrust and Monopoly, United States Senate, 89th Congress, 2nd Session, Part 1 (Washington, D.C.: U.S. Government Printing Office, 1966), pp. 6–37.
* 1958 figures used.

In a large number of other industries listed, the product line is so narrow and the size of operations and the value of shipments are so small that the classification is not really meaningful. Such industries are so narrow and their cross elasticity with other products is so high that to term them concentrated industries is not realistic in any practical sense. Examples of such narrow product definitions included in these industry groups are: hatters' fur; suspenders and garters; cigar boxes; window shades; inorganic color pigments; fatty acids; hand and saw blades; watch cases; and tobacco pipes.

The industry groups characterized by a high percentage of industry shipments by the eight largest firms satisfy one or more characteristics set forth in the earlier list of ten factors giving rise to large-scale operations. In contrast, the industries in which the eight largest firms account for less than 25 per cent of shipments represent a different type (see Table 2-12). These are industries in which the small firms perform a more significant role: food and kindred products; apparel and other fabricated textile products; lumber and furniture products; printing and publishing industries; handbags and purses; stone; clay and glass products; fabricated metal products; toys and costume jewelry; machinery industries involving special dies and tools;

Table 2-12—List of Products for Which the Largest Eight Firms Account for Less Than 25 Per Cent of Shipments, 1963

INDUSTRY CODE	INDUSTRY	PER CENT OF LARGEST EIGHT COMPANIES
	Group 20: Food and Kindred Products	
2013	Meat processing plants	23
2015	Poultry dressing plants	20
2021	Creamery butter	19
2086	Bottled and canned soft drinks	17
	Group 22: Textile Mill Products	
2253	Knit outerwear mills	16
	Group 23: Apparel and Related Products	
2311	Men's and boy's suits and coats	23
2329	Men's and boy's clothing, n.e.c.	19
2331	Blouses	15
2335	Dresses	9
2337	Women's suits, coats, and skirts	11
2339	Women's outerwear, n.e.c.	22
2341	Women's and children's underwear	17
2351	Millinery	14
2361	Children's dresses and blouses	20
2363	Children's coats and suits	24
2369	Children's outerwear, n.e.c.	23
2371	Fur goods	8
2392	Housefurnishings, n.e.c.	24
2395	Pleating and stitching	13
2397	Schiffli machine embroideries	21
2399	Textile products, n.e.c.	22
	Group 24: Lumber and Wood Products	
2411	Logging camps and contractors	19
2421	Sawmills and planing mills	14
2426	Hardwood dimension and flooring	22
2431	Millwork plants	10
2499	Wood products, n.e.c.	19
	Group 25: Furniture and Fixtures	
2511	Wood furniture, not upholstered	16
2512	Wood furniture, upholstered	18
2514	Metal household furniture	20
2541	Wood partitions and fixtures	8
	Group 26: Paper and Allied Products	
2652	Set-up paperboard boxes	19
	Group 27: Printing and Publishing	
2711	Newspapers	22
2751	Printing, except lithographic	19
2752	Printing, lithographic	10
2789	Bookbinding and related work	17
2791	Typesetting	10
2793	Photoengraving	13

INDUSTRY CODE	INDUSTRY	PER CENT OF LARGEST EIGHT COMPANIES
	Group 29: Petroleum and Coal Products	
2951	Paving mixtures and blocks	21
	Group 30: Paper and Plastics Products, n.e.c.	
3079	Plastics products, n.e.c.	21
	Group 31: Leather and Leather Products	
3171	Handbags and purses	18
	Group 32: Stone, Clay, and Glass Products	
3251	Brick and structural tile	19
3271	Concrete block and brick	7
3272	Other concrete products	23
3273	Ready mixed concrete	7
	Group 34: Fabricated Metal Products	
3441	Fabricated structural steel	20
3442	Metal doors, sash, and trim	13
3444	Sheetmetal work	16
3446	Architectural metal work	19
3451	Screw machine products	8
3461	Metal stampings	19
3471	Plating and polishing	8
3481	Fabricated wire products, n.e.c.	19
3494	Valves and pipe fittings	22
3499	Fabricated metal products	22
	Group 35: Machinery	
3544	Special dies and tools	9
3559	Special industry machinery	18
3565	Industrial patterns	14
3599	Miscellaneous machinery	12
	Group 36: Electrical Machinery	
3679	Electronic components, n.e.c.	21
	Group 37: Transportation Equipment	
3799	Transportation equipment, n.e.c.	23
	Group 39: Miscellaneous Manufacturers	
3993	Signs and advertising displays	8
3999	Miscellaneous products, n.e.c.	22

Source: U.S. Bureau of the Census, *Concentration Ratios in Manufacturing Industry, 1963,* Report Prepared for the Subcommittee on Antitrust and Monopoly, United States Senate, 89th Congress, 2nd Session, Part 1 (Washington, D.C.: U.S. Government Printing Office, 1966), pp. 6–37.

and special industrial machinery. These industries have the common characteristics of the absence of any significant economic advantage to large-scale operations.

In these industry classifications, several factors have accounted for the dominant position of small firms. The activities in which local markets appear to have been important include the following categories:[2]

1. Local consumer markets.
2. Local business markets.
3. Local construction markets.
4. Metal service markets.
5. Source of raw materials.

The local consumer markets include the general categories of fresh foods such as meats, dairy products, confectionaries, bread and soft drinks, and newspapers. Several influences have diminished the position of small business in these markets. Improved preservation methods have facilitated large-scale production and distribution. This trend has been reinforced by a fundamental change in the patterns of urban transportation. When consumers were heavily dependent on public transportation systems, the pattern of retail distribution was very different. The downtown department stores were located at the core terminals of the transportation arteries. Benefiting from heavy traffic flows, the downtown department store could provide variety and depth of choice. At the same time a great network of small local outlets developed to serve the dominant convenience needs of consumers. The "Mom and Pop" store, particularly, provided services late at night and on weekends for those who wished to avoid the longer or inconvenient trip. This pattern of retail distribution was greatly altered with the increased use of the automobile. Increased mobility was further stimulated by the rise of government lending programs on housing, which enabled a family to locate in the suburbs with a small monthly payment and avoid the crowded conditions of the city. The automobile made it possible to go to both the place of work and to decentralized shopping facilities. The rise of the discount house was related in substantial measure to the availability of low-rent locations with ample parking facilities that could be readily reached by the automobile.

Thus a revolution has been wrought in many aspects of retail distribution. As a consequence, there has been a reorganization and regrouping of retail activities. The number of independent outlets has decreased. The supermarket is basically a response to the convenience of ready access by automobile. Chains of supermarkets have developed to achieve economies of purchasing and distribution.

The position of small business has been more favorably maintained in the other types of local markets listed. In newspapers there have been diverse trends. Some economies of scale and some advantages of combining activities have resulted in attrition in the number of metropolitan newspapers. On the other hand, the number of neighborhood newspapers has increased.

Similarly, the local business markets in commercial printing and signs and advertising displays have continued to represent areas of vigorous activity for small business. The reason is that these represent personalized or differentiated services.

In various aspects of the construction markets, small firms continue to dominate. This is because of its local nature. To move heavy equipment to a distant building site would be very expensive. In addition, there is a high labor content in the work. Thus, various types of economies of scale do not exist in the construction industry and, as a consequence, it continues to be dominated by small firms.

The metal service industries provide specialized functions performed in the interstices of broader industrial activities. Many of the small firms in the metal service markets are satellite firms. Their number is a function of the total amount of activity going on in the area and is thus closely tied to industrial development of individual regions.

The industries greatly influenced by the source of raw materials have characteristically been mining, logging, agriculture, fisheries, wineries, and related canning and other food preparation activities. These types of processing industries have in the past tended to be small-scale because of heavy transportation costs of raw materials as well as heavy storage costs. But again, technological and transportation changes have resulted in economies of scale and economies of decentralized canning operations guided by a large business firm.

In contrast to markets in which small business firms predominate because of geographic segmentation, there are a number of national markets in which small firms have historically played an important role. These include apparel, leather (excluding shoes), and furniture. The explanation for predominance of small firms in these small industry groups, even though the products are produced for national markets, differs for each product. For apparel and leather, styles change from years to year. In addition, there are no significant economies of scale in manufacturing. Because of the wide variety of sizes, shapes, and changing styles, national advertising to establish brand acceptance has not been feasible. With regard to furniture, transportation costs have been an important consideration, in addition to the wide variety of size, shapes, and styles. It is cheaper to ship the compact lumber near the consumption markets than to transport the bulky finished furniture. Thus, the furniture industry has many characteristics of the locally oriented markets described earlier in this section.

Small business has predominated in retailing because of many characteristics of easy entry. Capital requirements can be quite small, trade credit is abundantly available, and there is a wide variety of sources of assistance. In addition, experience can readily be acquired by employment in other retail establishments. The small business in retailing is characteristically a specialty shop. Thus personalized styles and personal service can be emphasized in competition with the large department stores and discount houses.

The service industries represent a large and rapidly growing sector in response to an economy of high income and increased leisure. The service sector now accounts for 11 per cent of national income generated and almost 17 per cent of total employment. One of the largest single segments in the American economy, it is not far behind the wholesale and retail trade, which accounts for 18 per cent of the number of persons employed. And both are not far behind manufacturing, which accounts for 26 per cent. The four areas of manufacturing, wholesale and retail trade, services, and government account for almost four-fifths, or 80 per cent, of total employment.

The service industry also has important local characteristics. Among the very rapidly growing segments of the service industries are hotels and motels, personal services (especially beauty and barber shops), shoe repair, garment repair, and laundry and cleaning service. Auto repair and services have grown with the burgeoning automobile industry. The electrical repair shops, including radio and television, have been areas of rapid growth as well. In the high-income, high-leisure economy, amusement and recreation services have grown substantially.

Thus we see that small business has had a characteristically predominant position in a number of identifiable industries—those in which the fundamental economic and management characteristics of small business have provided a relative advantage over large firms. The analysis of the industries in which small business predominates emphasizes that the fundamental economic position of small business is determined by basic economic factors. It is significant that the industrial distribution of small business is not haphazard. This is not a matter of decisions on the part of government to put small business in certain areas, or on the part of large business to pre-empt certain industries. The fundamental determinants are established by the economics of these industries. Thus the extent to which public policy can, on a sound economic basis, alter the position of small business is circumscribed. The position of small business and its future growth in the economy will be determined primarily by general economic and technological trends.

Trends Influencing the Future Position of Small Business

Twelve important developments will have an impact on the future of small business. These may be identified as follows:

1. Rate of total economic growth.
2. Differential industrial growth.
3. Energy sources.
4. Transportation.
5. Metropolitanization.
6. Technological change.
7. Business structure and organization.
8. Demographic characteristics.
9. Labor markets.
10. Management technology.
11. Franchising.
12. Leased departments.

The higher the general economic rate of growth in the economy, the more favorable the environment for small business. A faster rate of growth implies an accelerated movement to a high-income economy, so that the opportunities for the customized and specialized activities of small business are enhanced. Furthermore, general sales to capacity relationships are more favorable.

A second major economic trend is the differential growth of individual industries. As pointed out before, in the high-income economy, the service sector grows at a differentially faster rate. A high rate of growth of the service industries is favorable to the development of small firms.

A third major factor is the nature of energy sources. The decentralization of energy sources into small units is continuing. One major source of decentralized energy is the increased feasibility at low cost of nuclear energy. In addition, various types of energy cell devices are permitting the establishment of energy sources in remote areas at low cost. This permits further decentralization of industry and favors the establishment of small firms isolated to a greater degree by transportation factors than by energy factors. The general characteristics of the energy industry have long favored the establishment and successful operation of small concerns. We have for a long time taken it for granted that the opportunity of purchasing electric power in small quantities has been a factor that has favored the small concern. The price of purchasing energy in small quantities as compared to large quantities has not operated as a differential disadvantage to small business.

A fourth trend, related to energy sources, is found in the nature and cost of transportation. In general, improved transportation systems tend to widen markets. This reduces the geographical segmentation of business operations and tends to weaken the position of small business. On the other hand, the existence of a transportation system that permits small quantities to be picked up and delivered at competitive costs has favored small business. It has permitted specialization and contributed to broader markets for specialized small business activities. In addition, the development of low-cost air freight shipments has also extended the trend toward economical shipment of small quantities, which favors small business.

A fifth important social and cultural trend has been the metropolitanization of population. The increased mobility provided by the automobile has reduced the convenience advantage of the local neighborhood store. This has militated against the position of small business and has resulted in the disappearance of a large number of small retail outlets whose main economic function was that of convenience and service. On the other hand, the development of many regional shopping areas or centers has also produced a place for small business.

As satellite and service operations within larger shopping centers small business has benefitted. The large shopping area with ample parking space brings a large traffic flow to a particular area. Small businesses performing specialized, personalized services benefit from such traffic flows.

A sixth trend is that of the increased dynamism of technological change. New products and new industries have provided new opportunities for small business. In addition within the broader opportunities for technological differentiation, the opportunities for specialization in narrow product segments are multiplied for small business. Technological change has resulted in an increased development of both producer and consumer durable goods. Despite technological change, the durability of capital goods makes them of continued economic value to small business units. Existence of a market for second-hand equipment, particularly in the light manufacturing and service industries, has provided small firms with the opportunity of obtaining capital equipment either at a small investment cost or through leasing and has also made it feasible for small firms to be established with low initial investment outlays. Furthermore, the growth of consumer purchase of durable goods provides an economic base for a number of types of service activities by small firms. Such goods require maintenance and repair services. The localized nature of their distribution and the convenience of having the related services performed in the home or in local neighborhood stores has stimulated the establishment of small firms to provide such services. The existence of markets for consumer durable goods has resulted in a stock of used items. This, in turn, has given rise to secondary markets conducted primarily by small independent dealers.

Industrial organization, seventh in the list of trends, has influenced the development of distribution methods that have favored small business. Manufacturers in a number of lines of business have marketed products or services through independently owned outlets. The decentralization of retail selling into the hands of independent owners motivates a more rapid awareness and response to shifting consumer tastes and preferences than might be the situation if such retail outlets were managed by employees relatively far removed from the centers of corporate level decisions.

Related to industrial organization aspects, the assertion is often made that the position of small business is certain to decline over time because of acquisitions by large firms. If the economic position of small firms were exactly balanced with large firms, the share of the economy for each would remain the same. But it is reasoned, if some small firms are acquired by large firms, the share of the large firms will increase. By definition, acquisition of large firms by small firms would still eliminate small firms. But the foregoing overlooks an important motivational consideration. The opportunity to sell-out creates an important stimulus for small firms. Uncertain future profits can be transformed into certain capital values. Gains that otherwise would be subject to personal income tax rates can be subjected to the lower capital gains tax rates. Thus the existence of a market for the capital assets of small business can provide a powerful incentive to the creation of new small businesses. Disappearances by acquisitions may thus be more than offset by the stimulus to the formation of new firms.

The eighth set of trends relates to such demographic factors as the age distribution of the population, which influences opportunities for sales of various types of goods. The rapid growth of the toy industry in recent years has been related to a high growth rate in the preteen-age population, accompanied by a high-income society. The number of people in the 35–54 age bracket, from which independent owners of firms predominantly come, influences the supply of small firms for a given market demand. Another demographic factor is the extension and broadening of educational levels. When a large proportion of the population receives increased education and knowledge of both managerial and technical factors in our society, the fundamental competence for operating small business units is increased, favoring the health and survival of small firms.

A ninth important area is the nature of labor markets. Tendencies toward rigidity and inflexibility have been introduced into labor contracts. The raising of minimum wages and the adoption of industry-wide union contracts reduces the flexibility of small business, as does the rigidity of job classifications resulting from union agreements. However, such general regulations are more enforceable and more often enforced in large organizations. Although in theory they are applied without deviation to small firms as well, in practice these general requirements are softened or bent in their application to individual small firms. Thus, in the administration of inflexible wage relations, realistic custom introduces a necessary degree of flexibility for their application to small business units.

A tenth trend is the increased accumulation of improved management technology. An increased body of literature and knowledge of management methods has been developed in recent years, as the methods for conducting business operations have become more formalized. To some degree this trend has favored the large business firm because it can more easily adopt such a body of knowledge and put the principles into operation through policy and procedure manuals.

However, the knowledge is equally available to the owners of small firms. Knowledge that otherwise might have had to be acquired by experience can now be achieved in part by formal courses and by reading. Thus, a considerable portion of advanced management technology has been successfully assimilated by the owners of small business units.

The increased utilization of efficient management skills by small business has been furthered by the growth of franchising—the eleventh of the trends listed above. Basically, franchising is a system of relationships by which efficient management practices for specific industries can be transmitted to a wide number of independent owners of business operations. Management policies, accounting records, and financial controls can be formalized and transmitted in written documents or through training programs. It is no accident that the formalization of management technology should have stimulated an increase in the extent and use of franchising during the last decade.

Finally, there is the related trend of the development of leased departments. A specialist in a particular segment of retail operations can obtain a number of benefits by leasing a department in a larger department store or discount store operation. The leased department represents an independent operation. The entrepreneur can bring to his area of responsibility the benefits of specialization and experience that he may have developed. But in addition, he receives the benefit of the large flow of consumer traffic brought under one roof by the large number of goods and services offered there. The organization of a complex of retail goods and services provides the convenience to the consumer of a one-stop shopping effort to fill a variety of needs.

These trends will have an important impact on the future economic position of small business. Some of the trends will favor small business, others will diminish its relative role; the net effect will be considered in the following section.

Forecasting the Future Position of Small Business

The methodology for forecasting the quantitative position of small business in the economic environment of the future is well established. First, the relative position of small business in individual industries is determined. Second, the relative growth rate of individual industries is forecast. Third, changes in industry characteristics that will influence the relative position of small business firms are identified. The application of this methodology must be related to the fundamental trends outlined in the preceding sections of this chapter. Taking both broad categories of forces into account, an increase in the number of small firms can be forecast for some sectors and a decrease in others.

In general, small businesses in local consumer markets and in markets segmented geographically by sources of raw materials are likely to decline. This decline will be due to improvement in transportation methods and technologies of production.

In particular, the economies of scale have resulted in mergers and larger units of operation in the apparel industry. Some parts of the apparel industry will be favorably influenced by the high-income, increased-leisure economy. These will include sports and casual clothing as well as high-quality individualized clothing. Thus, economies of scale will decrease the total number of units in the industry, but the number of small firms will grow in particular branches.

The high-income economy will favor the growth of firms in the toy industry and in sporting goods. However, trends toward larger-scale operations in the manufacturing end of both of these industries may be accompanied by an increased use of supermarkets and discount houses in retail distribution. The position of small firms in these categories may therefore decline.

In the metal working industries the position of small business may be expected to expand. With the increased mechanization of industry and with favorable economic growth in the economy as a whole, there will be an expansion in the need for specialized functions to be performed by individual small business units.

Although increased mergers and integration of activities will continue to take place in retail trade, opportunities for small business will also continue to exist. In the high-income, increased-leisure economy, there will be ample opportunity for focusing on specialized services and individualized products. The role of the specialty retail establishment will continue to be an important one.

Over-all, therefore, there is not a clear indication that the position of small business in the years ahead will either increase or decline in relative importance in the economy. Its position in individual industries will shift, but the relative growth of industries and its relative share in the total economy will determine its position. Small firms will continue to benefit from supplying specialized services and from their flexibility, adaptability, and ingenuity.

Important in the future position of small business will be the development and application of management skills of small business firms. There is considerable competition at the margin between small firms and large. The relative future position of large firms as compared to small firms will largely depend on the effectiveness with which new developments in management technology are applied.

The total environment is certain to change. The relative position of large and small business will therefore depend in part on the effectiveness with which each adapts to the changing environment. However, the basic advantages of each category, large and small, are not subject to such massive shifts that the position of either is likely to change in any substantial degree in the years ahead.

3

The Effect of Size on
Profits in Manufacturing
Industries

Theodore A. Andersen

Almost half a century of data are now available on the effect of size on profitability. From these data it is possible to attempt some evaluation of how the small firm has been faring insofar as relative profitability is concerned. The objectives of this study are several. The first will be to provide a general assessment of the trends in the competitive position of small business. Secondly, attempts will be made to identify the particular industrial sectors where small business has performed relatively well and those where it has done relatively poorly. Reference will then be made to the characteristics of these specified industries which perhaps explain the performance of small business in those particular environments. Finally, some generalizations will be developed concerning the prospects of small business, largely on the basis of the empirical findings of this study.

Data Limitations

The strength of the conclusions reached by this study are of course affected by the degree of reliability of the data used. Unfortunately, the deficiencies in the data are numerous and, at times, serious. The major data limitations appear to be as follows:

First, new manufacturing companies tend to operate at a loss in their early years and they also tend to be small. Thus, one of the reasons why small companies show lower rates of return is that they are new. It would be desirable to analyze the rates of return, by size of company, for firms five or more years old. This probably would show smaller differences in the profit rates of the various-sized companies. Unfortunately, this type of data is unavailable so we have little basis for estimating how much effect the elimination of the relatively new companies from our data would have.

Second, the data on profits by size of manufacturing companies are classified into industry groups that are relatively large, with each encompassing a rather broad line of products. Thus, within an industry the competitive position of smaller firms can be expected to vary greatly, depending on which of the products within the industry they may be manufacturing. Therefore, in concluding that in given industries small firms fare poorly, we are undoubtedly oversimplifying the prevailing conditions as they affect the relative profitability of small firms. There certainly would be many exceptions to generalizations of this type.

Third, in the smaller firms the officers and owners are probably the same persons and therefore their interests are more likely to be the same than would be the case in the larger corporation. To avoid taxation and double taxation, there is more incentive in the small firm to underreport profits and to overcompensate officers through salaries and other means. As tax rates were increased in the 1930's over the 1920's and were higher after World War II and the Korean War than before them, so have the incentives to underreport profits been increasing. Because this is accomplished more readily by the small firms, it is to be expected that their reported profit margins would show declines over time relative to all firms in rough proportion to the rise in corporate income tax rates.

Fourth, because of the price inflation since World War I, difficulties are encountered in observing comparable-sized companies over a long time span. A company with $100,000 of assets in 1920, solely because of inflation, might have $200,000 of assets in 1960 with no change in the physical scale of operations.

Fifth, the classification of a company as small is necessarily quite arbitrary. An automobile manufacturer with assets of a billion dollars is relatively small in the United States economy, but a printing company, in a highly specialized branch of printing, may be properly classified as relatively large if it has assets of $25,000. Thus ideally it would be preferable to vary the definition of "small" among industries and among product lines within industries. However, lack of information prevents this type of classification of companies.

Finally, no single ratio exists for measuring profitability in a completely satisfactory way. This study uses, wherever possible, profits after taxes to net worth, instead of profits plus interest to total assets. There are several reasons for this approach. Larger size may make possible more advantageous use of debt financing, which would tend to raise the rate of return on net worth. Because one of the purposes of the study is to evaluate the possible advantages of larger size, including financial, the ratio of profits to net worth is the relevant measurement to use. Also, data on interest payments are inadequate, making it difficult to ascertain accurately the ratio of profits plus interest to assets. Some interest expense is incurred by selling accounts receivable at a discount, but this is not reported as such. Some firms obtain extra credit from suppliers and pass up purchase discounts rather than using bank credit, paying interest, and taking advantage of purchase discounts. In effect, by foregoing purchase discounts, they are incurring an unreported interest cost. In the case of leasing, interest costs may effectively be borne but not reported. The effect that size has on such practices is not known but, because of this uncertainty, the ratios of profits plus interest to assets may be suspect.

The seriousness of these data inadequacies is difficult to judge and varies, depending on what particular questions are being examined. Interpretations of findings presented in this chapter are subject to the weakness of the data bases.

Earlier Studies of Profit and Size

Major contributions to an understanding of the effect of size on rates of return have been made by Professors Crum and Stekler, and indirectly, by Ralph Epstein.[1] Although Epstein's analysis focused on the variance by industry of the rates of return of the larger corporations during the 1919–1928 period, he also made a similar analysis of some 1,500 smaller firms. Comparison of the two sets of findings makes possible some judgments about the performance of small business in this earlier period.

The findings of these three analysts provide some interesting contrasts. Epstein showed that the smaller firms were doing quite well relative to the larger ones, whereas Crum showed that during the depression of the 1930's the profit position of the smaller firms deteriorated much more sharply. For example, as shown in Table 3-1,

Table 3-1—Ratio of Profit Margins of Smaller Firms to Those of Larger Firms, 1922–1928

	1922	1923	1924	1925	1926	1927	1928
Rubber	206	140	137	79	188	178	977
Paper	213	140	65	104	165	133	216
Chemicals	141	176	171	109	116	177	85
Textiles	88	88	164	125	135	130	146
Food	116	123	113	142	107	99	96
Metals	141	119	110	89	86	116	122
Leather	110	98	113	149	76	95	96
Lumber	97	99	81	64	92	155	136
Stone, clay, glass	99	76	65	78	87	94	69
Special mfg.	68	50	74	77	58	79	75
Printing	61	66	68	77	63	68	57
All manufacturing	132	121	111	94	94	122	105

Note: The ratios for 1919, 1920, and 1921 were 92, 111, and 376, respectively.

Epstein found the profit margins of the smaller manufacturing corporations as a group to be higher than those of the larger firms for each of the years 1922 through 1928, except for 1925 and 1926. In marked contrast, Table 3-2, based on Crum's study, shows that the differences between the rates of return of the smaller firms and those of all corporations, expressed in percentage points, were substantial, particularly in 1931, 1932, and 1933.

Most of the differences between the results obtained by Epstein and those by Crum can be explained by the fact that the former's study was based on a sample of smaller firms and included only companies that operated at a profit.

Table 3-2—Differences in Percentage Points Between the Rates of
Return of Corporations with Assets of Under $250,000
and the Industry as a Whole, 1931–1936

	1931	1932	1933	1934	1935	1936
Tobacco	−17.9	−23.0	−11.6	−16.0	−17.2	−16.8
Leather	−14.4	−15.8	−11.8	−10.1	−11.3	−10.2
Paper	−9.3	−10.7	−4.4	−4.4	−4.2	−4.2
Lumber	−12.7	−11.9	−9.3	−9.0	−6.5	−5.8
Primary metals	−18.3	−15.1	−10.8	−7.8	−8.1	−6.7
Textiles	−15.1	−16.4	−11.3	−8.3	−8.2	−7.7
Stone, clay, glass	−11.6	−12.6	−9.8	−10.9	−9.5	−7.9
Rubber	−5.5	−12.9	−11.6	−0.3	−10.3	−5.9
Printing	−11.2	−13.0	−10.6	−6.4	−8.1	−6.6
Chemicals	−9.8	−12.4	−7.3	−6.4	−8.2	−7.0
Food	−7.8	−11.6	−11.0	−7.6	−10.4	−7.3
All manufacturing	−12.8	−15.2	−10.0	−8.3	−8.9	−7.2

Crum's sample of the larger firms, on the other hand, included both deficit and income firms. For the years 1922 and later, this difference is believed to be of lesser significance because the number of large com-

Table 3-3—Comparative Rates of Return for Net Income Corporations

	Corporations with Assets Under $50,000 (Per Cent)	All Corporations (Per Cent)
1931	11.9	7.9
1932	9.4	6.0
1933	9.0	6.2
1934	11.3	8.3
1935	11.4	9.9
1936	13.7	10.1

panies that operated at a deficit was little more than 3 per cent in any one year, and in only one year, 1928, was it as high as 3.7 per cent. It should be remembered, however, that many small firms operate at a loss and if this deficit group were included, the ratios for the smaller firms would have been much lower. In general, when only net income firms are considered, the smaller firms show higher rates of return than do the medium- and large-sized companies. This was true even during the early 1930's, as is shown in Table 3-3.

Stekler's study concerned the relative profitability of the smaller firms in the 1947–1957 period. One of his significant findings was that these firms on an over-all basis held their own between the 1947–1951 and 1955–1957 periods insofar as their relative profitability is concerned. This is shown in Table 3-4. However, among industries there was substantial change: ten industries showed the position of smaller firms to be worsening, in eight cases they were improving, for electrical machines there was no change, and for all manufacturing the ratio im-

Table 3-4—Profit Ratio of Firms with Assets of Less Than $250,000, Expressed in Index Form (Profit Ratio of Total Industry = 100)

	1947–1951	1955–1957
Food and beverage	45	74
Tobacco	8	52
Textile	21	negative
Apparel	40	69
Lumber	63	46
Furniture	62	59
Paper	75	72
Printing	101	94
Chemical	56	64
Petroleum	142	50
Rubber	106	96
Leather	26	38
Stone, clay, glass	86	67
Primary metal	80	92
Fabricated metal	97	88
Machinery	80	94
Electrical machinery	47	47
Transportation	33	65
Scientific instruments	81	72
All manufacturing	66	74

Source: H. O. Stekler, *Profitability and Size of Firm* (Berkeley, Calif.: Institute of Business and Economic Research, University of California, 1963), p. 53.
Note: Profit data is adjusted to compensate for possible excess officers' compensation. Profit ratios are measured by comparing profits after taxes plus interest to assets.

proved from 66 to 74. For the ten industries showing declines, the average drop was 19 index points; for the eight industries showing increases, the average rise was 21 index points. This indicates that changes in relative positions were substantial.

Epstein, Crum, and Stekler were all concerned with the problem of excessive officers' compensation, and the latter two developed some estimates of its impact on rates of return. Crum found that if profits and officers' compensation were combined, their ratio to net worth was higher for the smaller companies than the industry average (Table 3-5).

Stekler estimated the amount of officers' compensation that was believed to be excessive and then added this computed excess to reported profits. This adjustment had the effect of increasing by about 4 percentage points the rates of return of the smaller firms, but for firms with assets of $5 million or more it had very little effect (see

Table 3-5—Fate of Return Counting Full Compensation of Officers as Profits (Per Cent)

Asset Size Class (000's)	1931	1932	1933	1934	1935	1936
Under $50,000	4.9	−6.1	4.8	15.5	22.0	31.1
$50–100	3.7	−3.1	3.8	8.9	11.3	17.2
100–250	1.3	−3.2	2.0	5.6	8.3	13.2
250–500	0.5	−3.1	1.0	4.0	6.4	10.1
500–1,000	−0.5	−3.4	0.6	3.0	5.2	8.6
1,000–5,000	−1.2	−3.1	−0.4	2.4	4.4	7.1
5,000–10,000	−0.7	−3.0	−0.8	2.0	3.7	6.4
10,000–50,000	0.3	−2.0	−0.2	2.9	4.8	6.2
50,000–100,000	2.4	0.5	1.1	3·2	4.5	6.3
100,000 and over	—	—	—	—	—	4.8
All companies	1.1	−1.3	0.7	3.2	5.0	6.8

Table 3-6). This method used by Stekler for measuring excess officers' compensation was as follows: The ratio of officers' compensation to sales was computed for each asset-size class in each industry for the no-net-income firms (firms operating at a loss). It was believed that the firms operating at a loss would have little or no incentive to overpay officers. These ratios were than applied to the sales in the corresponding asset-size classes in the same industries to arrive at estimated normal officers' compensation. The difference between actual compensation and the computed "normal" compensation was added to reported profits, with the results already referred to in Table 3-6.

This adjustment assumes that officers in profit-making firms are not worth more than those in companies operating at a loss. It also assumes that to spend relatively more on management is an unnecessary drain on profits. Because these assumptions are not believed to be valid, the increase in profits accomplished when adjustment is made for excess officers' compensation is viewed as excessive. The concern of this study is generally with changes over time in the relative profitability of the smaller firms, rather than the actual level of the rates of return.

Therefore, no adjustment of profit rates has been attempted to correct for possible excessive officer's compensation.

Table 3-6—Comparison of Rates of Return After Taxes on Assets by Size Class for All Manufacturing Corporations, Before and After Adjustment for Officers' Compensation, 1947–1951 Average

Asset-Size Class (000 Dollars)	Rate of Return Unadjusted (Per Cent)	Rate of Return After Adjustment for Officers' Excess Compensation (Per Cent)
0–50	−5.1	−1.3
50–100	3.1	7.3
100–250	5.5	8.9
250–500	7.0	9.6
500–1,000	8.2	10.0
1,000–5,000	9.3	10.1
5,000–10,000	9.9	10.3
10,000–50,000	9.9	10.1
50,000–100,000	9.7	9.8
100,000–plus	9.2	9.2
Weighted industry average of all but largest class	8.9	9.8

The findings of Epstein, Crum, and Stekler cannot be compared directly because the bases of their data vary too much. However, it does appear that from World War I to the present, the small firms that operated at a profit have enjoyed rates of return above the industry average for net income firms. Secondly, the smaller firms were especially hard hit by the depression of the 1930's. Finally, in the first decade following World War II there were substantial changes among the major industries in the relative rates of return of the smaller firms. In many industries their position worsened substantially; in many other instances it improved significantly, but on an over-all basis gains were realized.

The Profit Performance of Small Business, 1947–1965

Almost two decades of post-World War II data are now available on the effect of size on rates of return. Because the economic disruptions of the 1930's were so great and the data of the 1920's were inadequate in many respects, these postwar data represent a large portion of the total information we have on the effect of size on profits. As such they warrant careful analysis. The data for the 1953–1965 period are particularly important because corporate income tax rates were quite stable throughout this period and a "buyers" market generally prevailed after the Korean War.

Tables 3-7, 3-8, and 3-9 show the profit performance of small business for the 1947–1960, 1947–1949, and 1958–1960 periods. After 1960

Table 3-7—Index of Profit Margins, 1947–1960
Corporations with Assets of Less Than $250,000

	1947–1960 Index	1947–1949 Index	Rank	1958–1960 Index	Rank
Petroleum	90.8	121.7	1	127.4	1
Printing	65.4	85.3	2	43.8	4
Fabricated metals	47.3	20.5	14	23.2	7
Stone, clay, glass	44.0	83.5	3	14.2	10
Machinery, nonelectric	40.7	19.1	15	19.1	8
Paper	32.9	37.1	5	60.7	2
Beverages	30.0	1.7	17	34.9	5
Chemicals	27.3	22.1	12	34.6	6
Scientific instruments	25.8	25.5	11	10.9	11
Motor vehicles	21.8	27.7	10	44.4	3
Rubber	14.0	37.4	4	(44.7)	17
Food	11.2	20.7	13	18.0	9
Machinery, electrical	1.1	37.8	19	(3.7)	12
Tobacco	(1.5)	(3.9)	18	(5.8)	13
Lumber	(2.5)	31.3	7	(68.3)	18
Furniture	(23.9)	29.7	8	(125.9)	19
Primary metals	(36.0)	33.4	6	(16.7)	15
Textiles	(41.6)	12.9	16	(27.5)	16
Leather	(47.2)	(59.0)	20	(129.9)	20
Apparel	(66.7)	27.9	9	(12.8)	14
Transportation equipment, excluding motor vehicles	(98.2)	(152.1)	21	(282.6)	21
All manufacturing	16.9	28.0		25.9	

Note: Indexes in parentheses reflect deficits.

the annual Statistics of Income reports for corporations excluded data on net worth by size of firm; also, the asset-size classes were changed. Therefore, for the 1960–1962 period, the ratios of net profits to total assets for firms with assets under $100,000 are shown. Also, for manufacturing firms with assets under $1 million, profitability data through 1965 are available.

In Tables 3-7 and 3-9 reference is made to the index of profit margins. The index is computed by dividing the profit margins (profits

Table 3-8—Index of Profit Ratios, 1960–1962
Manufacturing Corporations with Assets Under $100,000

	1960	1961	1962	1960–1962 Average
Petroleum	216.0	0.0	0.0	72.0
Printing	10.9	14.9	0.0	8.6
Machinery, nonelectrical	(5.3)	(87.2)	10.6	(27.3)
Stone, clay, glass	(31.9)	(56.8)	(17.1)	(35.3)
Food	(27.3)	(27.9)	(51.3)	(35.5)
Textiles	(118.2)	0.0	0.0	(37.4)
Fabricated metals	(71.4)	(45.5)	0.0	(39.0)
Beverages	(85.1)	0.0	(43.4)	(42.8)
Paper	54.2	0.0	(184.1)	(43.3)
Apparel	(46.4)	(74.2)	(23.3)	(48.0)
Primary metals	(184.4)	0.0	0.0	(61.5)
Chemicals	(77.6)	(44.4)	(87.3)	(67.8)
Motor vehicles	(124.4)	0.0	(93.3)	(72.6)
Rubber	(191.7)	(54.5)	(122.0)	(122.7)
Scientific instruments	(22.8)	(413.7)	(158.2)	(164.9)
Leather	(250.0)	(204.3)	(208.8)	(221.0)
Lumber	(250.0)	(272.2)	(227.3)	(229.8)
Electrical machinery	(128.9)	(261.5)	(343.6)	(244.7)
Furniture	(370.0)	(248.1)	(229.0)	(282.4)
Transportation equipment	(2287.5)	(1400.0)	(263.9)	(1317.1)
All manufacturing	(57.1)	(70.0)	(55.8)	(61.0)

Source: *Statistics of Income,* Internal Revenue Service, 1960, 1961, 1962.
Note: Indexes in parentheses reflect deficits.

after taxes as a percentage of net worth) of the various asset-size classes by the profit margins of the industry as a whole and then multiplying the result by 100. Thus, if the rate of return for the industry was 10 per cent and for a given asset-size class 12 per cent, then the index would be 120 for that asset-size class.

Where the index is reported as a negative number, this means that the profit margin of the smaller firms was less than that of the industry, and it was also negative. Following is an example of how the index has been computed:

Assume that industry profit margin is 2%:
when profit margin of class size is 2% then index = 100
$$\begin{aligned}
1\% \; '' \quad '' &= 50 \\
0\% \; '' \quad '' &= 0 \\
-1\% \; '' \quad '' &= (50) \\
-2\% \; '' \quad '' &= (100) \\
-4\% \; '' \quad '' &= (200)
\end{aligned}$$

Table 3-9—Index of Profit Ratios, 1960–1965
By Asset-Size Classes

Asset-Size Class ($Millions)	1960	1961	1962	1963	1964	1965
Under 1	59.5	63.4	87.7	80.0	99.6	110.0
1–5	60.1	68.6	81.1	71.7	84.7	89.0
5–10	73.3	77.6	78.5	80.2	83.0	88.2
10–25	79.6	78.8	80.3	80.2	83.6	91.5
25–50	88.4	86.7	87.5	80.7	85.8	90.0
50–100	92.0	94.3	88.7	86.8	90.7	90.0
100–250	98.4	95.8	92.3	96.8	96.1	96.5
250–1,000	101.9	105.7	95.4	94.1	94.2	95.2
1,000 and over	119.0	122.9	121.0	124.6	115.5	109.8

Source: Quarterly Manufacturing Reports, FTC–SEC, 1960–1965.
Note: The index was computed by dividing the profit ratio (profits after taxes as percentage of net worth) of each asset-size class by the same ratio for all manufacturing in like years and multiplying by 100.

The following conclusions can be drawn from the data on the profit performance of the smaller manufacturing corporations since World War II:

1. The smaller firms did better when a sellers market prevailed and they showed their worst performance during business recessions (see Figure 3-1). Thus they did relatively well in 1947, 1948, during the Korean War, and from 1961–1965, years when the economy was expanding rapidly. During the recession years, 1949, 1954, 1958, and 1960 their average rate of return was −1.4 per cent against 6.6 per cent for all industry in these same years.

2. The industries where the position of small business enjoyed the greatest relative success were petroleum and printing. In the petroleum industry the smaller firms generally refrain from engaging in the wholesale and retail distribution of petroleum products where rates of return are relatively low. This enables the smaller firms to enjoy profit margins that are generally close to the rate for the over-all industry. Printing, to a large extent, is a job-shop type of industry, which probably explains the favorable performance of small business in it.

3. The smaller firms did poorest in the transportation equipment industry (excluding motor vehicles and parts) and in the leather industry. The manufacture of transportation equipment, such as aircraft, ships, and locomotives, obviously requires a great deal of engineering so that smaller firms are handicapped in competing

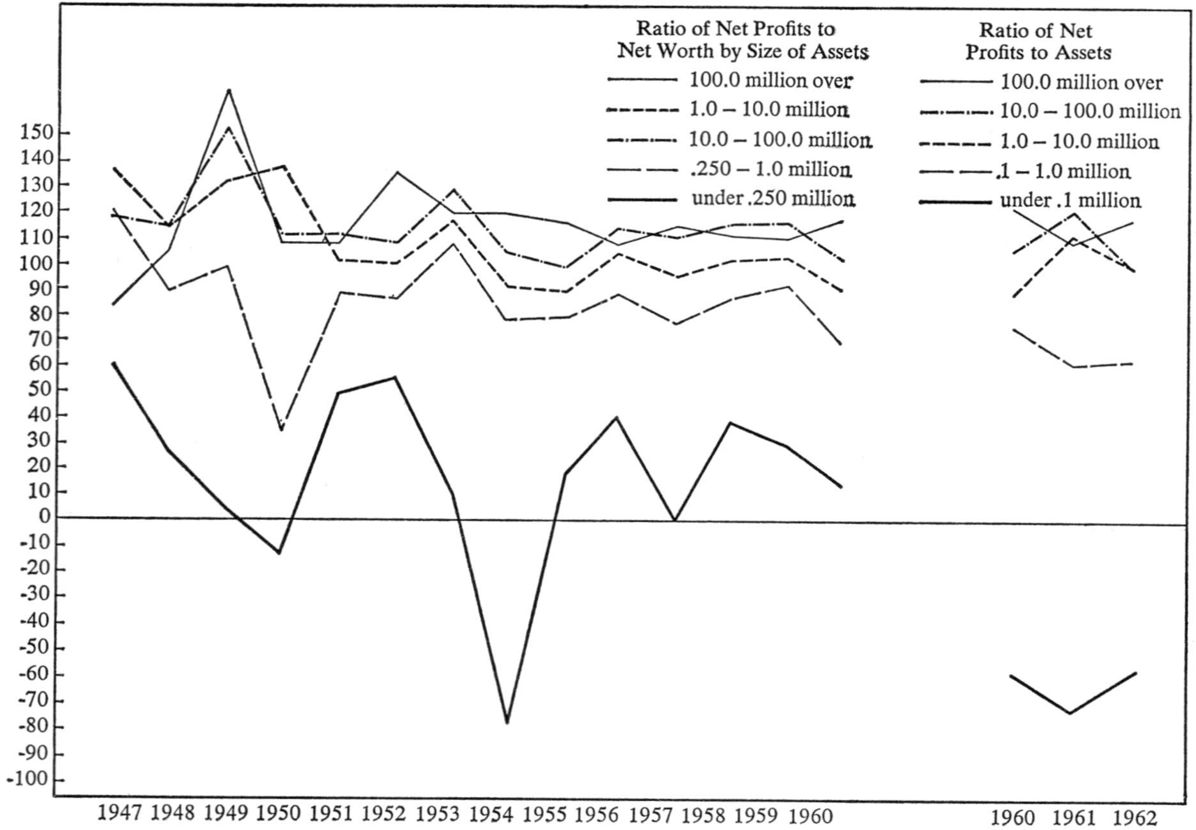

78

Ratio of Net Profits to
Net Worth by Size of Assets
——— 100.0 million over
– – – 1.0 – 10.0 million
—·—· 10.0 – 100.0 million
– – – .250 – 1.0 million
——— under .250 million

Ratio of Net
Profits to Assets
——— 100.0 million over
·········· 10.0 – 100.0 million
– – – 1.0 – 10.0 million
– – – .1 – 1.0 million
——— under .1 million

1947 1948 1949 1950 1951 1952 1953 1954 1955 1956 1957 1958 1959 1960   1960 1961 1962

150
140
130
120
110
100
90
80
70
60
50
40
30
20
10
0
-10
-20
-30
-40
-50
-60
-70
-80
-90
-100

Figure 3-1—Total Manufacturing

in this field. The major manufacturing item in the leather industry is shoes, and apparently there are particular cost advantages of large-scale production that explain why the smaller firms do so poorly, profitwise.

4. In most industries, the relative position of small business has fluctuated very sharply, probably because of the highly dynamic nature of the business environment. The frequent changes in prices, costs, investment rates, products, services, and technology, to mention just some of the major influences, have caused the relative profitability of the smaller firms to show almost continuous change in most industries since World War II. Also, at times waves of mergers of the unsuccessful firms can improve the profitability record of the class of small firms. At other times, the starting of many new firms, which are generally small and usually operate at a loss for at least their early years, may cause the profitability record of small firms to worsen.

Conclusions

Viewing the 1919–1965 period as a whole, there are only a few significant generalizations that can be made with some reliability. One reason for this difficulty is the considerable variance in the profit performance of the smaller manufacturing corporations. Perhaps if more data were available a more definite identification could be made of the industries where the relative profit position of the smaller firms has been improving or worsening. As it is, however, few such clear trends are apparent.

Tables 3-10, 3-11, and 3-12 show for selected periods the performances of small business, by industry, from 1922 to 1962.

From examination of these data it appears that small firms do better in general in industries where the job-shop type of operation is common and where engineering costs are not unusually heavy. Examples are printing, fabricated metals, stone, clay and glass, and the nonelectrical machinery industries. Where long production runs of somewhat standardized products are involved—such as tobacco, lumber, iron and steel, textiles, and clothing—the smaller firms had the poorest record. In strategic planning, the entrepreneurs of the smaller firm should consider the optimum scale of product research, product

Table 3-10—Ratio of Profits After Taxes to Net Worth, 1922–1960

Industry	1922–1928	1931–1936	1939–1941	1947–1949	1958–1960	1947–1960
Apparel			2.14	3.3	−0.5	−0.4
Beverages			12.27	0.3	2.5	2.0
Chemicals	13.0	−1.14	4.18	3.2	3.5	3.3
Electrical machinery			5.86	−4.9	−0.2	0.0
Fabricated metal products				2.5	1.3	5.8
Food	12.1	−2.72	1.86	2.5	1.3	1.2
Furniture and fixtures			2.29	3.9	−5.2	−0.1
Leather	13.7	−6.96	0.96	−2.9	−6.0	−0.2
Lumber	11.7	−10.76	4·66	6.9	−2.9	2.0
Motor vehicles			−1.71	4.3	4.6	3.3
Machinery, nonelectric			6.56	3.1	1.7	4.1
Paper	11.8	−1.30	5.11	6.7	4.6	3.9
Petroleum			3.51	8.7	8.3	6.2
Primary metals	12.1	−5.94	9.17	4.9	−0.4	4.1
Printing	14.0	−4.33	0.93	11.0	3.9	6.8
Rubber	11.7	−8.43	9.19	3.6	−2.9	2.3
Scientific instruments				1.2	1.0	2.5
Stone, clay, glass	12.2	−7.50	3.47	9.8	1.0	5.0
Textiles	11.6	−9.17	1.21	2.9	−0.1	−0.2
Tobacco		−2.24	−3.14	−0.2	—	−0.2
Transportation equipment, excluding motor vehicles			−5.10	−7.3	−4.2	−4.3
All manufacturing	12.1	−5.58	3.34	3.7	1.7	1.9

Table 3-11—Index of Profits, 1922–1960

Industry	1922–1928	1931–1936	1939–1941	1947–1949	1958–1960	1947–1960
Apparel			29.3	27.9	−12.8	−66.7
Beverages			97.8	1.7	34.9	30.0
Chemicals	139.0	−493.6	35.8	22.1	34.6	27.3
Electrical machinery			41.3	37.8	−3.7	1.1
Fabricated metal products				20.5	23.2	47.3
Food	114.0	−683.2	24.2	20.7	18.0	11.2
Furniture and fixtures			32.4	29.7	−125.9	−23.9
Leather	105.0	−166.4	13.7	−59.0	−129.9	−47.2
Lumber	104.0	−258.8	107.1	31.3	−68.3	−2.5
Motor vehicles			neg	27.7	44.4	21.8
Machinery, nonelectrical			58.9	19.1	19.1	40.7
Paper	149.0	−211.2	69.0	37.1	60.7	32.9
Petroleum			90.7	121.7	127.4	90.8
Primary metals	112.0	−326.3	95.5	33.4	−16.7	36.0
Printing	66.0	−444.0	14.1	85.3	43.8	65.4
Rubber	272.0	−348.2	102.8	37.4	−44.7	14.0
Scientific instruments				25.5	10.9	25.8
Stone, clay, glass	81.0	−343.6	37.9	83.5	14.2	44.0
Textiles	125.0	−328.0	16.5	12.9	−27.5	−41.6
Tobacco		−22.3	neg	−3.9	−5.8	−1.5
Transportation equipment			neg	−152.1	−282.6	−98.2
All manufacturing	111.0	−455.3	36.8	28.0	25.9	16.9

Table 3-12—Industry Rankings, by Relative Profitability, 1947–1962

Industry	1947–1960	1939–1941	1947–1949	1958–1960	1960–1962
Petroleum	1	5	1	1	1
Printing	2	15	2	4	2
Fabricated metals	3	—	14	7	7
Stone, clay, glass	4	9	3	10	4
Machinery, nonelectric	5	7	15	8	3
Paper	6	6	5	2	9
Beverage	7	3	17	5	8
Chemicals	8	10	12	6	12
Scientific instruments	9	—	11	11	15
Motor vehicles	10	17	10	3	13
Rubber	11	2	4	17	14
Food	12	13	13	9	5
Electrical machinery	13	8	19	12	18
Tobacco	14	18	18	13	—
Lumber	15	1	7	18	17
Furniture and fixtures	16	11	8	19	19
Primary metals	17	4	6	15	11
Textiles	18	14	16	16	6
Leather	19	16	20	20	16
Apparel	20	12	9	14	10
Transportation equipment, excluding motor vehicles	21	—	21	21	20

engineering, production, and marketing for a given type of business. If this scale is quite large in any, some, or all of these categories, then it may be disadvantageous for small business to attempt to enter or remain in such fields. If, on the other hand, the scale of such operations need not be large, and if there is rapid product and technological change, or there is the necessity for conforming to highly varied customer requirements, then small firms may operate with significant advantages. There appear to be enough products falling into the latter categories to provide continuous and widespread opportunities for the success of small manufacturing businesses. What is required of small business is (a) careful long-range planning to identify the constantly changing opportunities for small business and (b) the ability to adapt readily to a highly dynamic business environment.

After allowing for the possible underreporting of profits by small business and the fact that many such firms are relatively new and hence less profitable, it still appears that in general the rates of return for the smaller firms are below the averages for their industry. This condition has prevailed for many decades, however, and evidence could not be found to support the conclusion that the competitive position of the smaller firm is generally worsening.

4

The Failure Rates of Business

O. D. Dickerson and Michael Kawaja

Dun and Bradstreet reports the failure rate of businesses as having ranged between 4 and 154 per 10,000 concerns in the 1920 to 1965 period.[1] On the other hand, a study conducted in Providence, R.I., in the early 1960's found that only 41 of 81 retail and service firms survived more than two years.[2] Such wide variations in the reported failure rates of business concerns are common in the literature on business survival patterns. The purpose of this chapter is to organize the available data on failure rates in a manner that will help to explain such variations and so shed light on the factors which explain the different failure rates reported.

Business failure rates are worthy of study for at least three important reasons. First, failure rates affect the start-up rate of new businesses and hence potential competition. Second, business failures involve personal losses and economic waste. Third, a better understanding of the causes of failure can improve knowledge of the training required for successful business operation, a knowledge that is of interest to business educators as well as to entrepreneurs.

The Availability of Data

The authors originally set out to develop an actuarial treatment of the mortality functions of small businesses in the United States to provide answers to such questions as: What is the life expectancy of a small business? What trends have been observed in these life expectancies? How does life expectancy vary by size of firm, age of firm, and field of endeavor? A search of the literature revealed, however, that the data necessary for such computations do not exist, at least in usable form. Few of the published data were specific to small business. Furthermore, none of the comprehensive studies gave a breakdown by age of firm, which is probably the most important single variable. And, finally, the results of the studies that have been made are not comparable largely because of differences in the definitions of critical terms, such as *birth* and *survival* of firms.

The research effort was therefore shifted to focus on an analysis of such data as do exist on mortality and survival rates with a view to classifying these data in a meaningful manner.

Variations in Failure Rates

Failure rates fluctuate cyclically and vary by region, industry, age, and size of firm. These variations are examined in this section.

CYCLICAL VARIATIONS

As may be seen from the time series data given in Table 4-1 (and illustrated in Figure 4-1), failure rates of business concerns exhibit no long-term trend but vary in a cyclical pattern with peaks and troughs corresponding roughly with those of general economic activity. The absolute number of failures and total liabilities of failing concerns followed a similar cyclical pattern whereas the average liability per failure exhibited a marked uptrend beneath the cycles. Since the series is in current dollars, not constant dollars, this is not surprising.

Table 4-1—Failure Trends, 1920–1965

Year	Number of Failures	Total Failure Liabilities	Failure Rate Per 10,000 Listed Concerns	Average Liability Per Failure
1920	8,881	$295,121,000	48	$33,230
1921	19,652	627,401,000	102	31,926
1922	23,676	623,895,000	120	26,351
1923	18,718	539,387,000	93	28,817
1924	20,615	543,226,000	100	26,351
1925	21,214	443,744,000	100	20,918
1926	21,773	409,233,000	101	18,795
1927	23,146	520,105,000	106	22,471
1928	23,842	489,559,000	109	20,534
1929	22,909	483,252,000	104	21,094
1930	26,355	668,282,000	122	25,357
1931	28,285	736,310,000	133	26,032
1932	31,822	928,313,000	154	29,172
1933	19,859	457,520,000	100	23,038
1934	12,091	333,959,000	61	27,621
1935	12,244	310,580,000	62	25,366
1936	9,607	203,173,000	48	21,148
1937	9,490	183,253,000	46	19,310
1938	12,836	246,505,000	61	19,204
1939	14,768	182,520,000	70	12,359
1940	13,619	166,684,000	63	12,239
1941	11,848	136,104,000	63	12,239
1942	9,405	100,763,000	45	10,713
1943	3,221	45,339,000	16	14,076
1944	1,222	31,660,000	7	25,908
1945	809	30,225,000	4	37,361
1946	1,129	67,349,000	5	59,654
1947	3,474	204,612,000	14	58,898
1948	5,250	234,620,000	20	44,690
1949	9,246	308,109,000	34	33,323
1950	9,162	248,283,000	34	27,099
1951	8,058	259,547,000	31	32,210
1952	7,611	283,314,000	29	37,224
1953	8,862	394,153,000	33	44,477
1954	11,086	462,628,000	42	41,731
1955	10,969	449,380,000	42	40,968
1956	12,686	562,697,000	48	44,356
1957	13,739	615,293,000	52	44,784
1958	14,964	728,258,000	56	48,667
1959	14,053	692,808,000	52	49,300
1960	15,445	938,630,000	57	60,772
1961	17,075	1,090,123,000	64	63,843
1962	15,782	1,213,601,000	61	76,898
1963	14,374	1,352,593,000	56	94,100
1964	13,501	1,329,223,000	53	98,454
1965	13,514	1,321,666,000	53	97,800

Source: Dun and Bradstreet, Inc. *The Failure Record Through 1965*, New York, 1966.

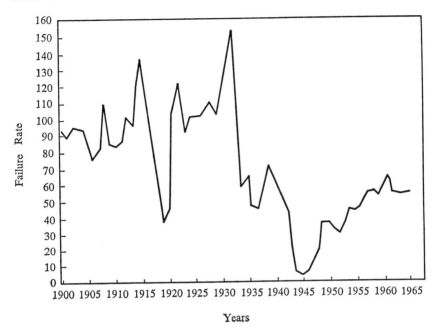

Figure 4-1—Rates of Business Failures
(Failure Rates per 10,000 Firms, 1900–1965)

Sources: Federal Reserve System, Report to the Committees on Banking and Currency and the
Select Committee on Small Business, *Financing Small Business*, Parts 1 and 2, 1958, p. 212; Dun
and Bradstreet, *The Failure Record Through 1965*, p. 3.

FAILURE RATES BY REGION

Failure rates vary by region from a low of around 29 firms per
10,000 listed concerns in the North Central states to slightly over 120
per 10,000 listed concerns in the Pacific states in 1965. By state, the
range is from a low of 8.2 in Vermont to a high of 211.7 in Utah.

Between 1940 and 1965, as shown in Table 4-2, failure rates re-
mained relatively steady or declined in New England, Middle Atlantic,
South Atlantic, East North Central, West North Central, and East
South Central states. They increased dramatically in the West South
Central, Mountain, and Pacific regions.

There are no data that would permit categorical statements to be made as to the causes of these geographic variations in failure rates. However, it is probable that the relatively high and increasing failure rates of the Pacific region are explainable, at least in part, by a higher start-up rate of new business in this dynamic region, since as will be shown in a later section, these new businesses have higher failure rates than older businesses.

Table 4-2—Failure Rates by Region
(Failure Rate per 10,000 Listed Concerns)

Region	1940	1965
New England	65.4	49.1
Middle Atlantic	116.0	70.2
South Atlantic	47.4	47.4
East North Central	51.8	42.9
West North Central	25.8	28.8
East South Central	32.7	31.2
West South Central	30.5	46.0
Mountain	40.0	75.0
Pacific	65.0	120.5

Source: Dun and Bradstreet, Inc., *The Failure Record Through 1965,* New York, 1966.

FAILURE RATES BY LINE OF BUSINESS

National Studies. Available national studies indicate that lines of business may be ranked from high to low by percentage of newly established or acquired firms surviving two years or more, as follows: (1) wholesale trade; (2) finance, insurance, and real estate; (3) contract construction; (4) manufacturing; (5) mining and quarrying; (6) service; (7) transportation, communication, and other public utilities; and (8) retail trade.[3] Exactly the same ranking results where lines of businesses are classified as to median age of firms.

It seems probable that this ranking is very similar to that which would be obtained if lines of business were classified on the basis of the proportion of businesses that are very small. However, there is no really convincing statistical evidence on this point. The only available breakdowns of lines of business by size distribution show size of business by the number of employees, and the data do not clearly support the hypothesis that there is a higher concentration of small firms in retailing than in wholesaling, and so on. There are two factors that may explain this. First, the number of employees is a poor basis for size classifications, and second, the industry groupings are probably too broad to be very useful. Undoubtedly, on average, some lines of retailing are conducted on a larger scale than some lines of wholesaling or manufacturing. Thus, the data on failure rates based on a more detailed breakdown of types of business which show substantial overlaps in the range of failure rates in manufacturing and retailing may be consistent with the hypothesis that the above rankings of broad industry classes by failure rates would be approximately the same as the rankings of these industry classes by the proportion of firms that are very small.

State Studies. A study of Alabama firms by Paustian and Lewis supports the general ranking of industries based on the national data and specifically concludes that "there appears to be a greater propensity to fail in the industrial groups where small business composes a larger proportion of the firms than in groups with a larger proportion of large firms."[4] This supports the hypothesis based on the scant nationwide data that variations in industry failure rates are explained in large part by typical size of firm.

Failure Rates by Age

The problem of definitions of terms is particularly acute when one attempts to determine from existing studies the exact differences in failure rates by age of firms. The age of failing firms depends entirely on definitions of both "births" and "deaths." For example, some studies define failure only as bankruptcy or insolvency that results in losses to creditors. The vast number of businesses that "die" by merger or acquisition are not included. Other studies include mergers or acquisitions in their failure classifications. Still others add firms whose doors have closed because of inability to provide the owner with what he regarded as an adequate return on his investment, regardless of whether the firm's demise involved a loss to creditors. The definition of "birth" varies even more widely. For example, the Dun and Bradstreet rates apparently are based on a definition of "birth" as becoming listed in the *Dun and Bradstreet Reference Book.* "Failure" apparently refers to bankruptcy or insolvency that results in liabilities to creditors. The vast number of businesses which "die" without actually becoming insolvent are not included, nor are the many firms which do not survive long enough to obtain a listing. This results in understating both births and deaths, but relatively greater understating of deaths and death rates. This is pointed up by the following quotation:

> Business failures, representing the most drastic effects of the wear and tear of our economy, are actually only a fractional portion of the total turnover in business population. In recent years over 400,000 concerns have been started annually, between 350,000 and 400,000 have been discontinued, and a slightly larger number have transferred ownership or control. On every business day, more than 5,000 listings in the Dun & Bradstreet Reference Book are changed; new names are added, discontinued businesses are deleted, credit and financial ratings are revised, both upward and downward, and name styles are altered.[5]

As an illustration of the opposite pole, Pfeffer and Neumann, defining "birth" as obtaining a name and "survival" as lasting long enough to make a profit or alternately surviving long enough to recoup early losses, produced violently lower survival probabilities.[6] Paustian and Lewis, who defined both "birth" and "death" in terms of listing in the Alabama Department of Industrial Relations, obtained rates of failure much higher than Dun and Bradstreet but much lower than Pfeffer and Neumann.

Because of the critical importance of definitions of "birth" and "death" rates and the general lack of uniformity in the definitions of these terms used in available studies, no attempt has been made here to compare the results of existing studies. Rather, the analysis has been limited to a separate review of each of the significant studies on failure rates by age of firm.

National Studies. In the late 1940's and early 1950's extensive studies were conducted by the Business Structure Division of the Office of Business Economics on failure rates by age of firms for different industries. These studies found that, for all the lines of business studied, failure rates decrease and survival probabilities and expected future life increase with increasing age of firm (see Figure 4-2). This presents a situation comparable to that found in mortality rates during the early years of human life. Businesses have a high "infant mortality" rate. All other national studies support this general finding that life expectancy increases with age. The Dun and Bradstreet studies, for example, indicate that the second, third, and fourth years are critical, and after the first year the percentage of firms failing each year de-

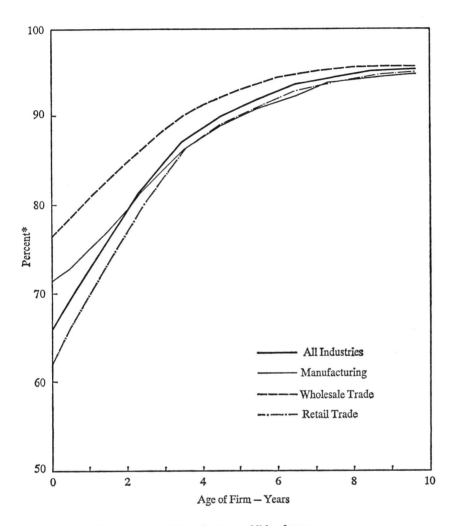

*Percent of firms in operation surviving at least one additional year

Figure 4-2—Life Expectancy by Age of Firm

Source: Betty C. Churchill, "Age and Life Expectancy of Business Firms," *Survey of Current Business,* December 1955, p. 15.

clines smoothly. As indicated above, it is suspected that most first-year deaths never get into the Dun and Bradstreet list.

State Studies. Studies conducted in a number of different states all support the finding that the early years of a firm's life are crucial. As noted earlier, Mayer and Goldstein in their study of 81 Rhode Island firms found that only 41 survived the first two years. Twenty-eight of the forty unsuccessful firms failed within their first 11 months, with the number of failures distributed approximately evenly among each of these 11 months. Kinnard and Malinowski found that for the manufacturing firms in the Hartford, Conn., area the first five years were critical, with the highest failure rates being in the second and fifth years.[7] Similarly, Hoad and Rosko, who studied new small manufacturers in Michigan, found that of 95 firms which started business during the year ending June 30, 1960, eight failed in the first six months, ten in the second six-month period, 11 in the third six-month period, and three in the fourth. Three more failed during their third year. Thus, within three years, 35 of the 95 firms failed. Thirty-seven were judged to be successful, 22 were marginally successful, and three were dormant.[8] Pfeffer and Neumann, who analyzed failures among California life insurance companies according to their stage of development, also found that the largest proportion of failures occurred at the earliest stages of the firm's life.

FAILURE RATES BY SIZE

The findings discussed to this point indicate that new firms have a much higher failure rate and hence a shorter life expectancy than do older firms. Since new firms are typically small relative to the size of firms in their industry, this suggests that the failure rate of small firms is higher than the 53 per 10,000 given in the Dun and Bradstreet reports. More specifically, from the descriptions of the samples of firms used in each of the state studies cited earlier, it can be seen that the relatively high failure rates found in the state studies are for firms that are small relative to the average of all firms in their industry classes.[9]

National Comparisons. The only available national data that deal specifically with the size distribution of unsuccessful firms measures size by the amount of the firm's liabilities. They indicate that the majority of unsuccessful firms have liabilities of less than $100,000, and the bulk of these have liabilities of less than $25,000.[10]

However, these data may be grossly misleading for at least three reasons. First, the size distribution of all firms may be such that most firms (successful and unsuccessful) have liabilities of less than $100,-000. Thus, even if failures were evenly distributed percentagewise among the size classes, most failures (in percentage terms) would have liabilities of less than $100,000. To be meaningful, these failure statistics must be compared with data on the size distribution (by the same liabilities measure) of all firms—and these are not available. Second, by most definitions, failing firms are those which have "excessive" liabilities. This suggests that measures of the liabilities of unsuccessful firms may at best be of limited value. And third, as a firm approaches failure, its size (probably by all measures, including liabilities) is likely to shrink, again suggesting the inadequacy of liabilities as a measure of firm size for purposes of computing failure rates.

State Studies. Individual state studies provide a better basis for conclusions on failure rates by size of firm, although they too are somewhat unsatisfactory. Studies conducted in Rhode Island and Connecticut found higher failure rates among smaller firms (where the size of firm was measured by the number of employees).[11] Because both studies were limited to relatively small geographic areas— Providence and Hartford—they eliminate the variation due to regional differences. Further, the Connecticut study was limited to manufacturing firms; hence the number of employees is a more reliable measure of firm size for this study than for the Rhode Island study. The Rhode Island study dealt with a wide variety of service and retail firms; thus the differences found in failure rates among small and large firms may be due to differences in the lines of business studied as well as to the size of firm, but the available data provide no way of sorting out the relative importance of these factors.

A study of survival patterns in Illinois also found higher failure rates among smaller firms (4 per cent for small firms compared to 10 per cent for large firms).[12] However, the conclusions of this study are of questionable value since the size classifications of firms were derived by asking each of the respondents in the sample to rate its size relative to other firms in the same line. That is, the classifications were based on subjective criteria, which may have varied largely from respondent to respondent.

In summary, therefore, the Connecticut study of manufacturing firms that varied in employee size from less than nine to more than one thousand is the most reliable of all existing studies on the size distribution of failing firms, and it found substantially higher discontinuance rates among smaller firms than larger ones.

Causes of Failure

The examination of variations in failure rates sheds some light on the causes of failure. For example, it was found that failure rates are higher in periods of depression than in an economic boom. Thus, in a sense, one "cause" of failure is the general level of economic activity. The only available national studies which deal specifically with the causes of failure are those conducted by Dun and Bradstreet. Unfortunately, with the exception of disaster, the Dun and Bradstreet classifications (for example, neglect and lack of experience) are largely arbitrary or too vague to yield meaningful conclusions. Like the national studies, the state studies which focus specifically on causes of failure also use largely arbitrary breakdowns, although they do provide a better perspective on the significance of education, relevant experience, and capitalization, as determinants of failure rates.

Three state studies dealt specifically with an analysis of the problem of causes of failure in a scientific manner, and they broke these down into two broad categories: education and experience, and capitalization. The main findings of these studies may be summarized as follows:[13]

1. The rate of closures bears an inverse relationship to the age of the firm's owner.

2. The survival experience of women business owners differs little from that of male owners.

3. Owners with less formal education (measured in terms of years of schooling) have a higher rate of business discontinuance.

4. There is little relationship between previous experience in the

same line of business taken by itself and the discontinuance rate. Of course, this does not mean that not having worked in a line of business is a positive factor inducing success, but it does suggest that skills developed in an occupation are insufficient preparation for the successful conduct of a business enterprise.

5. Various combinations of education and experience were studied and it was found that inexperienced and uneducated managers are the least likely to succeed, whereas educated and experienced managers have the highest success rate.

6. Individuals who previously owned a business have a much lower failure rate than those who have never been in business before. Thus the single experience factor which appears to matter most is not experience in the same occupation but rather whether the person has had *entrepreneurial* experience.

7. Management teams of two, three, or four persons have a much higher success rate than single managers.

8. In general, the larger the amount of invested capital, especially in the $1,000–$25,000 range studied, the lower is the failure rate. Further, the source of initial capital appears to have a bearing on failure rate. Lower failure rates were found among firms which had a higher proportion of initial capital in equity form.

Conclusion

This chapter has sought to organize available data on the failure rates of business concerns with a view to explaining the variations in the reported failure rates commonly found in the literature on business survival patterns, thus shedding light on the factors that explain these different failure rates. The main findings are as follows:

1. Business failure rates fluctuate cyclically, with peaks and troughs corresponding roughly to those of general business conditions.

2. Failure rates vary by region, with the highest rates being found in the western states.

3. Failure rates vary significantly by line of business, with the highest rates found in retailing.

4. The life expectancy of a business firm increases with its age.

5. The larger the size class of firm, the lower is the failure rate.

6. The single experience factor that appeared to matter most in determining success of a new firm is not experience in the same line of business but rather experience in owning a business, whatever its kind.

7. The larger the amount of capital initially invested, and the higher the equity-to-debt ratio, the lower is the failure rate.

Part II

CAPITAL
MANAGEMENT THEORY
FOR SMALL BUSINESS

5

The Cost of Capital
to the Small Firm

Eugene F. Brigham

Widely recognized as one of the fundamental concepts in the field of finance, the cost of capital underlies the vitally important capital budgeting process and provides the key to questions of proper capital structure and appropriate financing decisions. Further, the cost of capital framework should also be useful for research designed to explain small businesses' financing decisions and problems.

Cost of capital theory is a relatively new concept and is still in a state of flux. Competing hypotheses relate to several specific aspects of the theory, and as yet empirical tests have not resolved these conflicts to everyone's satisfaction. In addition to theoretical problems, formidable measurement difficulties are encountered when one attempts to estimate the cost of capital for an individual firm.

Special problems arise when the cost of capital concept is applied to the typical small business. As a rule, the small firm's securities are privately held, which makes it difficult to use market data when calculating the cost of the various types of capital. Also, smaller firms do not have as wide a range of choice in selling securities as theorists typically assume; consequently, they reach barriers to expansion (or, strictly speaking, discontinuities in their cost of capital schedules) more often than do larger firms. Finally, smaller firms are generally closely identified with one individual or a small group of individuals, making it necessary to give explicit recognition to such matters as the marginal utility of wealth, control of the firm, and the problem of separating the firm's earning power from that of its owner-manager.

Valuation

Cost of capital theory is based on the capitalization of income method of valuation, which states that the value of any business asset is equal to the sum of its discounted cash flows. The equation may be stated as follows:

$$V = \frac{R_1}{(1+r)^1} + \frac{R_2}{(1+r)^2} + \cdots + \frac{R_N}{(1+r)^N} = \sum_{t=1}^{N} \frac{R_t}{(1+r)^t}$$

Here, V is the theoretical value of the asset; R_t is the net cash flow expected in each year, t; r is the appropriate discount rate; and N is the asset's expected life.[1] If the asset in question is a 20-year bond paying $40 interest annually and $1,000 on maturity, and if the current rate of interest on bonds with this same degree of risk and liquidity is 5.5 per cent, then any standard bond table shows that V equals $819.40.

Although in theory the same principles apply to the valuation of common stocks as to bonds, two features make their analysis much more difficult. First is the degree of certainty with which receipts can be forecast. For bonds (and preferred stocks) this forecast presents very little difficulty because the interest payment (or preferred stock dividend) is known with relative certainty. But in the case of common stocks, forecasting future earnings, dividends, and stock prices is exceedingly difficult, to say the least. The second complicating feature is that, unlike interest and preferred dividends, common stock earnings and dividends are generally expected to grow, not to remain constant. Hence standard annuity formulas cannot be applied, and more difficult conceptual schemes must be used.[2]

RISK AND RATES OF RETURN

The discount factor (r) in the equation above is the rate of return an investor receives if he buys the assets for a price V, holds it for N years, and receives R_t dollars each year. If R_t and N are estimates of future values rather than actually realized figures, then r is also an estimate. Depending on the degree of certainty with which N and R_t can be forecast, the investor is more or less assured of receiving his estimated rate of return. If, for example, the asset is a bank time deposit or a Treasury bill, R_t can be estimated quite accurately and thus r is reasonably well known *ex ante*. If, on the other hand, the asset is the bond of a weak company or the note of an individual, there is a chance of default and thus some doubt about the *ex ante* yield. If the asset is a share of stock, future cash flows—dividends plus capital gains—are even less certain, and there is still more uncertainty about r's final outcome.

As risk is typically defined, greater uncertainty about future returns generates higher risk. For example, one can be quite certain of his rate of return if he buys short-term government bonds but much less sure if he buys common stocks; consequently, common stocks are considered to be more risky than bonds.

Although some individuals are gamblers by nature and seem to prefer more risk to less, investors as a group are risk averters. Given risk aversion, securities with higher risk must also sell on the basis of higher *ex ante* yields. For example, a 9 per cent return might be acceptable for the stock of an automobile parts manufacturing firm, whereas a more stable and predictable electric utility stock might sell on a 7 per cent yield basis.

One might also observe that different degrees of risk are incurred by individual firms within particular industries. For example, a firm that has a strong research and development program, excellent recruitment and management training programs, and broad geographic diversification will be regarded as less risky than another firm that has none of these features and will sell on a lower yield basis. If small firms, because of less product or geographic diversification, lower R&D expenditures, greater management succession problems, or any other reason, are considered to be more risky than large firms, then investors will require a higher rate of return on small firms' securities.

MARKETABILITY AND RATES OF RETURN

Investors also value flexibility, or maneuverability. If one becomes disenchanted with a particular investment, or if he needs funds for consumption or other investments, then it is highly desirable for him to be able to liquidate his holdings. Other things being the same, the higher the liquidity, or marketability, the lower an investment's required rate of return. Accordingly, one would expect to find listed stocks selling on a lower-yield basis than over-the-counter stocks, and publicly owned stocks selling at lower yields than stocks with no established market. Because investments in small firms are generally less liquid than those in large companies, we have another reason for expecting higher required yields among smaller companies.

HISTORICAL RATES OF RETURN

Equity Yields. Equity yields differ among firms because of differences in inherent risks and marketability, but they also differ for an individual stock over time. If the demand for funds is particularly heavy and at the same time the supply is restricted, the law of supply and demand requires that the price of funds—the interest rate on debt or the required rate of return on equity—be higher than when supply and demand conditions are reversed. In the late 1940's, for example, many corporations were expanding and seeking funds to finance this expansion, but many investors were expecting a serious postwar depression and were not interested in purchasing stocks. The result was a very high required rate of return on equity issues and low stock prices and P/E (price/earnings) ratios.

As it became clear that the booming economy was not headed for a depression, investors began putting more money into the equity markets. Simultaneously, productive capacity began to catch up with demand, lowering corporate demands for funds. The net result was a pronounced decline in required rates of return and a much higher level of stock prices and P/E ratios. On the average, P/E ratios of industrial stocks were about 7.5 in 1949 but up to 20 by 1958, and at the 1961 peak stocks were selling for over 24 times earnings.

Average P/E ratios change for either of two reasons: changes in required rates of return or changes in growth expectations. For example, the 1949 to 1961 increase in P/E ratios may have been caused by either declining required equity yields, higher growth expectations, or a combination of the two.

Various financial researchers investigating returns on publicly owned stocks over long periods have found them to average about 7.5 per cent. When measured from stockmarket lows, returns are relatively high; conversely, when the market is high in the base period, stockholder yields are relatively low. For example, had one bought a portfolio of stocks at the average price prevailing in 1949 and held them until 1964, his return would have been about 16 per cent.[3] The same group of stocks, bought during the high market in 1961, would have yielded a little over 6 per cent by 1964.

Some rough averages of estimated stock yields on firms subject to different market conditions are shown in Table 5-1. To the extent that the future approximates the past, and that investors base expected future returns on those realized in the past, the figures in the table should give some idea of stockholders' required rates of return under different market and risk conditions.

Table 5-1—Estimated Rates of Return on Common Stocks (k values)

| | STOCK MARKET CONDITION | | |
	High	Normal	Low
Low risk	6.5	7	9.5
Average risk	7	8	12
High risk	8	12	20

Source: J. Fred Weston and Eugene F. Brigham, *Managerial Finance* (New York: Holt, Rinehart and Winston, 1966), p. 306.

These yields refer to marketable stocks of large corporations. No comparable data are available on unlisted or privately owned firms, but there is every reason to think that such data would show considerably higher returns for unlisted securities than those given in the table. With higher risk (resulting from less diversification, greater problems of management succession, and so on) and less liquidity, it is difficult to imagine any other pattern of returns.

Debt Yields. Debt yields also vary over time and with the characteristics of the individual loans. Many different statistics could be presented to support this assertion, but Table 5-2 illustrates it sufficiently. The year 1958 was a period of monetary ease; 1962 might be characterized as "normal" for recent years; and 1966 was a period of extremely tight money.

Table 5-2—Bank Rates on Short-Term Business Loans in 19 Large Cities

	SIZE OF LOAN ($ THOUSANDS)			
	1–10	10–100	100–200	200 and over
1958	5.5	5.0	4.6	4.1
1962	5.9	5.5	5.2	4.8
1966 (June)	6.4	6.3	6.0	5.7

Source: Federal Reserve Bulletin, August 1966, p. 1202.

Interest rates on loans decline as the size of the loan increases because of the fixed costs of making and servicing loans. In addition, part of the decline occurs because small firms make small loans, and small firms are inherently more risky than large ones. But at any rate, it is clear that returns on debt, like those on stock, vary over time and with the characteristics of the borrower.

Cost of Individual Capital Components

The valuation process and the concept of expected rates of return were discussed in the preceding section. Now to be considered is the cost of capital, which is based upon these valuation concepts. First, the cost of different kinds of capital—bonds, preferred stock, and common stock—are examined. Then the various capital components are combined to form a weighted, or over-all, cost of capital.

Debt Capital

If a firm borrows $100,000 for one year at 6 per cent interest, its before-tax dollar cost is $6,000 and its before-tax percentage cost is 6 per cent. As a first approximation, the cost of debt is defined as the rate of return that must be earned on debt-financed investments to keep the earnings unchanged. If a firm borrows and invests the borrowed funds to earn a before-tax return just equal to the interest rate, then the earnings available to common stock remain unchanged; therefore, the cost of debt turns out to be the interest rate.

It should be emphasized that the cost of debt is applicable to *new* debt, not to the interest rate on old, previously outstanding debt. The cost of capital is used in a decision-making process—the decision to obtain capital to make investments—and the fact that a firm borrowed at high or low rates in the past is irrelevant. Also, it should be noted that the definition is merely a first approximation; it will be modified later to take into account the fact that because interest payments are deductible the Federal government pays a portion of the cost of debt.

PREFERRED STOCK

The cost of preferred stock is defined similarly to that of debt: it is that rate of return which must be earned on preferred stock-financed investments to keep the earnings available to common shareholders unchanged. This required rate of return is the preferred dividend (D_p) divided by the net price that the firm realizes from the sale of a new issue of preferred stock (P_n):

$$\text{Cost of preferred stock} = \frac{D_p}{P_n}$$

For example, if a firm sells an issue of $100 par value preferred stock with a $6 dividend and nets $95 per share after underwriting commissions, then its cost of preferred stock is 6.3 per cent ($6/$95).

TAX ADJUSTMENT

Because of the differential tax treatments of interest payments and preferred dividends, the definitions of the cost of debt and preferred stock are incompatible as they stand. Cost of capital calculations may be made on either a before-tax or an after-tax basis. Ultimately, however, business decisions must consider after-tax effects; therefore, only the cost of capital after taxes will be considered.[4] The cost of preferred stock is already on an after-tax basis as defined, but a simple adjustment is needed to arrive at the after-tax cost of debt. Because interest payments are tax deductible, the government in effect pays a share of the interest cost of profitable corporations; therefore, the cost of debt capital is reduced as follows:

$$\text{After-tax cost} = (\text{Before-tax cost}) \times (1 - \text{Tax rate}).$$

For example, if the before-tax cost is 6 per cent and the tax rate is 48 per cent then the after-tax cost is as follows:

$$(0.06)\ (1 - 0.48) = (0.06)(0.52) = 3.12\%$$

Had the tax rate been 50 per cent—as is usually assumed for ease of calculations—then the after-tax cost of debt would have been one-half the interest rate.

COST OF EQUITY

The cost of equity capital is defined as the minimum rate of return that must be earned on equity-financed investments to keep the value of the existing common equity unchanged. In other words, if 7 per cent is a corporation's cost of equity capital, then an equity-financed investment raises the price of the firm's stock if—and only if—the internal rate of return on the investment exceeds 7 per cent. This required rate of return (k) is the estimated yield. Unlike interest rates on debt, which are well defined, equity yields are merely estimates.

Equity funds are obtained from two basic sources: retained earnings and the sale of newly issued stock. Are the costs of equity obtained from these two alternative sources the same? In general, the answer is that they are not. In the first place, the flotation costs incurred when stock is sold are avoided when equity is obtained by retained earnings; this lowers the cost of retained earnings vis-à-vis new outside equity. Second, the difference in tax rates on capital gains and dividend income makes retention attractive and lowers the cost of retained earnings.

If the stockholders' before-tax required rate of return k is equal to 8 per cent, for example, then the cost of equity capital from depreciation and retained earnings is less than k. Under certain assumptions the cost of depreciation and retained earnings turns out to be as follows:

$$k_d = k_r = (1 - T)k$$

Here, k_d is the cost of depreciation-generated funds; k_r is the cost of retention-generated funds; and T is the tax rate paid on capital gains. If a firm's stockholders pay a 30 per cent marginal tax rate on normal income and a capital gains tax on one-half that rate, and if k is 8 per cent, then the cost of depreciation and retention-generated funds is as follows:

$$k_d = k_r = (1 - 0.15)8 = (0.85)8 = 6.8\%$$

New outside equity obtained from the sale of stock (k_e) has a higher cost:

$$k_e = \frac{k}{(1 - F)}$$

Here, F is the percentage cost of floating new stock issues. If k is 8 per cent and F is 15 per cent, the cost of new outside equity is as follows:

$$k_e = \frac{8}{(1 - 0.15)} = \frac{8}{(0.85)} = 9.4\%$$

The costs of internally generated equity and new outside equity are averaged in proportion to their usage, and the resulting weighted average cost of equity is used in the calculation of the over-all average cost of capital.

"FREE" CAPITAL

Certain forms of capital—most notably trade credit, accrued taxes and wages, deferred taxes, and unearned income—have no explicit cost. If discounts are involved, trade credit can have a very high explicit cost. If terms are 2/10, net/30, and the discount is not taken, then the additional 20 days of credit carries an implicit interest rate of 36 per cent. There may also be intangible costs involving supplier ill-will if trade credit is not paid promptly. Should funds by these sources be considered free and, therefore, be assigned a zero cost? By far the most common approach is to net such funds out against cash outflows in the capital budgeting process and to ignore them in calculating the cost of capital. As an illustration, consider a retail firm thinking of opening a new store. According to customary practices, the firm should (1) estimate the required investment outlay, (2) estimate the net receipts (additions to profits) from the new store, (3) discount the estimated receipts at the cost of capital, and (4) accept the decision to open the new store only if the present value of the expected revenue stream exceeds the investment outlay. The estimated accruals, trade payables, and other costless forms of credit are deducted from the investment before making the calculation.[5] The other approach is to take the investment outlay at its full value and to include the costless sources when calculating the cost of capital.

Weighted Average Cost of Capital

The marginal concept is often used erroneously in connection with the cost of capital. Suppose a particular firm's after-tax cost of debt is 2.5 per cent (the interest rate on new debt issues is 5 per cent); its estimated cost of equity is 8 per cent; and the decision has been made to finance next year's projects by selling debt. The argument is frequently advanced that the cost of these projects is 2.5 per cent because debt will be used to finance them. This position contains a basic fallacy. To finance a particular set of projects with debt also uses up some of the firm's potential for obtaining new low-cost debt. At some point, as expansion takes place in subsequent years, the firm must use additional equity financing to prevent the debt ratio from becoming too large. On this basis, the firm must be viewed as an on-going concern, and its cost of capital must be calculated as a weighted average of the various types of funds it uses—debt, preferred stock, and equity.

THE CALCULATING PROCEDURE

Before discussing the proper set of weights to employ in computing the weighted average, it is useful to look briefly at the calculating procedure. The right-hand side of the balance sheet is shown in column 2 of Table 5-3. The dollars are converted to percentages in column 3, and column 4 gives the after-tax costs of the different types of capital—debt, preferred stock, and equity. Column 5 is the product of columns 3 and 4, and summing column 5 gives the weighted average cost of the firm's capital: 0.0605, or 6.05 per cent.

THE WEIGHTING SYSTEM

Although both financial theorists and corporate financial managers disagree over particular aspects of debt policy, there is general agreement that firms do have optimum capital structures. *Optimum* is defined as the capital structure that minimizes the average cost of capital.

Determining an actual firm's optimum capital structure requires both analysis and judgment, and it is up to a firm's financial management to decide on the best capital structure for its company. Once this decision has been reached, the weighting system for the average cost of capital calculation is also determined.

Table 5-3—Computing the Weighted Average Cost of Capital

(1) Capital Components	(2) Balance Sheet Figures	(3) Per Cent of Total	(4) Component Cost (Per Cent After Taxes)	(5) Column 3 Times Column 4
Debt	$ 30,000	30	2%	0.0060
Preferred stock	5,000	5	5%	0.0025
Net worth	65,000	65	8%	0.0520
Total	$100,000	100		0.0605 or 6.05%

Effects of Size on the Cost of Capital Components

A firm's size can affect its over-all cost of capital by affecting either the cost of individual capital components or the capital structure. In this section effects on individual components are considered; effects on the capital structure will be discussed in the following section.

EFFECTS OF SIZE ON THE COST OF DEBT

For several reasons smaller firms must pay somewhat higher interest rates than larger firms. First, a small firm with the same financial structure as a larger one is, nevertheless, somewhat more risky; this additional risk requires a higher interest rate, or risk premium. Second, the cost of making and servicing loans includes an element of fixed costs; this also means that lenders must set higher interest rates on small loans. Finally, smaller companies have fewer opportunities to shop for credit, so they do not always get the lowest cost money available.

Federal Reserve Survey. The evidence supports these contentions. Table 5-2 can be interpreted as showing lower interest costs to larger firms. Tables 5-4 and 5-5, which deal more directly with the question,

Table 5-4—Interest Rates on Business Loans to Borrowers Classified by Size of Borrower

All Borrowers by Size of Assets ($ Thousands)	1955 SURVEY			1957 SURVEY		
	All Loans	Unsecured	Secured	All Loans	Unsecured	Secured
Less than 50	5.9	6.0	5.9	6.5	6.5	6.5
50–250	5.1	5.2	5.1	5.7	5.7	5.7
250–1,000	4.7	4.5	4.7	5.4	5.2	5.4
1,000–5,000	4.2	3.8	4.4	5.1	4.8	5.2
5,000–25,000	3.8	3.6	4.1	4.7	4.5	4.8
25,000–100,000	3.4	3.3	3.7	4.3	4.2	4.5
100,000 and over	3.1	3.1	3.1	4.1	4.1	4.1
All borrowers	4.2	3.7	4.6	4.9	4.5	5.2

Source: *Federal Reserve Bulletin,* September 1959.
Note: Average rates are computed by weighting by dollar volume of loans made at each rate.

present interest data from the 1955 and 1957 Federal Reserve Loan Surveys. Table 5-4 shows the average interest rates paid on bank loans by borrowers in different size classes. Data is given for secured, unsecured, and total loans, and for both 1955 and 1957. The salient features of the table are that small companies pay substantially more for bank credit and that, in general, secured credit is more expensive than unsecured credit. Table 5-5 shows that small firms use secured credit much more frequently than do larger ones.

Why is secured credit more expensive than unsecured, and why do small firms use security so much more often than larger ones? Offhand, one might think that a secured loan would be less risky than an unsecured one, and that this would lead to a lower cost for the one that has security. If everything else were held constant this would be true, but other factors are decidedly not the same. The security used for most business loans is either accounts receivable, inventories, or fixed assets, and significant costs are involved in making and servicing such loans. Also, companies that must use secured credit are, generally, more risky than unsecured borrowers. Part of the higher cost of secured loans reflects this risk differential. Small firms, being inherently more risky than larger ones, are frequent users of higher-cost secured credit.

Table 5-5—Percentage of Secured Loans to Business Classified by Size and Type of Business

Business of Borrower	All Borrowers	SIZE OF BUSINESS IN ASSETS ($ THOUSANDS)			
		Under 50	50–250	250–1,000	1,000 and Over
Manufacturing and mining	37.5	78.0	75.0	26.0	11.1
Wholesale commodity	60.5	72.1	71.7	47.0	65.8
Retail	63.6	74.8	72.7	61.6	49.7
Sales finance	17.8	74.3	78.5	5.2	0.8
Public utilities	46.7	90.6	85.0	34.6	27.3
Construction	67.9	72.1	72.6	26.8	51.4
Real estate	87.1	89.1	88.1	82.8	62.8
Service	70.0	81.8	81.9	26.2	11.1
Other nonfinance	71.5	82.4	78.3	54.9	52.3
All business	50.3	78.4	76.5	28.2	17.5

Source: Federal Reserve Bulletin, September 1959.

Financial Lease Costs. Leasing is frequently an alternative to borrowing, and evidence shows that here, too, the smaller firm must pay more for funds. In a 1964 survey of specialized leasing companies

Table 5-6—Implicit Interest Rates in Standard Lease Contracts (As of April 1964)

Net Worth of Leasee	Implicit Interest Rate in Lease Contract (Per Cent)
Under $200,000	11.5
$200,000–$1 million	8
$1–15 million	7
$15–50 million	6
Over $50 million	5

Source: Eugene F. Brigham, "The Impact of Bank Entry on Market Conditions in the Equipment Leasing Industry," National Banking Review, September 1964, p. 24.

and commercial bank leasing departments, the author found typical lease rates ranging from 5 per cent for very large firms to 11.5 per cent for relatively small companies. These data are shown in Table 5-6.

In summary, the evidence is quite clear that smaller firms pay more for credit than do larger ones; however, it is not entirely clear that this cost differential results from size alone. The higher cost of debt may be due primarily to the fact that small companies use more leverage than larger firms. Another possibility is that small firms are found in more risky industries and that this accounts for the observed relationship between size and interest rates.

EFFECTS OF SIZE ON THE COST OF EQUITY: PUBLICLY OWNED COMPANIES

As we have seen, the cost of equity is vastly more difficult to measure than is the cost of debt. Equity returns are not contractual as are those from notes or bonds; therefore, their *ex ante* estimation is a great deal more subjective. This estimation is always difficult, but for stocks that have an established market and a history of dividend and price data it is possible to make reasonable estimates of the cost of equity capital. For privately owned firms the problem is more complex because of some difficult conceptual problems and a lack of data upon which to base estimates.

One approach to extending the cost of capital concept over the full range of firms involves making estimates of the effects of size on costs over the segment of firms on which reasonably good data is available, and then extrapolating the trend down to cover the smaller firms. This has some clear and obvious dangers; any conclusions reached must be regarded as first approximations only. Nevertheless, this procedure, admittedly with caution, is followed here with regard to the cost of equity.

Size and the Required Rate of Return. Whereas reasonably good data are available to show how the cost of debt varies with size of firm, there is no comparable information for the required rate of return on equity. The studies upon which Table 5-1 is based do not classify returns by size of firm; in any event, the firms are all listed on the New York Stock Exchange and are large in an absolute sense. There is, however, some information bearing on the relationship between size of firm and returns on equity capital.

The first bit of evidence on the relationship between size and required rate of return is the return on net worth data contained in the FTC-SEC *Quarterly Reports.* Table 5-7 summarizes this information. Objections can be raised to using these data to make inferences about the size/return relationship,[6] but to the extent that objections are not overriding, there is evidence that smaller manufacturing firms are less profitable than larger ones. Investors, to the extent that they are aware of this fact and take it into account in their own calculations, must be expecting to make lower returns on investments in smaller firms. Although it may be hard to accept the position that investors will invest in small firms expecting lower rates of return than they would get in larger ones, it is also difficult to believe that investors are fooled, year after year, into making commitments in small firms. Some possible reasons for investing in small firms are offered in a subsequent section where the cost of equity for privately owned firms is considered.

Table 5-7—Profit Rate (After Taxes) on Stockholder Equity as Percentage of Rate for Firms of $1–5 Total Assets ($ Millions)

Year	Under $1	$1–5	$5–10	$50–100	$100–250	$250–1000	Over $1000
1956	89.6	100	100.9	111.3	108.5	124.5	140.6
1957	84.3	100	94.4	124.7	125.8	132.6	179.8
1958	72.4	100	169.0	251.7	255.2	255.2	327.6
1959	81.4	100	97.1	135.7	150.0	141.4	184.3
1960	79.4	100	101.6	146.0	161.9	150.8	206.3
1961	50.0	100	216.7	383.3	366.7	438.9	527.8
1962	76.6	100	98.3	125.0	141.7	145.0	201.6
1963	53.2	100	129.8	155.3	178.7	176.6	257.4
1964	105.7	100	110.0	125.7	138.6	138.6	197.1
1965	126.8	100	103.2	110.7	119.3	118.2	161.2
1966	134.5	100	109.1	108.2	112.7	110.9	130.0

Source: FTC-SEC, *Quarterly Financial Report for Manufacturing Corporations*, first quarter of each year.
Note: The corporate tax rate on income less than $25,000 was cut from 30% to 22% in 1964. Although the tax rate on income over $25,000 was also cut (from 52% to 48%), the tax changes were most beneficial to very small firms. This probably explains the marked improvement in the profitability index of the "Under $1 million" size group after 1963.

A recent and elaborate study is provided by Miller and Modigliani's investigation of the cost of capital in the electric utility industry.[7] Although this study is limited for present purposes in that few if any electric utilities would ever be classed as small business, the largest firms in the sample were several times as large as the smallest. Did k decline as size of the firm increased? To quote from this study: "The only mild surprise is the virtually negligible contribution of size (to k)."[8]

Another study dealing with electric utility companies and extending down to relatively small unlisted firms also found size of firm to be unimportant as a determinant of the cost of equity capital, other things being held constant.[9] This study showed, however, that listed companies have an advantage over unlisted firms, and because only the larger firms have the option of listing their stocks, there is some decline in the cost of capital as size increases.

A fourth study, by Archer and Faerber, examined 238 manufacturing firms that issued stock during the years 1960–1962.[10] Measured by assets, the firms ranged in size from under $100,000 to over $100,000,000, and the sample included all types of manufacturing companies. Archer and Faerber's conclusions regarding the effects of size on the required rate of return match those of the preceding studies: "Given the model and period being studied, no support has been found for the hypothesis that the size of the firm has a significant impact upon the cost of external equity to the firm."

The evidence, then, suggests that little relationship exists between a firm's size and its required rate of return on equity capital—at least for firms that are large enough to be publicly owned. This last statement is an important qualification, but before considering whether or not the evidence of these studies can be used to draw inferences about required returns on privately owned companies, the relationship between flotation costs and firm size is examined.

The Effects of Size on Flotation Costs. The cost of new outside equity is dependent upon both the required rate of return and flotation costs and may be defined as follows:

$$k_e = \frac{k}{(1-F)}$$

Here, k_e is the cost of new outside equity; k is the basic required rate of return; and F is the percentage cost of floating new outside equity issues. Even though k may not vary with size of firm, if F falls as firm size increases, then k_e will also fall.

Available evidence suggests a pronounced decline in F as size of firm increases. Archer and Faerber stated that "the costs of flotation of a public sale of common stock were found to be significantly related to either the size of firm or the size of the issue. The size of the firm no doubt limits the size of the issue, and the two are closely correlated as expected. That small issues would involve higher issuance costs might be anticipated intuitively."[11]

This statement is borne out rather dramatically by the SEC statistics presented in Table 5-8. The costs of floating new equity issues averaged 27 per cent for issues under $500,000 but dropped to 5.4 per cent on issues of $20 to $50 million. Archer and Faerber do not provide comparable statistics, but they do make the statement that for their sample "flotation costs varied from 5.25 per cent to 44.32 per cent." Undoubtedly their range is much wider because the SEC figures are averages, not individual firm's costs, and the average is necessarily between the extremes. Accordingly, it seems that the two studies are reasonably consistent with one another.

Table 5-8—Costs of Flotation, 1951–1955
(Costs Expressed as Percentage of Gross Proceeds)

Size of Issue ($ Millions)	DEBT			PREFERRED STOCKS			COMMON STOCKS		
	Under-writing Com-mission	Other Ex-penses	Total Costs	Under-writing Com-mission	Other Ex-penses	Total Costs	Under-writing Com-mission	Other Ex-penses	Total Costs
Under 0.5	—	—	—	—	—	—	21.0	6.0	27.0
0.5–0.9	7.5	4.0	11.5	8.7	4.0	12.7	17.1	4.6	21.8
5.0–9.9	1.0	0.8	1.8	2.9	0.8	3.7	5.3	0.9	6.2
20.0–49.9	0.8	0.5	1.3	2.8	0.4	3.2	5.0	0.4	5.4
50.0 plus	0.9	0.3	1.2	2.1	0.4	2.5	—	—	—

Source: Securities and Exchange Commission, *Cost of Flotation of Corporate Securities, 1951–1955* (Washington, D.C.: U.S. Government Printing Office, June 1957).

As with the values for the basic required rate of return, available flotation cost figures relate only to the cost of raising new money from the general public; there are no statistics on the cost of procuring equity funds from private sources.

In summary, then, among firms large enough to be publicly owned, size has relatively little impact on the required rate of return, but it does have a substantial impact on the costs of selling new issues of common stock. If, under normal market conditions, very large firms in the "average" risk class have k equal to approximately 8 per cent— and this is a reasonable estimate—then very small publicly owned companies probably have k values in the neighborhood of 10 per cent. In other words, if the average investor is willing to buy the stock of a giant food chain such as Safeway Stores or A&P on the basis of an expected return of 8 per cent, then he is probably willing to buy a small local chain's stock on the expectation of a 10 per cent yield. If, however, Safeway or A&P were to sell new common stock, they would have a cost of new equity of about 8.4 per cent, but the local chain could easily have a cost in the neighborhood of 13.5 per cent.[12] Thus, the cost of new outside equity could easily be 60 per cent higher to the small firm.

EQUITY COSTS FOR THE PRIVATELY OWNED FIRM

Extrapolations beyond the range of observations upon which the trend is based are always dangerous. In the present instance, extrapolating relationships between size of firm and cost of equity capital below an asset size of about $100,000 means moving from publicly owned to privately owned firms, and intuition leads us to expect profound changes as we move from one market segment to the other. Clearly, then, the most we can hope to accomplish is to formulate some very rough estimates of equity costs for the small, privately owned firms. In doing this, reliance must be placed partly on judgment and intuition, and partly on the data for publicly owned companies.

The Required Rate of Return. Is it reasonable to expect k, the required rate of return, to be higher for privately owned firms than for publicly owned ones? There are actually several reasons for expecting this condition to exist. First, because privately owned firms tend to be small, and because small firms tend to be riskier, there should be a higher cost of equity for closely held companies. Second, the liquidity question becomes extremely important when we move into the sphere of the private firm. In the case of a proprietorship or a one-owner corporation, the sale of the business generally requires that the buyer have not only money to invest but also a willingness and ability to run the business. This severely restricts the number of potential purchasers and limits the liquidity of an investment in such a company. If the firm is a partnership or a corporation owned by several stockholders, the problem of disposing of a minority interest can be even more serious; in this case, liquidating the investment requires finding someone who must be personally involved with the operations of the firm in order to protect his interests but who will not be able to control it. Regardless of the size of the firm, these problems are all mitigated by public ownership, leading us to anticipate lower new equity costs for publicly owned firms.

Risk, and especially liquidity, doubtless increase the cost of equity to the small firm. However, another factor—the ability to buy control with a relatively small investment—may tend to reduce it. One often hears of the advantages of "working for yourself"; can these advantages be translated into cost-of-capital terms, and might they not tend to reduce the required rate of return for small firms? To give a concrete example, suppose someone is choosing between two alternative investments, each requiring an outlay of $25,000. The first is the common stock of a large, listed corporation on which the investor expects a return of 10 per cent consisting of dividends and capital gains. The second is all the stock of a small business, and on this the investor expects an 8 per cent return consisting of dividends, capital appreciation, and incremental salary. Is it not possible that a rational, well-informed investor might choose the latter in spite of its lower expected return, greater risk, and much lower liquidity simply in order to "be his own boss"? If so, and if this feeling is strong among many investors, then it is possible that the cost of capital could be lower for certain smaller firms.

Even though the above ideas have some validity, this position should not be pushed too far. For although the owner-manager may be willing to invest his own funds at a lower return, it is most unreasonable to believe that other investors would be willing to assume minority positions in a small business except at a higher return than they could obtain elsewhere on safer, more liquid investments. Also, it is unreasonable to think that the owner-manager himself would be willing to accept submarginal returns on unlimited increments of investment. Although he might invest $25,000 at 8 per cent to buy himself a job as his own boss, he would probably not be willing to put additional funds into the business except at higher expected returns.

Flotation Costs for Privately Owned Firms. Archer and Faeber used both seasoned (previous public market) and unseasoned firms in their sample—55 per cent unseasoned, 45 per cent seasoned—but they do not indicate any difference in flotation costs for these two classes. They stated that "the unseasoned issue might be expected to involve larger flotation costs because of the somewhat greater uncertainty on the part of the underwriter as to proper pricing of the issue," but they did not test this proposition. Intuitively, however, their statement is appealing, and in the absence of evidence to the contrary it does seem likely that firms going public for the first time would incur higher flotation costs.

No statistics whatever are available on the costs of raising equity funds privately; therefore, anything said on the subject is necessarily conjectural. On the one hand, it might be argued that stock sales by private firms are much the same as direct placements in the term loan market and that, consequently, flotation costs, except possibly for certain finders' fees, are minimal. On the other hand, one might question the adequacy of such a narrow definition of flotation costs, and it could be suggested that including a value for the owner's own search time causes flotation costs to be quite high for the private firm.

DIFFERENTIAL PERSONAL TAX RATES AND THE COST OF RETAINED EARNINGS

It has been shown that the differential tax rates favoring capital gains generally cause the cost of retained earnings to be lower than the required rate of return on new outside equity. In the case of widely held corporations, problems associated with determining the applicable stockholder tax rates may result in a disregard for this consideration, but this is certainly not the case for the privately owned firm. Many small businesses are owned by relatively wealthy individuals, and withdrawing cash from the business through either dividends or salaries results in their having very high personal income taxes. Such individual owners may find it more advantageous to retain profits in the business and reinvest them at relatively low rates of return rather than to withdraw cash, pay taxes, and invest the proceeds at higher external rates.

It has been argued that such external investments—either entire companies through merger or marketable securities—could be made within the firm rather than by its owner as an individual. To some extent this is true, but search costs, antitrust considerations, funds availability, and administrative problems connected with running the acquired firm limit the acquisition of other small businesses, and Section 531 of the Internal Revenue Code (the restriction on the improper accumulation of earnings to avoid payment of dividends) limits the acquisition of marketable securities.

Are tax considerations likely to be more important to the small, privately owned firm than they are to the large, publicly owned firm? In many instances they probably are, and this could be an important reason for the finding that smaller firms have lower rates of return on net worth than larger ones.

DIFFERENTIAL CORPORATE TAX RATES AND THE
COST OF CAPITAL

Corporate income under $25,000 is taxed at 22 per cent; income over $25,000 is taxed at 48 per cent. This has obvious and important implications for the investment policies of large and small firms. If a firm earning less than $25,000 has a required rate of return equal to 10 per cent after corporate taxes, then it must earn 12.8 per cent before taxes $(10 \div (1 - .22))$ to provide the required after-tax yield. By contrast, a firm earning over $25,000 would have to earn 19.2 per cent before taxes to net 10 per cent after taxes. This is obviously an important investment incentive to small businesses, but it has little to do with the effect of size on the cost of capital when cost of capital is defined on an after-tax basis as it is here.

The Effect of Size on Capital Structure

TOTAL CAPITAL

Besides influencing the cost of individual capital components, size may also affect the over-all cost of capital by affecting the capital structure. Does capital structure vary systematically with size of firm? According to Table 5-9 such a tendency does exist within manufacturing firms; the smallest group obtains almost 50 per cent of its total funds from debt sources, but this figure falls to 33 per cent for the largest group. Current liabilities decline from 35.8 to 19.2 per cent over the size range, with most of this decline coming in trade accounts payable. Long-term debt increases somewhat as we move up the size scale, but not by enough to offset the decline in current liabilities. The net result is that larger firms, on the average, use significantly less debt than smaller ones.

In part, the greater reliance on debt, especially trade credit, by small firms results from their large investment in current assets, particularly inventories. In addition, there is strong evidence that smaller firms do not have ready access to long-term sources of funds, especially equity capital.

Table 5-9—Financial Structure by Size of Firm, Manufacturing Corporations, Fourth Quarter 1965 ($ Millions)

	Under $1	$1–5	$5–10	$10–25	$25–50	$50–100	$100–250	$250–1000	Over $1000
Short-term loans	5.2	6.4	6.5	5.5	4.2	4.1	4.1	2.8	1.0
Trade accounts and notes payable	19.0	13.2	9.9	9.0	7.7	7.1	7.3	7.0	6.9
Current maturities on long-term debt	2.3	1.8	1.5	1.3	1.1	0.9	0.7	0.6	0.4
Other current liabilities	9.3	10.3	9.5	9.4	9.8	10.2	11.3	12.1	11.0
Total current liabilities	35.8	31.6	27.3	25.3	22.9	22.3	23.3	22.6	19.2
Long-term debt[1]	14.0	11.8	12.6	14.9	14.9	17.7	17.8	19.3	14.3
Total liabilities	49.8	43.4	39.9	40.3	37.8	39.9	41.1	41.9	33.5
Stockholder equity[2]	50.2	56.5	60.1	59.7	62.2	60.1	58.9	58.1	66.5
TOTAL liabilities plus stockholder equity	100.0	100.0	100.0	100.0	100.0	100.0	100.0	100.0	100.0

Source: FTC-SEC, Quarterly Financial Report for Manufacturing Corporations.
1 Includes a small amount of "other noncurrent liabilities."
2 Includes a small amount of "reserves not reflected elsewhere."

INTEREST-BEARING CAPITAL

As was pointed out earlier, current practices call for including only interest-bearing debt in the capital structure when calculating the cost of capital; noninterest-bearing debt is netted out against required investment outlays in the capital budgeting process. However, it is still appropriate to exclude "free" capital when computing the cost of capital for purposes of comparing the costs of different-sized firms. Does not more extensive use of "free" trade credit by smaller firms tend to bias their cost of capital upward if trade credit is excluded from the calculation? The fact of the matter is that small firms in a given industry probably receive no more "free" credit than do larger firms in the industry. The small firms may make greater use of the trade credit by not taking discounts, not paying accounts on time, and so on, but this "extra" trade credit is by no means costless and may actually have a higher cost than either interest-bearing debt or equity. It is well known that a 36 per cent implicit interest cost is involved in the failure to take the discount when the terms are 2/10, net 30. It is also well known that when firms do not pay accounts promptly, they suffer reductions in the availability of trade and other credit, poor service in periods of short supply, and so forth. These costs cannot be quantified, but they are certainly important and probably at least equal the cost of interest-bearing debt or equity.

If these arguments are approximately correct, then it is reasonable to compare average costs of capital computed without regard to "free" capital. Such capital structures, built from the data contained in Table 5-9, are presented in Table 5-10. Here we see that smaller manufacturing firms tend to use debt more extensively than do larger firms. At the low end of the size scale companies obtain almost 30 per cent of their capital from debt sources; at the other end of the scale the ratio is only 19 per cent.

Size of Firm, Rate of Growth, and the Over-All Cost of Capital

Clearly, calculating a firm's cost of capital is a rather complicated process involving highly subjective estimates of many critical variables. In this section illustrative cost of capital schedules are given for "small"

Table 5-10—Capital Structures of Manufacturing Firms ($ Millions)

	Under $1M	$1–5	$5–10	$10–25	$25–50	$50–100	$100–250	$250–1B	Over 1B
Short-term bank loans	5.2	6.4	6.5	5.5	4.2	4.1	4.1	2.8	1.0
Current maturities on long-term loans	2.3	1.8	1.5	1.3	1.1	0.9	0.7	0.6	0.4
Long-term debt	14.0	11.8	12.6	14.9	14.9	17.7	17.8	19.3	14.3
Total debt	21.5	20.0	20.6	21.7	20.2	22.7	22.6	22.7	15.7
Stockholder equity	50.2	56.5	60.1	59.7	62.2	60.1	58.9	58.1	66.5
Total "capital"	71.7	76.5	80.7	81.4	82.4	82.8	81.5	80.8	82.2
Percentage debt	29.7	26.1	25.5	26.6	24.5	27.4	27.7	28.1	18.9
Percentage equity	70.3	73.9	74.5	73.4	75.5	72.6	72.3	71.9	81.1
	100.0	100.0	100.0	100.0	100.0	100.0	100.0	100.0	100.0

Source: FTC-SEC, Quarterly Financial Report for Manufacturing Corporations.

and "large" firms. "Small" and "large" are undefined, but the small firm might be one with assets of $200,000–$300,000, and the large one might be a company listed on the New York Stock Exchange.

EFFECTS OF GROWTH RATES ON THE COST OF EQUITY

As we have seen, internally generated equity capital costs less than external equity because of flotation costs and differential tax rates on dividend versus capital gains income. This makes it necessary to calculate a weighted average of retained earnings and new outside equity for use in computing the over-all cost of capital. At low growth rates, retained earnings are sufficient to supply all the equity that is needed; at higher rates of growth it becomes necessary to bring in expensive external equity capital. Therefore, a relationship exists between a firm's rate of growth and its cost of capital. The nature of this relationship can be explained best by an example.

A hypothetical firm, Small Company, has decided that its optimal capital structure calls for 30 per cent debt, 70 per cent equity. The existing stockholders are all members of one wealthy family, and given their tax situation and outside investment opportunities, they have determined that the required rate of return on retained earnings is 8 per cent—the same as the current rate of return (after corporate taxes) on equity. New outside equity can be obtained in unlimited quantities *so long as equity is raised in sufficient amounts to maintain the 70 per cent equity base.* The firm's marginal tax rate is 22 per cent, and it has decided to pay no dividends provided retained earnings can be invested to yield more than 8 per cent after corporate taxes.

The firm's cost of capital before taxes,[13] or its "hurdle rate" for new investment, depends on the extent to which it must use new external equity, and this in turn depends upon its rate of growth. Under the assumptions of the example, retained earnings supply all the equity needed so long as the firm grows no faster than 8 per cent, the rate of return on the equity base. Beyond this growth rate, high-cost external equity must be obtained. The before-tax cost of retained earnings is 10.3 per cent; this rate of return, before the 22 per cent corporate tax, yields 8 per cent after taxes. The before-tax cost of external equity, on the other hand, is much higher:

$$k_e = \frac{k}{(1-T)/(1-F)} = \frac{20}{(1-.22)/(1-.3)} = 36.6\%$$

Table 5-11—Calculations of Hypothetical Firm's Cost of Capital

GROWTH RATE (%)	SOURCE OF EQUITY CAPITAL		SMALL FIRM			LARGE FIRM		
	Per Cent External	Per Cent Internal	Wted. Avg. Cost of Equity	Cost of Debt	Wted. Avg. Cost of Capital	Wted. Avg. Cost of Equity	Cost of Debt	Wted. Avg. Cost of Capital
8 or less	0	100.0	10.3	7.5	9.5	15.4	6.0	13.6
9	11.1	88.9	13.2	7.5	11.5	15.9	6.0	13.9
10	20.0	80.0	15.6	7.5	13.2	16.3	6.0	14.2
12	33.3	66.7	19.1	7.5	15.6	17.0	6.0	14.8
14	42.9	57.1	21.5	7.5	17.3	17.5	6.0	15.2
16	50.0	50.0	23.5	7.5	18.7	17.7	6.0	15.4
18	55.5	44.5	24.9	7.5	19.7	18.1	6.0	15.7
20	60.0	40.0	26.1	7.5	20.5	18.3	6.0	15.8
25	68.0	32.0	28.2	7.5	21.9	18.7	6.0	16.2
30	73.3	26.7	29.6	7.5	22.9	18.9	6.0	16.3
100	92.0	8.0	34.5	7.5	26.4	19.8	6.0	17.0
1,000,000	100.0	.0	36.6	7.5	27.9	20.0	6.0	17.2

Notes: 1. Per Cent External is found by the equation $(G - R)/G$ where G is the growth rate, and R is the after-tax return on existing net worth.
2. The following assumptions are incorporated in the calculations:
   a. $R = 8\%$.
   b. k_e is 8% for both the large and small firm on an after-tax basis. Marginal corporate income taxes are 22% for the small firm and 48% for the larger one. Dividing k_r by $(1 - T)$ for each firm produces the following before-tax values of k_r: k_r (small) = 10.3%; k_r large = 15.4%.
   c. New stockholders in the small firm require a 20% return after corporate taxes, and flotation costs are assumed to be 30%. Therefore, the before-tax cost of new outside equity for the small firm is:

$$k_o = \frac{k/(1 - F)}{(1 - T)} = \frac{20/.7}{.78} = 36.6\%$$

and for the large firm:

$$k_o = \frac{8/.78}{.52} = 20\%$$

   d. Debt as a percentage of total capital is assumed to be 30% for the small firm, 20% for the large one.

122

The percentage of equity that must be raised externally depends on the rate of growth, as follows:

$$P = \frac{G - R}{G}, G \geqslant R$$

Here P is the percentage of external equity, G is the rate of growth in assets, and R is the rate of return (after taxes) on equity. For example, if Small Company grows at a 15 per cent rate and earns 8 per cent on equity, then it must raise 46.7 per cent of its equity requirements externally. With 46.7 per cent of its equity costing 36.6 per cent and 53.3 per cent costing 10.3 per cent, the average cost of equity is 22.6 per cent. If growth increases to 20 per cent, 60 per cent of the equity requirements must come from external sources and the average cost of equity rises to 26.1 per cent.

Equity and debt costs must be averaged to determine the firm's over-all cost of capital. Using the 30–70 debt–equity weights, we find average before-tax costs equal to 9.5, 18.1, and 20.5 per cent for growth rates of 8, 15, and 20 per cent respectively.[14] The *marginal* cost of capital—the relevant figure for use as a hurdle rate in capital budgeting—is the weighted average of the *marginal* costs of debt and equity. In the example the marginal cost is constant and equal to the average cost at rates of growth up to 8 per cent; above an 8 per cent growth rate, it is constant and equal to 27.9 per cent. Marginal costs are the costs of increments of capital. Above an 8 per cent growth rate, increments of equity must come from outside the firm and cost 36.3 per cent for the small firm. By assumption, 70 per cent of all new capital is equity, and 30 per cent is debt costing 7.5 per cent. Therefore, the marginal cost of capital beyond an 8 per cent growth rate is the weighted average of 36.6 per cent equity money and 7.5 per cent debt money, weighted 70–30, or 27.9 per cent. These relationships are shown in Table 5-11.

Because of the lower corporate income tax, the small firm has a relatively lower before-tax cost of capital up to the limit of internal equity financing. This means that with the same relative investment opportunities the smaller firm should accept a larger percentage of its opportunities and grow at a faster rate *when investment opportunities are not especially plentiful*. However, the marginal cost of capital for small firms is very much higher than that for the large firm, and its discontinuity gap is much wider. Because of this the smaller firm should

not expand beyond its internally generated funds unless investment opportunities are truly exceptional.

Effects of Size on the Cost of Capital: Internal Equity Only

The Small Company in the preceding example is a very small,
privately owned concern with a marginal tax rate of only 22 per
cent; this implies that its taxable income is less than $25,000. Because
the before-tax cost of equity is defined as $k/(1 - T)$, the shift in
T as the firm's income passes the $25,000 mark produces a shift in the
cost of equity. In other words, a small firm with an income less than
$25,000 might have a marginal cost of capital (before-tax) equal to
15 per cent, whereas a slightly larger company might have a marginal
cost of 20 per cent.

Effects of Size on the Cost of Capital: External Equity Only

The cost of externally generated equity is defined as follows:

$$k_e = \frac{k/(1 - T)}{(1 - F)}$$

To the extent that the basic rate of return k, the marginal tax rate
T, and flotation costs F vary with size of firm, then the cost of external equity k_e must also vary with size. Because we are now concerned with *outside* equity, there are presumably no forces such as
the ability to work for oneself influencing the required rate of return. With k dependent solely on risk, liquidity, and the like, it can
be expected to decline with firm size until a reasonably large size
is reached. This usually leads to economies of scale in financing over
a wide range of sizes. Similarly, F declines with size, and this too
leads to economies of scale. On the other hand, T shifts upward
at the $25,000 income size, producing an upward shift in k_e.

Conclusions

The essentials of cost of capital theory have been described and
used to analyze cost differentials between large and small firms. Both
debt and equity costs have been seen to be related to risk, liquidity,

flotation costs, and the breadth of the market in which a firm obtains capital. On all of these counts small firms have disadvantages vis-à-vis large ones, and this leads to the conclusion that the cost of capital should decline as firm size increases.

There are, however, certain advantages to small size, at least within limits. First, smaller companies typically use somewhat more debt than larger ones, and this probably reduces their cost of capital over what it would be if all firms used the same capital proportions. Second, until their before-tax income reaches $25,000 small companies have a definite cost advantage stemming from their lower tax rates. And third, to the extent that investors are willing to accept a relatively low rate of return on their investment in order to "be their own bosses," owner-contributed capital in small businesses may have a relatively low cost.

Theoretical considerations, reinforced by the available empirical data, suggest several interesting points. First, very large and very small firms probably have a similar cost of capital *under certain conditions*. The conditions for this approximate equality are (1) that the small firm is at the 22 per cent marginal tax rate (or, if it is not taxed as a corporation, that the owners' tax rates are lower than 48 per cent), (2) that all equity is generated internally, and (3) that the small firm is managed by its owners. Whenever these conditions do not hold, the larger firm is likely to have a lower cost of capital.

The second point suggested by the analysis is that two important types of discontinuities exist in the cost of capital schedules for the smaller firms. For one, as a firm's profits grow, its tax rate experiences a jump that produces an upward shift in the cost of capital curve. The other discontinuity is related to growth. A certain rate of growth can be financed by internally generated equity, but beyond this critical level new outside equity is required. The higher cost of outside equity causes the entire cost of capital curve to shift upward at this particular growth rate, and the shift is much greater for small, privately owned firms than for large, public corporations.

6

Cash Budgeting in
Small Business

James N. Holtz

To describe how a specific firm should prepare a cash budget would be of limited interest, because each firm is rather unique. Those techniques and data required as inputs to the process which are useful and available to one type of firm may not be available to firms with a different operating structure or market environment. The principal difference between cash budgeting for a large firm and a small one is that the small firm may not be able to devote the accounting and financial resources required to construct and maintain a comprehensive budget system.

This chapter will focus on the theoretical constructs underlying the preparation of the cash budget. Several techniques will be presented which, although novel, can be adapted within the resource base of a fairly small enterprise.

The Financial View of the Firm

A firm can be described in various ways. An obvious description concerns the skeletal aspects of the firm: the steel, brick, and mortar. This view is essentially one of plant and equipment. A second view would emphasize the human aspects: the production and marketing personnel, the management team, and so on. The flows of materials and of information are still other noteworthy aspects of an enterprise. These views of the firm are well known and, when considered in combination, constitute what can be termed the physical environment of a firm.

The physical operations of the firm add utility—that is, form, place, or time—to a good (or a service). This process of product transformation, generally termed the *production function*, transforms various inputs into a more valuable output.

Various academic disciplines study and improve upon the management of each of these subsystems. For example: engineering studies systematic plant layout and design and product design; industrial relations studies the management of the flow of personnel; marketing studies the flow of goods to markets and the desires of consumers for product improvement; accounting designs better information flows; and so on.

There is, however, another conception of the firm or its operations in the financial environment. From this standpoint the firm is not brick, mortar, personnel, and material, but simply a pool of cash—cash that has been raised by the owners in some fashion and placed at the disposal of management. Management must make decisions to acquire assets at the physical level and then expend either cash or credit derived from a sound cash position to acquire these assets. Credit is simply a deferral of the expenditure of cash.

Once the physical assets are obtained, they are transformed and sold for cash or credit. Here credit is simply the deferral of the recovery of cash. The primary mission of the financial manager is to secure sufficient funds, on terms as favorable to the firm as possible, to implement the operating decisions of management. Stated as simply as possible, the financial officer is concerned with the requisition, the expenditure, and the recovery of cash. (In this chapter the terms *cash* and *funds* are synonymous.)

The preceding description of a firm is depicted in Figure 6-1. This diagram can be interpreted in the following manner: Cash (depicted by a circle) is expended for physical assets and leaves the control of the firm. The accounting department notes this expenditure and records it in T accounts. At this time the firm's cash is no longer lingering in the cash account but is invested in inventory, plant, equipment, and so on. The goods are transformed and sold for credit. At this time the accountant "moves" the investment from inventory to re-

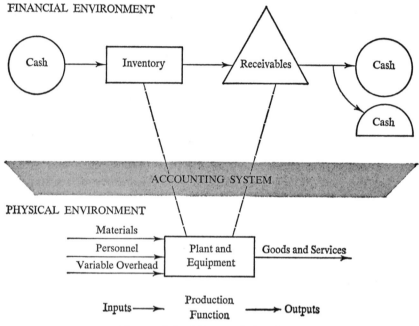

Figure 6-1—Views of the Firm

ceivables, where it lingers until it is collected. Hopefully the initial expenditure plus an increment of cash is recovered at that time. This sum is again available to be expended. The investment in plant and equipment is recovered over a longer time period through depreciation charges against taxable income and the eventual disposition of the asset.

A good understanding of the cash flow model of the financial activities of the firm is essential to the preparation of a cash budget, for all the cash budget does is embody the financial flows that have an impact on the cash account in a cash-inflow, cash-outflow format over a desired time horizon.

A reasonably descriptive cash flow model, diagrammatically presented in Figure 6-2, can encompass all financial expenditures of the firm. This model indicates that the firm assembled a pool of cash to begin operations in January. Cash was expended to acquire inventories in February. In March the initial inventories had been sold on account and these accounts were collected in April. They expended cash plus an increment of cash available to the management, which could "trickle down" and be expended for the desired nonworking-capital expenditures of the firm.

The model further indicates that the length of time required to recover an expenditure on working capital is three months; consequently, the working capital turnover period is three months. This means that three units of working capital must be employed for continuous operation of the firm. The concept of a unit of working capital is useful when a firm is beginning operations and in addition provides the rationale for the concept of the self-liquidating bank loan. However, when the firm has been in operation for a period of time, the individual units of working capital tend to become indistinguishable and the units are aggregated within one account (that is, inventories). It will be noticed that the balance sheet shows the location of the investment, which tends to destroy the image of the investment flow.

The incremental cash recovered in excess of working capital requirements is then available for other productive operations of the firm. Selling and administration expenditures are productive and must be made monthly. Expenditures for the acquisition of land, buildings, equipment, and other capital assets must be made from time to time. These expenditures, although desirable, are frequently postponable, so that management has some discretion concerning the timing of these cash outflows.

Expenditures on interest and taxes are legally mandatory and are not postponable, except under adverse conditions to the firm. Interest payments are contractual and usually the firm is not given more than a 90-day grace period before bankruptcy proceedings are instigated. Taxes are payable on specified calendar dates; and interest and other penalties are charged for delayed or partial payment. Additional

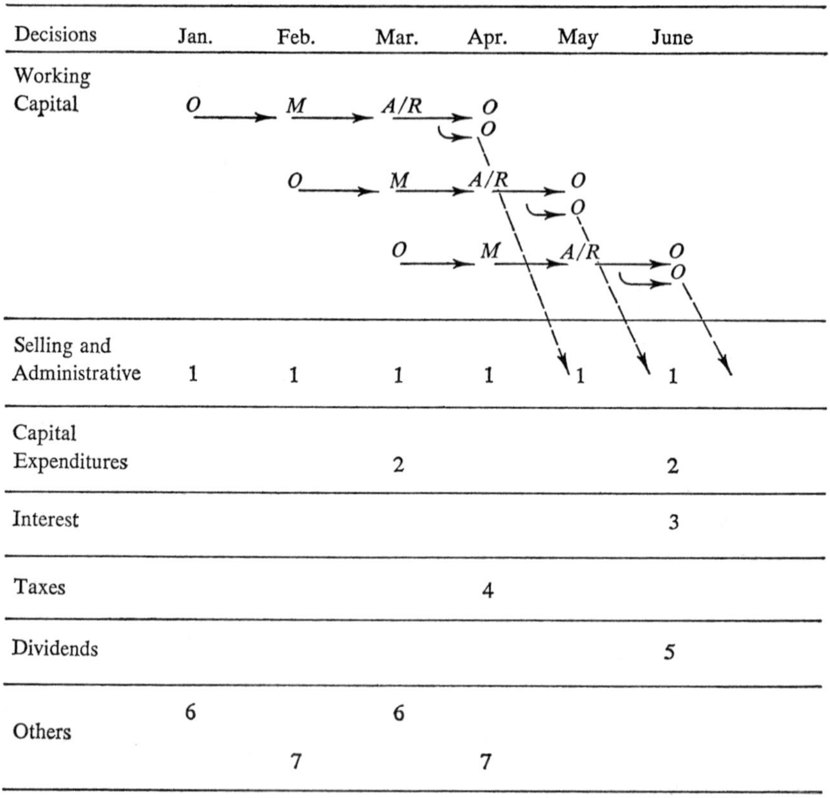

Decisions	Jan.	Feb.	Mar.	Apr.	May	June
Working Capital	$O \longrightarrow$	$M \longrightarrow$	$A/R \to$	O O		
		$O \longrightarrow$	$M \longrightarrow$	$A/R \to$	O O	
			$O \longrightarrow$	$M \longrightarrow$	A/R	O O
Selling and Administrative	1	1	1	1	1	1
Capital Expenditures			2			2
Interest						3
Taxes				4		
Dividends						5
Others	6	7	6	7		

LEGEND

O – Cash
M – Dollars lingering in Inventories
A/R – Dollars lingering in Accounts Receivable
1 – Dollars expended for Selling and Administrative Expenses
2 – Dollars expended for Capital Expenditures
3 – Dollars expended for Interest Payments
4 – Dollars expended for Income Taxes
5 – Dollars expended for Dividends to Shareholders
6 – Dollars expended for Other Operational Purposes
7 – Dollars expended for Other Operational Purposes

Figure 6-2—Trickle-Down Cash Flow Model

leeway for altering the timing of the tax payment exists through use of accelerated depreciation and other tax deferring techniques.

The payment of dividends to preferred and common shareholders, although desirable, is both optional and postponable, thus affording considerable leeway in the timing of these cash outflows.

There are numerous other classes of expenditures that are made by firms. Research and development, public relations, and legal fees are illustrative of these categories. In general, the relevant factor is the degree of control management has over the size and the timing of the outflows. It should also be remembered that some control is also exercised over the timing of the cash inflows.

This model then is descriptive of the nature and timing of cash flows and is consistent with the view of the enterprise as a pool of cash with emphasis on cash flows and a sufficient stock of cash. The essence of cash budgeting becomes forecasting the size and timing of the cash flows, assessing the degree of uncertainty in these estimates, and arranging for a suitable stock of cash on hand to meet the anticipated cash requirements of the firm.

Liquidity Versus Profitability

It is important to understand clearly the relationship between profits and liquidity because confusion frequently exists as to their precise relationship to decision-making in the firm. Retained earnings is a profit-oriented concept and does not fall out of the cash flow model.

Liquidity means cash. More generally, it means that the firm has at its disposal sufficient cash to meet foreseen expenditures. If a firm were perfectly liquid it would hold no physical assets, just the pool of cash. The cash budget is the primary mechanism utilized by the firm to assess the likelihood of attaining the desired degree of liquidity throughout the time period under consideration.

Profit is an accounting concept used to depict the earning power of the firm over a stipulated period of time. It is obtained by matching all relevant costs with the quantity of items sold during the period. At best, it is only an approximation of the earning power of a firm for that period. If a firm is interested in maximizing profits, it would not hold cash since cash must be expended before it can be recovered to make a profit. In fact, profits and liquidity are conflicting objectives. Generally, financial management attempts to maximize profits subject to the constraint of a desired level of liquidity.

The accountant's profit model and the cash flow model presented above differ in many respects. One major difference is in the recovery of funds lingering while invested in a fixed asset. The cash flow model includes expenditures for capital equipment—a substantial outlay for an asset that will last over a period of several years. The outlay for capital equipment affects profits, not in the period at which it occurs, but rather through a deduction for depreciation of that asset, which represents the loss in value of that asset during the accounting period.

A second major difference is that sales are instrumental in the determination of profit even though the sales may be for credit and not collected during that period. In fact, installment sales may require several years before the proceeds are collected in full. These and other distinctions between the cash flow model and the profit model demonstrate that there is a clear distinction between profits and liquidity. Profitability of expenditures is an important factor in decision-making, but liquidity is also important and is the sole concern of the cash budget.

A second clarification of concepts should be made before financial forecasting for a cash budget is discussed. Stocks must be distinguished from flows. A stock is a quantity of items at a point in time. One can speak of a stock of pencils, of chairs, of widgets. Stocks may exist in physical terms or in financial terms. One can speak either of the stock of widgets or of the financial investment in that stock of widgets. The balance sheet embodies the financial investment of a firm at a point in time.

A flow requires time. Sales, material used, labor applied, and funds alter, or flow, over a period of time. Flows also may be either physical or financial. The income statement, because it covers a period of time, embodies the flows within a firm.

Stocks change over time by only two devices: inflows and out-flows. The cash budget by neccessity reflects the interactions between the financial flows and the stock of cash in the firm over the relevant time horizon.

In a world of no uncertainty or risk few or no stocks would be required by a firm. The timing and the amounts of flows would be known with certainty and the inflows and outflows could be arranged to coincide. Every day the inflows would equal the outflows for that day and no stocks would be necessary. Stocks then, are held to insure that flows proceed as advantageously as possible for the firm.

In general, riskier enterprises, or those whose operations face considerable uncertainty, must hedge against this uncertainty by carrying more substantial stocks. Accordingly, the degree of confidence management possesses in their financial forecast will affect the size of the cash balance they must hold.

Financial Forecasting

All firms, regardless of size, face an uncertain future. The ability of a firm to comprehend the future depends on several factors. One, certainly, is the level of effort a firm can apply to this vital task. In general, larger firms are able to devote more resources to forecasting, but small firms compensate by having persons in charge of these financial forecasts who are more familiar with the over-all operation. A second factor is the nature and diversity of the firm's operations. A merchandising establishment usually has a simpler business structure than a manufacturing firm. Furthermore, the manufacturing process itself varies among firms and may be relatively simple in some and quite complex in others. In addition, some firms may be solely dependent upon one or a few buyers, whereas other firms sell to a large segment of the public.

These are among the factors that give each firm the unique operating characteristics that influence its methods of obtaining good financial forecasts. The critical feature of cash budgeting involves determining the level of desired stocks to hold in relation to the foreseeable flow of operations. This requires the preparation of a forecast of the "physical" environment affecting the firm and the translation of this environment into financial terms. A firm is more flexible—that is, it is more aware of its options—if it prepares operating and financial plans for several years in the future.

It is not feasible to prepare a cash budget for a prolonged time horizon, owing to the great uncertainties and numerous changes in the operations of the firm which will undoubtedly occur. Conventionally, the cash budget does not exceed a period of a year and is frequently constructed for a lesser time period. It is, however, important to be aware that the events which transpire after the last month of the budget planning period will require financing during the previous period before these events can be realized. Consequently, if any unusual events lie on that time horizon, the financial impact may occur in the planning period encompassed in the cash budget.

Certain factors must be identified if a realistic cash budget is to be generated. Obviously, the level of sales of the product line of the business has a major impact on the cash requirements. The firm may use macroeconomic models and multiple correlation techniques, the so-called "grass-roots" approach, or whatever means are at its disposal to obtain these sales estimates. The number of items sold times the anticipated price gives the revenue forecast. These revenues must then be adjusted for a reasonable amount of bad debts, which generally are based primarily on past experience. Once the revenues for the period have been computed, the timing of receipts must be ascertained, for only sales for cash have an immediate impact on the cash budget; sales where credit is extended do not affect the cash budget until they are collected. The timing of these factors can be coordinated in a schedule of accounts receivable. The combination of cash sales and collections on accounts receivable normally provides the largest consistent cash inflow over time to the firm.

It is necessary to acquire the inputs before they are sold (there are exceptions to this, but these can be considered in relation to the specific contracts). A merchandising firm acquires the product directly from its vendors; a manufacturing firm must produce the product from a spectrum of inputs. These inputs vary, depending on the nature of the product. Also, the inputs to manufacture the product vary as production of the product varies.

Management relates the two factors of manufacturing and sales in its decisions concerning inventory levels. Management may decide to manufacture at a rate corresponding to anticipated or actual sales, or to manufacture at a steady rate, irrespective of the current level of sales. In the former case, the levels of inventory are kept at a minimum, but the manufacturing process fluctuates as sales fluctuate, which may lead to inefficient production. In the latter situation, the level of inventory may either become abnormally high or low. If high, considerable sums may be lingering in that inventory and be subjected to sales risks; if too low, the anticipated level of sales may be jeopardized owing to lack of stock.

It was stated above that inputs vary as production varies. This statement is true subject to some frictions. There is a one-to-one correspondence between a quantity of materials used and a quantity of units produced (adjusted by scrap and so on). Labor, however, can be embodied in the product, and this relationship holds only if the production process has a continuous flow of material, or if the workers are paid on a piece-rate basis. Labor provides a service; it stands ready to produce, but if there are no materials, that labor service is dissipated. Other inputs such as tools, gloves, and rags are consumed in a production process, but not in any directly observable one-to-one correspondence with production.

Such factors as production supervision and electricity are consumed largely in relation to output, but some slippage does exist. For example, a foreman may supervise anywhere from two to perhaps forty workers; foremen, consequently, are added discontinuously with output. Electricity powers both lights and motors; the plant, however, is lighted irrespective of production levels, but motors are driven more in proportion to the level of production; these factors must be estimated on an individual basis, utilizing the information available.

Along similar lines, a building has an effect upon production, owing to capacity constraints. A given scale of plant can accommodate production from one unit to its maximum capacity. Frequently, capacity can be augmented by operating more than one shift, working seven days a week, and so on. Additional production can be obtained in several ways. One is, of course, to build an additional plant. Others include modifying the existing plant, acquiring new equipment, temporarily leasing additional facilities, subcontracting some in-house production, and so on.

Other activities of the firm are undertaken without the current level of sales or production in mind, yet they have an impact on the cash budget. The decision to undertake an expanded advertising campaign is aimed at establishing good public relations, which hopefully will stimulate future demand for the product. Expenditures with a more remote applicability to current sales involve the establishment or expansion of a research effort to improve existing products or foster development of new products.

Finally, after all physical activities have been formulated and quantified in dollar terms, a financial plan must be derived to support management's plan of action. This financial plan is constructed by considering the availability of capital and the cost-of-capital for the firm. As a result of the financial plan, management may be required to pay interest and sinking funds on debt and dividends on various classes of stock. These cash payments, when expended, feed into the cash budget.

Tradeoffs Between Flows and Stocks

The section on flows and stocks above indicated that in a world of certainty, actions could be taken by management to match inflows exactly to the outflows, with the result that no stock balances would be necessary. Firms, however, do not operate in a world of certainty; they face uncertainty and its attendant risks. To hedge against this environment, stocks of inputs and outputs must be held. The determination of optimal levels of stocks with their attendant financial impacts have been improved in the past decade through the application of such operations research techniques as queuing theory, linear and nonlinear programming, and transportation problems.

These mathematical applications of economics essentially attempt to equate marginal revenues with marginal costs; the objective is to maximize profits. The significant factor for cash budgeting is that each physical parameter is known with certainty; the cash requirements bear the residual brunt of these compounded uncertainties.

It is enlightening to conceive of the stock of cash as consisting of three "funds." The first fund is held to satisfy the transactions demand for money; that is, a sum of cash is necessary to pay bills, acquire inputs, and take care of all the factors described above. A second fund, the precautionary fund, is held because the transaction demand is not known with certainty. The uncertainty faced by a firm can be thought of as cone shaped (Figure 6-3), with more certainty about tomorrow, less about next month, and even less about events beyond a year. The larger the angle (a), the more uncertain the future; the more uncertain the future, the more cash must be held to hedge this uncertainty.

The third fund covers the speculative demand for money. This fund exists to enable the firm to take advantage of bargains that appear from time to time. For example, an opportunity to buy the products of a financially weak firm at submarket prices may appear. Management must have the cash if it is to be able to take advantage of these opportunities.

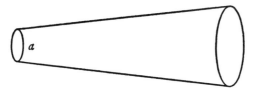

Figure 6-3—Uncertainty as a Function of the Future

Each flow in the cash budget can be visualized as requiring a transactions fund and a precautionary fund in production geared to the timing of purchases and to uncertainty. Each of the specific transactions funds can be aggregated into a total transactions fund. The precautionary funds are not usually additive for it is possible, although unlikely, that all flows will be affected in the same direction. One can expect that if sales fall, purchases and dividends can be cut back and the cash impacts from the individual factors can be offset to a degree. If an analysis is made of the degree of offset that can be anticipated, the precautionary funds can then be "added."

The speculative fund can be added to the combination of the transactions and precautionary funds. The result is that a fund of cash exists to meet all foreseen and some possible unforeseen events.

Shortcut techniques exist to approximate cash requirements. A considerable number of ratios and a set of applicable standards for these ratios have been evolved over time to guide financial suppliers of capital in approving the credit worthiness of the firm. These are the current, debt-to-equity, turnover, and other well-known ratios. These ratios can also be used by management to determine cash needs at a future point in time. For example, an examination of recent operations may indicate that the level of inventories is approximately 20 per cent of the cost of goods sold. If sales of $2,000,000 are expected, and the profit margin is 25 per cent, then cost of goods sold would be approximately $1,600,000 and an inventory stock of $320,000 should be maintained. This same ratio technique can be applied to the other working capital assets.

The level of investment in building must be predicated on capacity considerations, but adjusted by foreseeable depreciation that will occur. Once the level of investment in assets has been forecast, the level of current liabilities to be carried can be derived through utilization of appropriate current ratio constraints. Then, long-term debt levels are obtained through the debt-to-fixed-plant ratio. And finally, the equity portion of financing is derived by use of the debt-to-equity ratio and the appropriate standards for the firm.

Some error is inevitable in the above approach because a linear relationship is assumed to exist between the level of sales and the level of current assets. In practice, a nonlinear relationship is more appropriate, owing to the composition of the stock balance. The transaction portion of the stock to be held presumably is linear with sales; however, the precautionary portion is not directly related to volume, and the speculative component is relatively fixed, irrespective of volume variations. Consequently, when aggregated, a curvilinear relationship is generally obtained. These relationships can be obtained via correlation techniques or approximated through the use of simple scatter diagrams. These latter financial forecasting techniques are described in most basic business finance texts.

Break-Even Charts

Another technique for ascertaining the cash impact of operations can also be determined through the use of break-even charts. Actually, two break-even points are of interest: (1) the profit-and-loss, and (2) the cash. Both of these points can be obtained from the same chart if the chart is constructed in the following specific way.[1]

The first step is to divide all operating costs and revenues of the firm into those that are essentially variable with the level of production and those which are essentially fixed for the period under consideration, irrespective of the level of output. Second, the costs must be further structured along the lines of those requiring a cash expenditure and those not requiring an expenditure of cash during the period. At this point, there are the following five categories: (1) revenues (sales); (2) variable cash costs (materials, payrolls); (3) fixed cash costs (administrative expense); (4) variable noncash costs (can usually be overlooked except where depreciation expense is a function of output); and (5) fixed noncash costs (depreciation, depletion, amortization).

The chart is then constructed by placing all cash costs first, then adding on noncash costs (Figure 6-4).

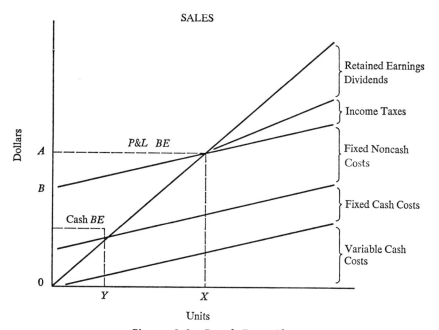

Figure 6-4—Break-Even Chart

In the illustration, at X units of production, both A dollars of sales are generated and costs are incurred; consequently, that is the *profit and loss break-even point.* Note, however, that at Y units of output, only B dollars are (1) actually expended and (2) recovered through sales; consequently, that is the *cash break-even point.*

This chart illustrates that output between 0 units and Y units will result in both an accounting loss and a drain of corporate cash. Output between Y and X units will result in an accounting loss, yet the cash account will be increased. Output greater than X units will result in both an accounting profit and increased accumulation of cash. This is further clarification of the distinction between profitability and liquidity.

This break-even chart must not be misinterpreted. The cash break-even point obtained in this fashion is a result of only the operations of the firm that are represented in the income statement. Other cash transactions, especially those affecting the balance sheet (that is, debt repayment, capital expenditures, and so on) are not included in this chart. Interest can be included as a fixed cash cost. Then one would have the profit-and-loss break-even point after interest. Taxes could be accommodated with a different interpretation of the meaning of the break-even points. This break-even presentation only partially reflects the total financial activities of the firm.

Methods of Treating Uncertainty

The obvious fact that firms operate in an uncertain environment was stressed above. The conventional literature on cash budgeting states this fact, then proceeds with a presentation and a discussion of single point estimates for each flow, which provides little help to management in assessing the impact of uncertainty upon the financial operations of the firm.[2] Actually, the flexible budget system for mass production operations is a good tool for assessing uncertainty because a separate budget is constructed which simulates several possible levels of operations. In the literature on cash budgeting, however, this procedure frequently is not tied directly to the cash budget. It certainly would be advantageous to provide management with some feel for the *range* of impact that various levels of operations can have on the cash account.

The flexible budget system, although an improvement over the preparation of a single budget, still lacks a statement of the likelihood of occurrence for each output level and for the inherent uncertainty involved in each line estimate. In other words, the cash manager probably assumes that the levels of operations underlying each of the budgets are equally likely, or postulates some subjective probability distribution of occurrence for each level, on the basis of his experience. Then he arranges for lines of credit and other financial contracts on the basis of his subjective feel for the uncertainty.

Actually, it is reasonable to assume that all levels of output are not equally likely. On the other hand, it may be advantageous to document this subjective probability distribution that his decisions are predicated on, so that others in management and financial lenders may have a chance to comment on its realism. It would be useful for management to have some technique for quantifying the uncertainty surrounding the precautionary demand for money (or for any other stock).

Management could, with some additional effort, estimate the degree of uncertainty in each of their estimates. These uncertainties undoubtedly could be described by some class of known probability distributions. A computationally simple and relatively inexpensive approach adapted from PERT (Program Evaluation Review Technique) could then be employed to quantify this uncertainty.

PERT attempts to quantify the range of uncertainty encountered by engineers in estimating the time required for completion of events in a complex project. The estimator is asked to furnish three time estimates; the most likely time to completion (m), an optimistic time (a), and a pessimistic estimate of the time to completion of the event (b). It is then assumed that the estimation process is best described by a beta (β) distribution, and a formula has been devised to approximate the mean and the standard deviation of the beta distribution. The formula for the mean is as follows:

$$\frac{(a + 4^m + b)}{6}$$

The formula for the standard deviation is as follows:

$$\frac{b - a}{6}$$

PERT advocates feel that this simple procedure results in a better expected value of the time to complete an event; at the same time the standard deviation gives management a feel for the range of uncertainty in the estimate. The remaining aspects of PERT are largely inapplicable for our purposes.

This approach in the context of cash budgeting would be somewhat as follows: The responsible manager would, for example, estimate that a sales volume of $10 million most likely will be realized, at worst $8 million and at best $18 million would result. Converting these sales estimates into the PERT formula would yield the following:

$[8 + 4(10) + 18]/6 = \$11,000,000$ as the most likely level of sales, and $[\$18,000,000 - 8,000,000]/6 = \$1,667,000$ as the standard deviation.

The financial manager would then estimate sales of $11 million, rather than the $10 million previously estimated, and could anticipate that the standard dispersion of estimates would vary from the mean by $1,667,000.

The use of the beta distribution and the accuracy of the formula can be questioned at first, but as management gains experience in this estimating approach, the procedure and formulas can be adjusted to reflect this experience. This approach should result in overcoming a forecasting bias, and hopefully the consistent effort applied in the planning stage should result in better management.

Summary

This chapter has attempted to provide management with some useful features of cash budgeting without going through the mechanics and presentation of an actual cash budget. The procedure was to present the theoretical construct—namely, the flow of funds in a firm—that is the foundation for the cash budget.

The distinctions between profits and liquidity, stocks and flows were emphasized. It was pointed out that liquidity is the primary concern of the cash budgets and liquidity constraints affect the profit potential of the firm. Stocks were described as being a negative factor to a firm in the sense that the firm should attempt to hold as low a level of stocks as possible, and these only to facilitate the operational flows.

The primary mission of financial forecasting is to determine the physical environment of the firm, estimate the inherent uncertainty, and translate these estimates into financial terms. Several techniques for forecasting financial requirements were briefly described. A major emphasis was placed upon management's devoting considerable effort to quantifying the degree of uncertainty in the future of the firm; for small business in particular, the use of an approach similar to that employed in the PERT technique was advocated. Considerable experimentation with the formulas will be required, for to the author's knowledge the technique has never been applied in practice.

Part III

APPROACHES TO FINANCIAL PLANNING FOR SMALL BUSINESS

7

Approaches to Long-Range Planning for Small Business

George A. Steiner

There is little doubt that the great majority of small businesses do little if any long-range planning. Furthermore, there is considerable resistance to doing much if any long-range planning. Although the virtues of such planning have been rather well "sold" to most of the largest corporations, the job remains to be done among the small business community.

Any expansion of long-range planning among smaller enterprises might best proceed upon three platforms. First, the small businessman must be convinced that long-range planning is worthwhile. Second, he must develop a genuine desire to practice such planning as a way of life. Third, he must adopt methods and principles suitable to his situation. This chapter will deal with these three bases.

What Is Long-Range Planning?

Simply stated, long-range planning is a process of thinking systematically about the future and of making current decisions on that basis. Implicit in this concept is the idea of examining future consequences of present decisions, as well as choosing from among future alternative courses of action as bases for making current decisions. Long-range planning, therefore, is action oriented. It is not speculation without current impact.[1]

Every businessman thinks ahead. This is not new. What is new in long-range planning today is looking ahead systematically. This means a more or less methodical, organized, and consciously pursued process. Managers have found that more formalization of the long-range planning process produces better results.

There is nothing in this concept that implies comprehensive or exhaustive inquiry into the future. Rather, the process actually used in a company should be adapted to the particular circumstances existing in the company.

WHY SO FEW SMALL BUSINESSMEN MAKE LONG-RANGE PLANS

The typical small businessman is apt to give one or more of the following responses when asked why he does so little or no long-range planning: "That's for big companies, not me." "Why should I? I'm doing O.K." "You can't forecast the future, so how can you do long-range planning?" "The future is tomorrow. I can't see tomorrow, so I'll take advantage of today." "Long-range planning is too time-consuming for me. I simply do not have the time, even if I wanted to do long-range planning." "I am in a cash squeeze and that's all I can think about now." "It's too complicated, my business is simple, and I know what the problems are." "My business is too small to formalize planning." "I can do all the planning I need in my head. Anyway, I don't want to discuss my plans with anyone. Why give someone a chance to find out and lose my competitive advantage?"

The average small businessman is faced with many barriers to long-range planning. He is pressed for time. He has most of the problems of an executive in a medium-sized company but without the help available in the larger companies. So, he is constantly fighting "brush fires" and, as anyone who has followed business planning knows, these momentary pressures drive out long-range planning. He is a doer; he is a man of action. There is probably more of an inverse than a positive correlation between successful doers and competent planners. Personally, the small businessman is a "loner." He usually starts alone and has had a habit of doing things himself.[2] Typically, too, the small businessman has kept secret his ideas, plans, and intentions. It is not easy to overcome this history of secrecy and share future plans with others. He also may be reluctant to discuss plans that may not materialize, because he does not want to be thought foolish or inept.

Finally, the literature on long-range planning is getting large, but most of it is not very helpful to the small businessman. He needs detailed guides to tell him how to go about long-range planning. These are not easy for him to find. The result is that he feels lost in trying to start the effort.

These are all reasons that have some substance; but not one of them, nor all of them together, is enough to justify a businessman's avoiding systematic long-range planning.

THE NEED FOR LONG-RANGE PLANNING IN A SMALL BUSINESS

There is no question that larger companies have found great value in long-range planning. Indeed, most of them have instituted formal programs and have assigned staff to work on them. The testaments to the value of such planning are many. For example, a study made in 1964 of the 13 fastest growing companies in the United States revealed that all gave high priority to long-range planning and managed to inspire most levels of managers to think about the future.[3] A deep study of the causes of failure of ten small businesses (seven with less than 150 employees and an average life of 21 years) showed that every company lacked planning.[4]

The matter of forecasting the future seems to bother many businessmen. There is no question about the fact that no one is given the talent to foresee the future. Forecasting is making a judgment of the future upon the basis of present knowledge. The more accurate the forecast, however, the better a plan will be, other things being equal. But, planning can be effective even if a forecast is not too accurate, provided, of course, that the forecast is made more accurate as time moves on and if plans are changed to fit the changing forecast. Whether they realize it or not, all businessmen forecast. The only issue is how well they do it. If a manager, for example, decides not to purchase a new machine, he is in effect forecasting that his profits would not be increased in the future by the net contribution to profits that can be made by the purchase. On the other hand, if he buys the new machine, he is forecasting that its net contribution to profits will be plus rather than minus.

There is confusion about the meaning of forecasting and planning in the minds of some businessmen that must be cleared. Forecasting is not planning, nor is a forecast a plan. It is only one assumed factor in planning. Planning is determining what a manager wants in the future and developing methods to get it. This can be facilitated by a hospitable environment, but often it can be done reasonably well despite an inhospitable environment. Forecasting may tell which type of environment can be expected; planning will determine how to take advantage of it or prevent it from taking advantage of the firm.

Answers to some of the other reasons given for failure to plan ahead are obvious. Certainly, if long-range planning is important, a businessman simply must and can find time to do it. Actually doing long-range planning is simpler than many businessmen imagine, so complexity is no argument against doing it. The businessman who rejects future planning because he is doing so well today could not be more misguided. Rates of product obsolescence are getting faster rather than slower, production methods which today give a businessman an advantage may be obsolete tomorrow, and customers are often very fickle. Prosperity today is no assurance for profits tomorrow.

Long-range planning can be done without fear of revealing trade secrets. Also, doers can adjust to planning. Finally, there are techniques for long-range planning that can be fitted to just about any situation. They will be effective, too, if a few fundamental principles are followed.

Long-range planning is essential for a small as well as a large business if for no other reason than that it permits the managers of any size business to take better advantage of the opportunities which lie in the future and to overcome the threats which the future holds. This is the essence of entrepreneurship. Long-range planning should sharpen and stimulate this function. There are very few small businesses that have the financial reserves to underwrite the unexpected loss that occurs in an unforeseen shift from dependence on a single obsolete product or a few major customers. This sort of crisis may be avoided, however, merely by recognizing that it can happen if action is not taken to avoid it. But planning has other advantages for a small businessman. For example, he will find banks and other sources of cash much more willing to finance his needs if he has a well-designed long-range plan. Also, he may be able to "go public" much more easily and without fear of losing his business. And he may be sure of perpetuating his business upon his retirement.

Long-Range Planning in Small and Large Enterprises

The basic nature and purposes of long-range planning are the same for all businesses, irrespective of size. But this statement is true only at a relatively high level of abstraction. How different-sized companies go about starting and maintaining their long-range plans, what problems are encountered, what is done with plans, who works on the plans, what type of analysis is made at different stages of the process, and what is written and what remains unwritten, vary enormously from one company to another. What is sensible for one company may be complete nonsense for another.

Larger organizations have many advantages over small enterprises in undertaking long-range planning. Most obvious is the fact that they have the resources to employ full-time staff to help make the studies needed for long-range planning, to aid the line executives in making decisions associated with and growing out of planning, in reviewing plans made throughout the organization, and in helping to administer the entire process. Specialists can be hired for certain jobs or brought into the company on a full-time basis. Larger companies generally have more resources to implement plans. Their risks are spread over many rather than one or two products. Their world is larger and they can afford to make more mistakes. Top management may make broad strategic plans and have lower-level managers make them operational.

This all does not mean that large companies have few problems in long-range planning; they do. Nor is it true to say that smaller companies have more difficult problems in this respect than larger companies. It is more accurate to say that they both have problems but the problems differ. For example, a small dress manufacturer with skilled designers may have much less difficult long-range planning problems than, say, a major airline faced with having to decide which among a variety of new generation airplanes to buy. The decisions made in the long-range planning process of each may be just as fateful to the life of the enterprise.

Usually, however, the small businessman does have hard long-range planning problems. Although risk problems vary a great deal among small businesses, there is a tendency for risks to be more concentrated than in larger enterprises. Furthermore, the financial problems of a small businessman usually restrict his ability to spread risks. The small businessman often makes a few products, which are subject to wide changes in demand that are completely beyond his control. He has difficult problems in forecasting such market changes, not to mention his future costs of material and labor. And if he does accurately forecast dark clouds on the horizon, and does see the precise action needed today to avoid these hazards, financial problems usually arise in his taking action. To add new products, develop new customers, or in other ways to reduce his risks, requires capital frequently beyond his reach.

Within the size range of firms that may be labeled small business there are differing long-range planning requirements, problems, and acceptable methods. Availability of staff to help do long-range planning, for example, is a major problem for small business. If the total number of employees is under 25, there may be very little delegation of authority from the president-owner, who may hold all planning in his hands. When the number of employees grows from around 25 to 100, there must be some delegation of authority, and the president-owner may depend upon others in his organization to help him plan for the future. As the number of employees rises from 100 to 500, divisions may be established and full-time staff specialists hired to help executives do long-range planning.

There are, of course, other differences in planning problems among different-sized businesses. These illustrate the point. But, irrespective of size, all are obliged to plan ahead if they are to prosper in the long run. And all must tailor planning methods to their own environment.

WANTED! A LONG-RANGE PLANNING PHILOSOPHY

More important than procedures of planning is the attitude of the chief executive of the company toward planning. No procedure is worth much to a firm if the chief executive is not interested in long-range planning. He must develop an appropriate frame of mind, a philosophy, an attitude which embraces long-range planning as a way of business life. He must develop an open-mindedness which accepts the need to look frankly at the weaknesses (and strengths) of his business, to discover what his business really is, to accept the challenge without fear of looking into the future, and to make current decisions on the basis of what is found.

As the business grows, the small businessman must widen his philosophy to understand the advantages of and the ways to engender more widespread planning among his managers. Mr. Charles G. Mortimer, retired Chairman of the Board of General Foods Corporation, has commented on the importance of a chief executive's motivating his people. A major way for a growing business to follow his advice and reap the benefits of such motivation, as described in the following passage, is to institute effective long-range planning:

> More than anyone else, a chief executive should know the value of spreading the spirit and feeling of belonging. And this makes it incumbent upon him not only to provide appropriate monetary incentives for his people, but also to initiate and extend all down the line the concept that the people who work for *his* company are investing their business lives as truly as stockholders are investing their money. It is a basic philosophical fact that people with a sense of investing themselves, people who know that their management regards them as investors of their business careers, will produce better products, render better customer service, and give fuller measure of value to the public than people who are merely working to earn a living.
>
> When this happens, the effect is to increase the profitability of the company. And that, of course, is 'the name of the game.' That is the chief executive's first basic responsibility—to increase profitability and build a firm foundation for future growth. Creating constructive attitudes among employees will help him do this and is well worth the time it takes.[5]

Before a chief executive can do this, however, he must construct a right frame of mind for himself.

A Conceptual Model for Business Planning

Before discussing a variety of different possible approaches to long-range planning, it is useful to set forth a simple conceptual frame of reference for types of business plans and steps in their development. Figure 7-1 is a simplified sketch of different types of plans needed in a business. It shows also the general flow of action in the process of planning. A very large number of companies have systems that fit this model. The structure is exceedingly flexible and can be adapted to just about any size of business, style of management, type of business, or stage in the development of organized planning. So long as a manager is really interested in long-range planning, this conceptual model can be made operational and can be accommodated to the resources he wishes to devote to planning. It can be applied to a very small company equally as well as to a very large enterprise.

To the left of the chart are the premises that go into any planning effort. First are the basic purposes of the firm. These are usually expressed in broad and general terms. It has only been in recent years that many companies have written their basic purposes. But it is not necessary to express them on paper so long as businessmen think about them, for they are the starting point in long-range planning. Of major significance, too, are the values, ideas, and philosophies which a businessman holds. These permeate, of course, all the man does and are major determinants of all decisions he makes. For example, a businessman who is motivated to create a large business from a small one will go about his long-range planning in a far different manner than one who wishes to work more or less alone to invent new products in his own small laboratory.

Planning also must be based on an assessment of the evolving environment of the future both within and outside the firm. The possible number of elements to be examined is very great, and the art of long-range planning involves an ability to choose for deep examination those of major importance to the firm. Some of the more important ones will be discussed later in this chapter.

Upon these bases the over-all objectives, strategies, and policies of the firm can be set forth. They can be few in number, or many. They can concern any element of the business. The more concrete and important they are, however, the better the plans are likely to be. The time dimensions of objectives, strategies, and policies extend from the infinite to the immediate future, depending upon the subject. For example, a firm may set as its objective: "to be the top quality producer of microelectronic products in the industry." This has no time limit. On the other hand, a strategy "to hire a chief engineer by next month" has a short time dimension.

Medium-range plans cover a fixed time dimension set by a manager. A great many smaller companies consider two years to be a suitable period for medium-range plans but four- and five-year ranges are more frequent for larger companies. In this set of plans, one finds more quantitative expectations for such parts of the business as sales, profits, finance, production, research, and facilities.

The short-range plans usually refer to near-term quarterly or monthly budgets and plans, such as cash budgets, raw material schedules of purchases, production schedules, and shipment schedules, or any elements for which plans and controls are important.

To the right of the diagram are actions needed to complete the process. Organization for implementation means assuring that arrangements are made to operate on the basis of plans. Operations then take place, during and after which reviews of performance are made.

Operational Versus Analytical Steps in Planning

There are two ways to consider the steps of planning—analytically and operationally. The analytical steps are those which have been set up as the preferred procedures in all problem solving. Although they may be expressed in many different ways, fundamentally they take the following form for business planning: establish objectives; prepare basic premises; determine alternative courses of action to achieve objectives; examine different alternative courses of action; choose alternatives to be followed; put the plan into action; and review plans periodically.

These steps are implicit in the accompanying diagram (Figure 7-1) and are fundamental in all effective planning. But a businessman may not follow this sequence at all. The sequence of operational steps in planning may be much different from the analytical steps. For example, it is rare to find a planning program proceeding from one step

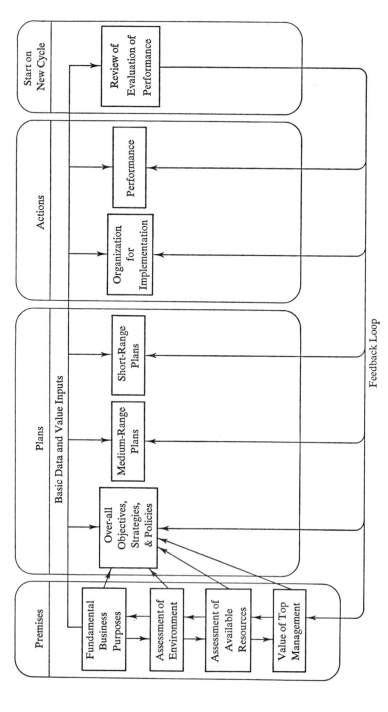

Figure 7-1—The Structure and Process of Planning for a Business

to the next without retracing or overlap—the process is highly iterative. A tentative goal may be changed after examining various alternative courses of action to achieve it. The original tentative goal may be found to be too high or too low.

In the following sections are presented a number of operational steps for planning. Although they differ markedly, they will be more easily performed if both the conceptual model of planning structures and the analytical steps are kept in mind. Precisely what sequence is followed and what depth of analysis is employed will depend upon many considerations: size of business, nature of top management, available help, type of business, nature of problems facing the business, and whether long-range planning is just beginning or has been in operation for some time.

The Suggested Operational Approaches

With this background, specific approaches can be presented. The following suggestions begin with the simplest and conclude with complex methods. These approaches are not mutually exclusive. All of them can, for example, be incorporated in the advanced, sophisticated systems. All the approaches have actually been used with success by small businessmen.

ASKING QUESTIONS

Columella is as correct today as he was centuries ago when he said, "The important part of every business is to know what ought to be done." However, this is not as easy as it sounds. Consider the case of the small businessman whose sales grew rapidly but whose receivables did not turn over quickly enough to finance his current needs. He had to borrow; but because he was not well established, he had to pay high interest rates for his loan, and this wiped out his profit. This man was not asking the right questions.

A survey of over 100 small manufacturers concluded that "the hardest part of planning seems to be getting started."[6] An elemental way to get started in long-range planning is to begin by asking some basic questions. A good place to begin is with objectives. It is most naïve to say, "Our objective is to make a profit—period." Of course it is, but maximizing profits involves a variety of objectives and the solution to many problems. Following are some suggested major questions to stimulate the habit of looking ahead to achieve desired profit and other objectives:

1. What business am I in?
2. What is my place in the industry?
3. What customers am I serving? Where is my market?
4. What is my company image to my major customers?
5. What business do I want to be in five years from now?
6. What are my specific goals for profit improvement?
7. Need I have plans for product improvement? If so, what?
8. What is my greatest strength? Am I using it well?
9. What is my greatest problem? How am I to solve it?
10. What share of the market do I want? Next month? Next year?
11. Are my personnel policies acceptable to employees?
12. How can I finance growth?

This list can be expanded easily. But for those very small businessmen—and some large ones as well—who are preparing such lists and are answering the questions, this is one excellent way to get started toward some systematic long-range planning. It does not take much thought to see how a decision about any one of these questions can have an important impact on most of the others. It is worthwhile, therefore, to do more than speculate idly about such questions. What is most useful is to get at the major issues, think about them continuously over time rather than spasmodically, and to set forth specific plans of action for those areas thought through.

KEYS TO SUCCESS

Every business, both large and small, will succeed or fail because of a limited number of strategic factors. There is no better way to get started in long-range planning than for a businessman to try to discover those that will be responsible for his future success. It is because finance is such a critical factor to most small businessmen that this area is traditionally the prime subject of analysis, both for small businessmen and scholars who are interested in small business problems. But other factors may be just as or more strategic than finance. For example, imagination may be the single most strategic factor in the success of a toy company or an advertising firm. Quality may be the most important factor in the success of a company producing components for a sophisticated aerospace product. Cost control and cost reduction may be the keys to the success of a company producing standard metal stampings for an automobile manufacturer.

Elements such as these should come to light in a more comprehensive long-range planning program. But, if no such program exists, a very small businessman may start his long-range planning with a list of those few strategic factors which will be responsible for his future success. Once they are identified they should, of course, be the subject of deep thought and appropriate action.

Check-off Lists

Some firms use check-off lists to guide their planning. These lists cover such important elements of planning as sales and marketing, research and development, products, plant and property, personnel, organization, finance, and competition. The items in the lists cover major questions that must be asked and point to types of information that should be examined. The following list of questions concerning the addition of new products illustrates this approach. Absolute measurement for many of the questions is difficult, if not impossible, to calculate. Simple ratings, therefore, may be and usually are checked for each question such as: excellent, good, average, poor, unsatisfactory.

Relationship to present operations

1. Does the product fall within the manufacturing and processing know-how of the company?

2. Will the product benefit by the present research and engineering activities of the company?

3. Does the product fit into the lines now handled by our sales organization? Will it permit more efficient utilization of our present sales organization?

Character of the Product

1. Will the product capitalize on our engineering strength?

2. Is there a reasonable volume potential?

3. Can the product maintain a high degree of distinctiveness in comparison with competing products?

4. Will the product contribute to the company's reputation?

Table 7-1—Master Planning Form

Item	CHANGE		Comment
	NY	YAN	
Research and development			
Products			
Product mix			
Service			
Supplies			
Suppliers			
Inventory			
Subcontracts			
Storage and handling			
Quality control			
Space			
Leasehold improvements			
Equipment			
Employees			
Fringe benefits			
Customers			
Sales outlets			
Terms of sale			
Pricing			
Transportation			
Advertising			
Promotion			
Packaging			
Market research			
Financing			
Insurance			
Investments			
Management reports			
Management procedures			
Management organization			
Governmental environment			
Economic environment			
Industrial environment			
Competition			
Community environment			

Instructions:

NY = next year; YAN = year after next. All changes are estimated in relation to the preceding year.

If a quantitative change is anticipated—i.e., change in size or amount—use the following symbols: L = large, M = medium, and S = small. Quantitative changes are assumed to be increases unless preceded by a minus sign.

If a qualitative change is anticipated, use the following symbols: l = large, m = medium, s = small.

Note that the notions of small, medium, and large changes are obviously subjective and will vary with the person using the form.

In general, a small change denotes a minimum level of change thought important enough to make note of. Most of the expected changes will probably fall in the medium category, indicating change of some magnitude. The large category will usually be reserved for changes of striking impact.

The notion of qualitative changes may need some clarification. This category of change would cover such items as a change in customer mix (which might or might not result in an increased number of customers). Using a new source of supply for raw materials and changing the media allocation of the advertising budget would also be examples of qualitative changes.

Commercial Considerations

1. Is the product necessary or desirable in maintaining completeness of line?

2. Does the inclusion of this product in the line have any effect on other lines?

3. Will it strengthen our position with distributors?

4. Will our name be of aid in marketing the product?

SIMPLIFIED MASTER PLANNING

Questions like these are helpful but more system is desirable. Roger A. Golde, a small business consultant, has devised a simple form to help the very small businessman organize his forward thinking.[7] It is shown in Tables 7-1 and 7-2 and is self-explanatory.

A manager-owner can work with Golde's form at odd moments, informally, with a minimum of help, if none is available or desired, or with much consultant aid, if that is appropriate and possible. This form has the great virtue of getting at major elements of success or failure of a firm. Working with it will raise questions and encourage decisions. For many small businessmen, starting with comparatively abstract concepts of goals and strategies is not easy. The more practical approach of Golde, however, should eventually lead to a better statement of objectives and strategies.

SELECTING CONCRETE KEY OBJECTIVES

Not all objective-setting need be abstract. An approach developed by Dr. Gunther Klaus, a well-known small business management consultant, is concrete and pragmatic, and it leads directly into systematic planning. He begins with a framework for decision, which is illustrated in Table 7-3. This particular exhibit concerns sales objectives, but it could also be used for profit. The assumption here is that, if sales are considered first, the profit objectives will emerge in logical fashion.

Dr. Klaus begins with an objective for sales as far in the future as it is practicable for the small business man to contemplate. In this case it is five years away, which may seem to be a long time for some small businessmen, but it is a proper time span for many. The central question is: What dollar volume of sales do I want five years from now? When that question is answered, it naturally raises a great many more. One is whether the present product line will permit the achieve-

Table 7-2—Hypothetical Completed Master Planning Form

Item	NY	YAN	Comment
		CHANGE	
Research and development	Mm		Start development of new altimeter for executive planes.
Products		−S	First sales of new altimeter.
Product mix		Ss	
Service		s	Slightly different for private planes.
Supplies		s	Needed for new altimeter.
Suppliers			
Inventory			
Subcontracts		S	Most of subassemblies will be subcontracted.
Storage and handling			
Quality control			
Space		S	Little bit of production space for new altimeter.
Leasehold improvements	M		Need for dust-free area.
Equipment	S		New test equipment.
Employees	S		Couple of technicians for development work.
Fringe benefits			
Customers		sS	Plan to hit owners of executive planes.
Sales outlets		Mm	Will need more sales representatives rather than own sales force.
Terms of sale			
Pricing			
Transportation			
Advertising		−M	Not so effective to private owners.
Promotion		m	Will switch to more demonstrations and trade shows.
Packaging			
Market research	S		Informal poll of private owners known by company.
Financing	S		Additional working capital for production.
Insurance			
Investments			
Management reports	I		Need for simple product costing system.
(Etc.)			(Etc.)

ment of that objective. If not, a number of other questions arise: Can the target be met by modifications? If so, what? If not, what new

Table 7-3—Sales Objectives

Area	First Year	Second Year	Third Year	Fourth Year	Fifth Year
Product modification					
New products					
Joint ventures					
New markets					
Acquisition					
Totals					BEGIN ←—— HERE

products can be produced? If this will not permit target achievement, should a joint venture be considered? Penetration of new markets? Acquisitions? Dealing with these questions opens up a decision-tree with many other branches. What manpower will be needed? What financing will be required? What will my costs be? Must some employees be sent to an executive training program?

This approach, like the preceding ones, is quite simple and is adaptable to different conditions and sizes of businesses.

THE PLANNING GAP

A modification of this approach is to identify the so-called planning gap.[8] Very simply, this approach calls for the establishment of tentative sales goals and the forecasting of current momentum—that is, what present and anticipated lines of business will produce in the future. The difference, as shown in Figure 7-2, is the planning gap. The issue, of course, is how will the gap be filled? (Similar charts can be drawn for profits, costs, personnel, floor space, and so on.) Asking and answering this question leads to the same sort of analysis as that discussed above.

RETURN ON INVESTMENT

Another approach is to concentrate on major elements entering into the return on investment calculation for a firm. The elements of this calculation are shown in Figure 7-3. Like the previous approach, a return on investment objective can be tentatively established for selected time periods. The analysis then begins by probing, in a fashion similar to that described above, what is necessary to achieve the

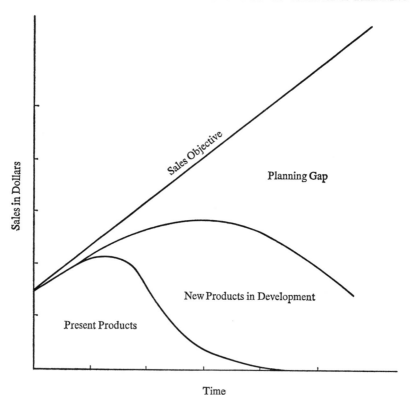

Time

Figure 7-2—The Planning Gap

objective. This approach is flexible in dealing with both short- and long-range factors in business life.

This approach has been for many years a central feature of the planning and control program of DuPont. It is, of course, usable by a small company. But a small company would find (as does DuPont) the approach more useful when accompanied by other elements of planning noted in Figure 7-4.

BREAK-EVEN ANALYSIS

The break-even point for a business is that point in production at which sales volume equals costs. At that point there is neither a profit nor a loss. Figure 7-4 shows a break-even analysis. A simple formula will also yield the break-even point:

$$\text{Break-even} = \frac{\text{Fixed Costs}}{100\% - (\text{Variable Costs/Sales})}$$

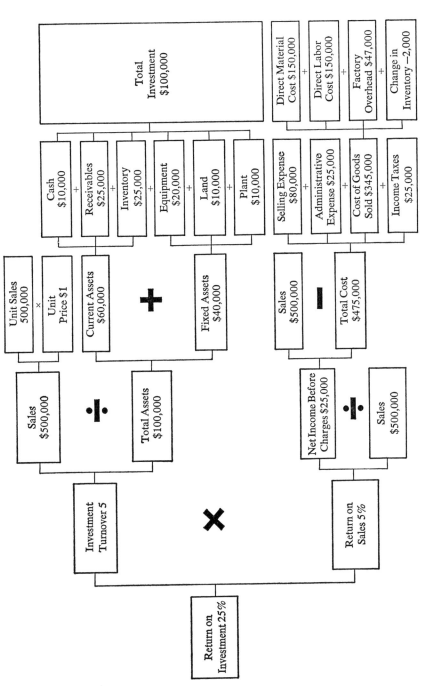

Figure 7-3—Return on Investment

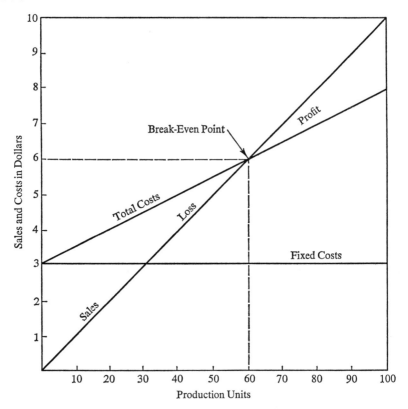

Figure 7-4—A Break-Even Analysis

The break-even analysis is a powerful tool to answer such very puzzling questions as: What is the impact on profit if fixed costs rise 10 per cent and sales decline by 10 per cent? Or if variable costs increase by 15 per cent and volume drops by 14 per cent? It is a simple method to get at some major issues important in the planning of a company. If the break-even analysis is used to ask a widening series of questions, as illustrated above, it can be the starting point for a long-range planning program.

Economists have criticized this tool because they rightly claim that costs are curves and are not linear as drawn on the chart. Furthermore, the technique assumes many things that may not be true, such as that productivity remains the same over time, or that fixed and variable costs can be separated. This is not the place to argue the merits of such criticisms. However, it is pertinent here to observe that within a "range of relevance" the functions of a break-even chart are rather linear. For many companies, for example, within a range of 10 to 15 per cent on either side of the break-even line, an assumed linear relationship can be accurate enough to form a solid basis for planning. Hence, this is a useful short- and long-range planning tool. Its value does decline, however, the longer the time span covered and the wider the ranges of output.

STANDARD ACCOUNTING STATEMENTS

Standard accounting statements are excellent bases for developing long-range planning. They can be very simple for a very small enterprise or developed in great and complex detail in a comprehensive planning program.

In a simple approach, and one which is indispensable to proper management in small as well as large enterprises, cash forecasts are prepared. What is involved is the identification and forecast of all important future sources and uses of cash available to the enterprise. Table 7-4 gives one elementary arrangement of items to be forecast to determine net cash flows. A number of different formats are contained in Schabacker's *Cash Planning in Small Manufacturing Companies*.[9] Most commercial banks have developed cash flow forms that are available to businessmen. These forms can be used, of course, to forecast cash flows for any period of time chosen—daily, weekly, monthly, quarterly, or over a number of years.

The revenue-expense forecast is not only a major planning tool but can be used also as a beginning point for long-range planning. Table 7-5 shows a simple revenue-expense forecast format. Here the effort is to identify and forecast all important elements of cost and revenues. The difference will show profit or loss and this in turn will provide information on the basis of which simple or sophisticated rates of return on investment may be calculated. Revenue-expense forecasts can and should be prepared for each important product of an enterprise as well as for the enterprise as a whole. These forecasts for individual products should extend over a period of time that includes at least the major part of the life span of the product.

An important feature of the revenue-expense forecast is that when

Table 7-4—Five-Year Forecast of Cash Sources and Needs
for a Small Business

Item	First Year	Second Year	Third Year	Fourth Year	Fifth Year
Cash sources:					
Opening balance					
Revenue from sales					
Depreciation					
Borrowing on facilities					
Borrowing on inventory and receivables					
Total cash sources					
Cash expenditures:					
Direct labor costs					
Materials purchase					
Payments to subcontractors					
New machinery and tools					
Increases in inventory					
Increases in receivables					
Increases in operating cash					
Payments on loans					
Factory burden					
Officers salaries					
Selling costs					
Taxes:					
Employer's share of Social Security					
Local property					
Income					
Total cash disbursements					
Net cash change					

depreciation is added to net profit, the result is cash gain from operations. As noted in Table 7-5, this does not, however, represent net cash flow. So, when simple revenue-expense forecasts are used in planning they should be accompanied by cash flow analyses.

Complete balance sheet and profit-and-loss statements constitute a more complicated basis for developing long-range planning. When a company gets to the point where it can develop such documents for the length of time for which organized future planning is done, it has demonstrated high capability in planning. As a consequence, the company might just as well develop a more comprehensive formal long-range planning program in which these documents are included as parts. This will not be illustrated.

Table 7-5—Five-Year Revenue-Expense Projection for a Small Business

Item	First Year	Second Year	Third Year	Fourth Year	Fifth Year
Sales revenues					
Product A					
Product B					
Operating expenses					
Direct labor					
Overhead					
Materials					
Selling expenses					
Depreciation					
Total					
Nonrecurring expenses					
Total operating expenses					
Interest and loan amortization					
Net profits before taxes					
Taxes					
Net profit after taxes					
Cash gain from operations (net profit after taxes plus depreciation reserve)					

Comprehensive Formal Planning of Centralized Companies

As companies grow in size and experience with organized long-range planning, it becomes possible and desirable to have a more complete planning program than has been discussed up to this point. The shape of the planning program follows more closely the conceptual model presented in Figure 7-1 and results in a comprehensive set of objectives and plans covering every major aspect of the business.

The following presents a brief description of an actual comprehensive planning program. The entire plan is, of course, too voluminous to include here. The data and substance are disguised to avoid identification. It is a five-year plan prepared by the president and his four major department heads, who worked mostly in the evenings and weekends to complete it. The firm had less than $2,000,000 annual sales and about 100 employees at the time the plan was prepared.

Corporate Plan for Magnetic Design, Inc.

I. *Corporate Purpose*

In this section the basic purposes of MDI are set forth. Two are given, which is about standard. The four modifiers, however, are a little unusual.

A. Two prime objectives of MDI
   1. To acquire reasonable and improving earnings through productive effort applied primarily to, but not limited to, the manufacture of magnetic devices and power supply equipment.
   2. To conduct the business in a manner that is constructive, honorable, and mutually profitable for stockholders, employees, customers, suppliers, and the general community.

B. These objectives are further amplified as follows:
   1. Earn a reasonable return on investment with due regard to the interests of customers, employees, and vendors.
   2. Expand sales while increasing profits.
   3. Provide top quality products for the federal government.
   4. Grow at a steady, stable rate.

C. Departmental purposes

The fundamental purposes of each major department of the firm are spelled out in this section. The departments are administration, marketing, production and engineering, and finance. It is a little unusual for departmental purposes to be specified at this point in a plan. They are usually blended into specific objectives set for their operations. Illustrating this section is the following for the production and engineering department:
   1. Manufacture and design company products with the quality, costs, and delivery schedules which will be attractive to prospective customers.
   2. Continuously be aware of developments that promise new and improved products for the company.

II. *Basic corporate five- and ten-year objectives*

A. The five-year annual sales and profit objectives are as follows:

Year	Sales	Pre-Tax Profits	Pre-Tax % Profits	Federal Tax	Post-Tax % Profit
First Year					
Second Year					
Third Year		[These are specified in			
Fourth Year		dollars and percentages.]			
Fifth Year					

B. The ten-year sales and profit objectives are as follows:

Ten years from now sales shall be $5,000,000 and earnings shall be $750,000 after taxes.

III. *Premises*

In this section the basic premises necessary for the plan are set forth. Here, of course, are forecasts of future markets, technology, competition, and evaluations of internal strengths and weaknesses. A framework of premises, with some illustrations from the MDI plan, follows:

A. External projections and forecasts

1. Survey of general business conditions, including a GNP forecast.
2. The market for company products, based upon general economic conditions for industrial products and estimates of government spending for company products.
3. Forecast of company sales based on the above two forecasts. In the case of MDI, the forecasts were made for each of the next five years. Because the company is in the Midwest, government spending for its products in the Midwest was estimated. Included were the Department of Defense, National Aeronautics and Space Administration, and the Federal Aviation Agency.

B. Competition

Because competition is keen for most companies, objective estimates of the strength of competition are important. After looking at what its major competition was likely to do, the firm looked at itself as follows:

1. Several state-of-the-art advantages have placed MDI several years in advance of competition in the magnetic devices equipment field. These are cryogenic magnets for commercial applications, and high reliability power supplies for long-endurance military application.
2. But, to realize fully the growth commensurate with the above advantages, several weaknesses must be overcome; namely, to develop an ability to construct crystals, and to develop sophisticated test procedures.

C. Internal examination of the past and projections

This section includes analyses of various parts of the enterprise, illustrated as follows:

1. Product line analysis
   a. Product(s) performance (sales volume, profit margin).
   b. Customer class served.

     c. Comparison with competitors' product(s).

     d. Comparison with substitutes and complementary performance.

     e. Possibilities for product improvement.

     f. Suggestions with regard to new products.

2. Market analysis
   a. Important factors in projected sales changes (product success, marketing organization, advertising, competitive pressures).
   b. New markets to be penetrated (geographical areas and customer classes).

3. Financial analysis
   a. Profit position.
   b. Working capital.
   c. Cash position.
   d. Impact of financial policy on market price per share.
   e. Prospects for future financing.

4. Production analysis
   a. Plant and equipment (maintenance and depreciation).
   b. Productive capacity and productivity.
   c. Per cent of capacity utilized.
   d. Suggestions for productivity improvements, cost reduction, how to utilize excess capacity, and plant expansion.

5. Technical analysis
   a. Research and development performance.
   b. Suggestions for improving research and development effectiveness.

6. Employees
   a. Employment and future needs.
   b. Technical manpower deficiencies.
   c. Appraisal of employee attitudes.

7. Facilities
   a. Evaluation of current facilities to meet new business.
   b. Machine replacement policy and needs.

IV. *Basic objectives, policies, and strategies*

This section of the plan conceptually covers every important area of the business, such as:

A. Profits.

B. Sales.

C. Finance.

D. Marketing.

E. Capital additions.

   F. Production.
   G. Research.
   H. Engineering.
   I. Acquisitions.
   J. Organization.
   K. Long-range planning.

This list can, of course, be expanded. As noted elsewhere, the more concrete the specification here can be, the easier it usually is to implement the plans. This is especially important for a small business-man so that he knows precisely what it is that is sought and the method to be employed to get there. For example, MDI marketing objectives were set forth as follows:

   1. Increase sales of magnetic devices 100 per cent in next five years. Increase sales of power supply equipment 200 per cent during next five years.

   2. Increase the total volume of industry sales from today's 25 per cent to 50 per cent of total sales in five years.

   3. Penetrate the Western market to the point where 10 per cent of company sales in five years will be there.

   4. Enter the foreign market within five years through a licensing agreement, a joint venture, or a manufacturing facility.

For each one of these objectives, the company prepared a detailed series of strategies ranging from a strategy to "sell custom designs directly to prime contractors in geographic regions where their main plants are located" to details such as special services to selected speci-fied customers, training programs for employees, and top management meetings with customers.

Possible inclusion of items which might be found in this section of the plan are many. To illustrate, strategies with respect to market-ing might, in addition to the above, include organization, use of dealers, possibility of distributing products manufactured by others, salesmen's compensation plans, and pricing policy.

Drawing a proper line of demarcation between the strategic plans and the detailed operational plans is very difficult. Ideally, the two blend together in a continuous line. In the case of MDI, this took place because those making the strategic plan also were the ones to implement it.

 V. *Detailed medium-range plans*

   In this section are the more detailed plans growing out of the above. For MDI these plans were developed for each of the next succeeding five years. The following were prepared:

 A. *Pro forma* balance sheet, yearly.

    B. Income statement, yearly.

    C. Capital expenditure schedule, yearly.

    D. Unit production schedule for major products, yearly.

    E. Employment schedule, yearly.

    F. Detailed schedule to acquire within three years a company with design capability in solid state magnetic devices.

VI. *One-year plans*

In this section were the next-year budgets. The first-year budgets for items A through F (in Section V above) were, in the aggregate, the same as for the first year of the five-year plan, but broken into quarterly time periods.

In addition to these budgets, the company had others, principally purchasing schedules for major components and raw materials, and typical detailed administrative budgets covering such things as travel and telephone.

Comprehensive Planning in Decentralized Companies

When divisions are established as profit centers a new dimension is added to the planning process. Usually, long-range planning is done for the entire company by the central offices when a company first begins formal planning. But, once the process is established, the central headquarters offices usually develop over-all company objectives, strategies, and policies and, upon this base, the divisions prepare detailed medium- and short-range plans. These are then presented to central management for review and approval. Sometimes the divisional plans are aggregated into one composite company plan. The structure and substance of the plans parallel that given in the foregoing plans for Magnetic Design, Inc.

HELP FOR THE CHIEF EXECUTIVE

One of the major problems of the chief executive in doing long-range planning is getting help. It is important for the manager-owner of a very small enterprise, the president of a medium-sized business, and the chief executive of a large business to recognize that considerable help is available. The executive needs only to understand what is available and learn how to use it.

His own staff is a prime resource. A manager always can do the planning himself. This is feasible and almost obligatory for a very small firm. As firms grow larger, however, it becomes both less possible and less desirable. Growth leads to more staff help. Following are some methods for using staff successfully.

First, the chief executive can conduct a freewheeling "think" session to get long-range planning started. Some companies take their top executives away from daily routine to some spa to engage in thinking and planning about the future. These sessions are useful to get the process started. Many companies conduct them as part of a well-entrenched planning program.

Second, the chief executive can first prepare objectives for the firm and then ask each functional manager to prepare plans for his own area of work responsibility.

Third, the chief executive can ask each functional manager to tell him what his plans are for the future, and then develop over-all objectives and strategies on the basis of them. Or, to initiate the process, he can ask each functional officer what he thinks ought to be done by the firm to get long-range planning under way.

Fourth, the chief executive can assign to one functional officer the job of starting planning. When it is progressing, this man can monitor the process.

Fifth, the chief executive can get together with his functional officers to form a committee to prepare strategic over-all as well as working plans for his company. This is what Magnetic Design, Inc., did. As the number of employees increases there may be great advantage to this method. A committee can offset some traits of chief executives, such as the desire for one-man authoritative control, making snap judgments, preoccupation with the short-run at the expense of the long-run, and secretiveness which hurts the firm more than it helps it. Committees of this sort, of course, bring to the front different points of view, which usually is healthy. Better communications are promoted, and individuals are likely to feel more intimately associated with the prospects and problems of the firm.

Sixth, when a firm gets larger it may be able to afford a small staff to devote full time to planning. Such staff is especially useful in decentralized, divisionalized companies. The staff helps coordinate work of the central headquarters' functional officers in the development of over-all firm objectives and strategies, aids the divisions in improving their planning capabilities, and helps the central headquarters management review the plans. Sometimes the director of such a staff will serve as the secretary to a corporate planning committee.

There are also, of course, outside sources of help for a president. Many consultants are available for all the major problems of the firm. This is well known and needs no further analysis here. One of the great neglected sources of help, however, particularly for the very small businessman, is his board of directors. Small businessmen should think seriously about the advantages of placing on their board one or more individuals with talents that can be used in actually performing long-range planning or advising the president about use of other outside consultants. University professors are one source often overlooked.

Summary

This chapter has sought to advance the practice of long-range planning in smaller enterprises. The many reasons that small businessmen give for not doing it, and barriers to its introduction and development, were presented and answered. It is a basic assumption of this chapter that many small businessmen do not engage in effective long-range planning because they are puzzled about how to begin the process and operate it so that it produces values greater than costs. Different possible approaches which have been successfully used in small firms have been presented. This discussion of practical approaches was begun with a conceptual model of business planning and a list of analytical and operational steps in planning. Practical approaches were described —the kinds of questions to ask, check-off lists of questions, simplified master planning, selecting concrete key objectives, the planning gap, return on investment, break-even analysis, standard accounting statements, and comprehensive planning of centralized and decentralized companies. Finally, a few comments were made about staff help that is available to any president to help him do a better job of long-range planning, which is, in the final analysis, his responsibility.

8

Strategic Decision-Making: Three Case Histories

Benjamin Z. Katz

Every small business is confronted with the need to make critical strategic business decisions that can contribute to success or disaster. No two of these opportunities for decision are exactly alike. The case histories discussed in this chapter are real, but the identity of the companies involved is disguised to protect the confidences of management.

In each case, a brief sketch of the company and its environment will be presented along with the central problem. To the extent possible, the situation as it existed at the point of decision will be described both before and after. Observations and inferences of general application will be offered, although the facts of each experience lend themselves to more than one possible interpretation.

Case 1. Technological Growth Company (TGC)

Unlike many small businesses started in the Southern California area in the past decade by a successful engineer-manager and an accountant friend as inside control man, TGC was a thoughtfully conceived, exceptionally well-planned, and even adequately capitalized company. This description merits the explanation that the founders were exceptional professionals, trained in science and commerce, who approached the formation of the company by studying models, exploring the many-faceted requirements for a successful business, and establishing a sound financial base from which to work prior to entering into the business venture.

In brief, their plan was to bring technical and financial management to already-developed products or processes in the scientific or technical realm of industry as opposed to, and to the exclusion of, the exploitation of consumer markets or products. This would present the best utilization of the founding father's talents and experience. In addition to personally investing equity capital for the first year, the founding principals obtained additional capital from a group of private investors on a small syndicate basis. After their initial commercial success with the production and marketing of an electronic component in a growing field in which it is difficult to qualify, they sought additional capital in the marketplace. Excellent preparation and presentation of their case included a sound plan and a successful beginning for profit implementation. They accepted a generous and continuing commitment from a Small Business Investment Company. Increased equity capital was to depend on performance by the company. A consideration to the SBIC was a convertible debenture, with the conversion price to be based on performance.

The company started in modest quarters and attracted previous associates and qualified personnel anxious to participate in a growth opportunity. One of the market requirement gaps identified for TGC by an inventor was in the information storage and recall field in the use of microfilm records. The leading company in the field at that time was so swamped with requests for mounting microfilm on aperture cards that there was a three to four month delay in sending microfilm to the factory to be mounted onto the computer data processing cards. The reason for such mounting was to enable prints or parts of documents to be classified, stored, and retrieved by a convenient and desirable method, tying in with existing information and data storage and retrieval systems. This had special applicability to engineering drawings and other design specifications, as well as usefulness in legal, accounting, and other fields.

The inventor of this better system, who was brought to TGC by an independent consultant, accepted the TGC offer because it gave him an opportunity to continue participation on an equity basis through a more generous royalty arrangement than had been previously offered, thus responding to his personal interest. An opportunity for conversion of the royalty into an option on TGC stock clinched the agreement.

What bothered the inventor was that, although TGC had the money, engineering skill, and production facilities, it did not have the marketing capability that he felt was necessary to put over his product. However, the TGC management recognized the advantages of a do-it-yourself system—a machine that individual companies could use to mount microfilm on aperture cards instead of being dependent on an outside service at a higher cost with substantial time delay.

The various marketing possibilities were considered and discussed. The boot-strap approaches of building sales by in-house salesmen, independent sales efforts, or through the use of manufacturing representatives were frankly discussed. The engineering-manager, who had been trained to a systems approach to problems, felt that one of the companies in the general field of information storage and/or retrieval and/or reproduction that had an existing marketing organization might be approached. The goal would be to have a "pro" take on the product either as an exclusive sales agency or perhaps as a joint venture, tying in the microfilm mounting machine with their other equipment. Although the inventor had trepidations about his "baby" being stolen, the company felt that the know-how protection of production processes was perhaps more important than any patent protection possibilities.

The final decision was reached when a marketing consultant convinced the inventor that his best protection was in product placement and acceptance in the market by getting there first and at a price that would discourage, if not preclude, competition. There was ample evidence and interest from market sampling to confirm to everyone involved that the need existed. But the requirement of a sophisticated, in-depth subsystem sale was the salient problem facing the company.

It was decided to contact a number of the major office equipment firms who might be interested in taking on the product for distribution and service. In this regard, it was recognized by the company that after sales, service would be an important feature, as the process was delicate, if not tricky. Even though a preproduction model was successful and operated on a satisfactory test basis, the technical mechanics were intricate and sensitive. The mechanical process was well guarded in a metal housing, but nonetheless it was felt that the process involving a transparent adhesive grip for the microfilm within the data processing card was prone to service problems. The fact that one of the biggest and best companies in the field was having three to four months delay and obvious difficulty in filling orders confirmed this concern, yet it also provided the opportunity for exploitation.

Should TGC, a fledgling innovator, approach the established giant in the industry, now attempting to fill the market need with their innovation? The management of TGC studied the company by talking with the trade and concluded that the only way the giant would be interested would be by acquisition. Also, the dilemma was recognized that in order to arrive at a price and evaluation, the process and machine would have to be disclosed to the most potent and logical competitor. The issue of approaching the giant was resolved in the negative. The basic consideration that the innovators wanted was to keep the new product and to process and produce it for a continuing profit rather than sell it. Furthermore, the giant company's reputation was found to be one of acquisition and control as opposed to joint venture with smaller company suppliers or junior partners.

Negotiations were undertaken with another giant company whose marketing and service organization was perhaps the best in the business and which was in the general office equipment field as well as data processing. Again, preliminary negotiations, as well as checking with the trade, revealed that the second giant's *modus operandi* was also to buy out as opposed to permitting joint efforts within the terms of basic parental corporate control and operational philosophy.

A reputable medium-large company in the reproduction field was next approached but negotiations were stopped abruptly when it was found that they were working on a similar solution to the recognized marketing need. Finally, a medium-large company with a leading position in the data reproduction field, which had grown rapidly in the past decade, showed an interest consistent with the small company's requirement of keeping the product. The company, whose name has become a household word, was interested in expanding and diversifying. It recognized that expanded use of its basic copying machine would result from the increased use of this auxiliary equipment, and make for more effective and increased use of its basic supplies. But this company, too, was hesitant about marketing a fledgling product, particularly when there appeared to be the potential of bothersome service problems. On the other hand, this company was willing, and ready, to invest in the further development and perfection of the machine with broader market testing, even though its initial offer for acquisition was refused.

The dilemma was resolved in an agreement whereby TGC would manufacture its own product in the name of the larger company, which would then market the product as its own and as part of its expanding service system. Thus, the desire of the innovators and owners was met by keeping their product production but distributing exclusively under a "private" brand.

The result was that a fledgling two-year-old company was able to obtain immediate national and international marketing and service coverages, complete with an ideal budget precommitted in terms of market research, product development, and advertising, along with after-sale service. At the same time, the innovator's profit was retained and kept within the company structure. The owners in this happy story realized a capital gain commensurate with the increase of sales from zero to several million in the first year of production. Management had the foresight not only to obtain the complete marketing services but financial and even engineering and design assistance for the increased production. This accomplishment was the basis for the move to bigger and better quarters and a solid foundation for the company's future growth. One result was the tripling of the conversion price on the convertible notes within the first year for the SBIC investor.

Success stories are generally happy lessons and it might be well at this point to ask what particular understanding helped to crystallize this desired solution. Perhaps the most significant was the realization on the part of the individuals who wanted to be on their own and make it on their own that they simply could not do everything by themselves. Equity was given for capital at the very beginning. Birthrights were traded for leverage in the process, and the sacred cow of complete management control was indeed sacrificed for a better market penetration and service requirement solution.

The functional approach to the financing requirements of a small business is important in this case. Just as in the production area a small business might look to its suppliers for part of its production financing requirements, so might it look to its distribution function for assistance in financing.

The rapid growth of franchising is a manifestation of this functional financing emphasis whereby the small firm may achieve capital for distribution through the franchising method. Similarly in joining with an established larger company for the marketing function under a private brand label arrangement, or as a complementary or auxiliary product line, the small manufacturer can very often obtain the necessary capital for complete marketing, including advertising, promotion, warehousing, and even after-sale service and the more direct salesmen costs.

Outside consultants were used effectively (if not freely) as critical requirements for expertise arose. Although it is true that large companies use outside consultants more often than small ones, this firm owes part of its successful growth to its decision to seek outside assistance when and as needed. The recognition by consultants of the psychological as well as profit needs of the innovators made possible the finding of a "partner" with whom they could live even though the idea of a "partner" was at first rejected.

It is tempting to end this vignette on these happy notes. Ultimately, however, the situation did not work out as well as it would have seemed had the story ended at this point. Although there was a sensational introduction and start in the marketing of the product, another lesson could have been anticipated and might have been learned.

Understandably, the fledgling company was most anxious to get started and recover investment in addition to realizing a profit on some considerable investment to date. This was especially urgent as they recognized the magnitude of the marketing and servicing job. It was noted earlier that one of the companies approached as a logical possibility was a similar medium-large company working on a similar product. The decision not to approach that company proved to be a wrong one because the first company that took it on ended up selling the product and market position to that company, who is doing an even better job with it! It took some time and cost to recognize that the particular service and market and subsystem fit better with the second company than it did with the first. A little more investigation of the integrity of the second company, which is exceptional, would have revealed that the innovators need not have been fearful of discussing their innovation with them just because they were working on something like it themselves. This fine medium-large firm had worked with many other small companies, even in acknowledged competition with them, on various research and development projects. Yet it has conducted itself in an exemplary manner, being considerate not only of "legal rights" but of confidence and profit rights. This company is also respectful of human rights and has enjoyed unequaled success in most of its endeavors. The point of the case is that in the pressing need for solutions to problems, the first or immediate answer, however attractive, should not preclude the consideration of a full range of choices.

Case 2. The Better Mouse Trap Company (BMTC)

An invention which provided a useful household good gave BMTC its start. Not only was the product a vast improvement on existing designs, but the exceptional technical capability of the inventor was translated into production equipment and assembly devices that yielded a very low unit cost. These key advantages helped gain a competitive edge for the new company and proved more important than the patent protection subsequently granted on its new product. The new company was a typical bootstrap "family-affair" enterprise with features common to many small businesses. The production and engineering man (the inventor) was both uninterested and untrained in business and finance. Therefore, another friend of the "family" undertook the financial aspects of management.

The company's product realized unprecedented success through its exceptionally low-cost production of a needed product that was well marketed through existing agency channels. The business chores were divided between the two principals. Each functioned almost completely independently of the other in his area of competence. The production and engineering man could be likened to the creative talents in the entertainment industry who often seem indifferent, if not disdainful, of financial considerations and problems. The second principal assumed responsibility for financial planning and control and managed everything from purchasing through accounting almost to the exclusion of his associate. A good marketing man helped gain trade and consumer acceptance. Brand name indentification and pricing structures helped build innovative profits and solid market acceptance.

The division of executive authority worked well for this firm and the production capabilities and inventive talents were put to use to create another new product, this time in the industrial field. Once again, the inventive contribution was significant, and along with superior production techniques, proved also to be exceptionally profitable for the company. At the same time, acceptance by the trade of a heavy duty version of the household product helped increase the acceptance of the product for the consumer market. Thus, the equivalent of the restaurant and hotel supply business became large users and demanded special versions of the basic household product, which added to the increasing financial return of the company. But all of this caused severe growing pains. Trade discounts resulted in profit pressures, but product acceptance was enhanced by the "professional" use and testimonials which were exploited.

The two principals in the company, each running separate parts of it, seemed to function fairly well in spite of the exceptional autonomy. As might be expected, however, a split developed as the one principal became more and more immersed in product development and production requirements while the other was forced to face the increased costs and cash drain of an expanding research and development budget not consistent with cash flow or profit projections. These terms and concepts were not common denominators of communication. As the two principals had been making more money than ever anticipated, and as the previous developments had paid off so very well in the marketplace, this situation continued, but at the cost of a festering resentment between the business manager and the inventor.

Application of a new electrical mechanical principle to a different aspect of the consumer market had attracted the interest of the inventor. He became heavily committed to costly research and development and the other principal assumed the operation of the entire company. A violent family squabble erupted when budget restrictions were attempted. This break occurred just as the company was moving into a new and larger plant, which required only 50 per cent financing when originally planned. Permanent financing by an insurance company was at a 60 per cent level. Just as two married individuals may become completely irrational and do things that are destructive to each other after years of successful marriage, so the two principals in this company not only split and separated but one attempted to undermine the other. As is often the case in a breakup of an original entity, one of the principals entered into destructive competition, including the raiding of personnel, price cutting, duplication of products, and marketing and production efforts. Costly litigation did not solve the problem and only after a ruinous price war, which attracted additional competition, did a truce evolve out of economic necessity.

BMTC, a company that had been exceptionally profitable, suddenly faced bankruptcy as a result of having drained all cash and personal reserves in what had become a vendetta. A partial solution was reached by splitting up of the business, with one principal taking that part of it in the consumer field and the other principal taking the other part in the industrial area.

After this experience, the inventor was understandably reluctant to take on a new business manager. Nonetheless, he did so, and in trying to prevent any possible recurrence of his previous experience, he chose a subordinate too weak and basically unsuited to the control job that was necessary. The inventor then undertook to learn the financial management end of the business, and being a person of exceptional intellectual endowment, he was able to do so, even while the business teetered on the brink of bankruptcy. The bank, which had had years of good experience with the company, advanced exceptional credit to it, but this was not sufficient to fill the hole left by the disastrous civil war that had preceded the request for increased credit. A review of the financing of the company at that juncture indicated that it had used about every conceivable means of obtaining the critical capital infusion. Accounts receivable were factored at the bank at an 80 per cent level. Chattel mortgages had been extended with a very high percentage of financing on equipment. Some inventory had been financed, and a blanket second mortgage on the plant and equipment was also taken as additional security to justify a level of borrowing higher than was warranted by the current condition of the company.

The most dangerous aspect of this situation, however, was the fact that the company had, prior to the split, obtained a computer for its data processing requirements and had gone through an expensive programming. Less than satisfactory results were obtained and considerable confusion resulted. This is not uncommon when a company shifts to a new data processing system. Confusion was added to disaster just as the breach in the previous organization was coming to a head. In addition to the manifold problems of the marketplace and unfair competition, there occurred this complete breakdown in the vital flow of accounting and control information and data.

Extension of the bank credit was made on the personal reputation and past performance of the founding inventor of the company, as opposed to the usual practice of lending on audited business statements, which simply were not available. Personal cash investment helped bolster a sagging confidence. Even a threatened suit against the computer company could not yield the necessary financial data promised through the computer with the alleged programming performance. Pro forma statements were attempted by a series of controllers. Cash flow projections were made by bookkeepers, and in desperation a simple debit and credit hand log and ledger system was reinstalled to give some feel for the missing financial data. Various outside consultants and services attempted to bridge this gap, but partly because of the lack of trust by the company head, these efforts were less than successful. In fact, the outsiders almost universally predicted an early demise and departed prematurely.

That this company is in business and is beginning to recover after so difficult a situation is cause for wonder for most people who were involved with it during those trying times. How did the company manage to survive? Pretty much the way an individual can tap unrealized resources in a moment of severe danger. The analogy of the adrenalin flow is apt.

The head of the company put back into it all of his own personal resources and tapped other available sources after a financial analysis pointed out where those might be. By instinct and philosophy he rejected the government's Small Business Administration agency but did attempt a loan from a private SBIC, which proved unfruitful. It became obvious that to achieve the needed maximum financing, the company would have to go to the higher rate of a factoring company as opposed to its bank. This was discussed with the bank and, in fact, was urged by it in order to reduce its considerable exposure.

Only the established acceptance of the company's product encouraged a factoring company to attempt to take on so difficult a challenge. In addition, there were considerable equities that the company could realize with a more venturesome credit institution. Calls were made on suppliers who had enjoyed good profits during the company's previous lush years for material financing and a hiatus on the past-due bills. The head of the company also called for capital loans to the company from the various manufacturing representatives and agents who had done well in product distribution. The response to this request lost a few good representatives who immediately ran for cover, but at the same time, yielded a surprising return from some of those distributors just as it had worked with suppliers from the production side.

Help came from an often overlooked source of funds, especially in a tight money market. During its expansion years, the company had built a fine plant and owned property in the value of several million dollars which was financed by an insurance company at that time at about 60 per cent of value. In the few intervening years the value of the property had risen approximately 20 per cent on a conservative basis. Thus, the existing financing on the property, even including the second mortgage extended by the factoring company behind the now-50 per cent insurance company first trust deed, only totaled approximately 65 per cent of the true current market value. Therefore, in spite of the company's weak credit situation, another mortgage loan was obtained on the basic real estate property value as distinguished from the credit emphasis for such a loan. A possible sale leaseback as a way of generating additional critical capital could not be consummated because of the questionable credit. The excellent location of the facility and the inherent value in the real estate attracted a "speculative" junior mortgage loan secured by a note and deed of trust up to 80 per cent or 85 per cent of the quick cash-out property value on an auction basis. This came from private individuals who were willing to assume the risk for the higher rate of return. It also made sense to the company as its insurance loan lock-in provision and prepayment penalties were actually more costly than paying the higher rate of interest and points on the smaller amount of the junior mortgage. Even though the costs, as a percentage, were higher, they still totaled less than the alternatively available first mortgage re-financing of the properties at higher first mortgage rates and yielded more of the urgently needed capital.

These additional sources of capital, however, were only life-blood transfusions to the company. Although it was still ailing, the owner refused to consider the possibility of sale or merger. His faith in the market position as well as the future acceptance of his product and his own capacity were boundless. Even further losses were sustained by the company during this turn-around period but the rate was sharply lessened. Costs were further reduced by shifting production to lower cost areas. Drastic and even forced reductions in personnel occurred while inventories were pared and some equipment sold off. A rebuilding process was begun in the marketing department with the inventor also wearing that hat (or rather, trying to!).

A return of better margins with new product varieties turned the company around the corner to profitability. During this difficult process, the head and manager of the company violated almost every management principle generally recognized for successful operation of a company. He refused to delegate authority. He did not hire, and then if he did, he almost immediately fired innumerable personnel. Counterbalance and controls gave way to intuition. This process may have left him with weak or less competent people, however loyal and dedicated. But the will and, indeed, the human resources of a dedicated individual should never be underestimated. The alternative costs that were involved in terms of the whole person and his family life, and the cost to subordinates' nervous systems, cannot be measured. The unquantifiable "capital" and energy of the extremely motivated man to make a point of his ability, or to make it in response to a seemingly overwhelming challenge, as opposed to maximizing profits, is a remarkable phenomenon. Some intuition was, after all, based on experience. The lack of department heads frustrated some creditors but also gained necessary delays for payments. Countervailing forces somehow came out in the company's favor.

It is generally recognized that maximizing profits is quite often not the reason the individual small businessman operates as he does. The right to self-determination can very often gain precedence. In this case, the necessity of proving the "experts" wrong was an important factor. This particular individual was highly motivated by noneconomic considerations. He achieved exceptional intellectual stature outside the business; however, more emphasis on the profit motive might have relieved his burdens and facilitated his nonmonetary goals.

This case points up the validity of Clarence Randall's observation that a business organization cannot consist of putting people in boxes but rather must match the personality and motivations of the key people to enhance effectiveness.

Another observation from this case is the strength of market acceptance and of marketing position in an established consumer brand name and product. Had this not existed, the company surely would have collapsed from its internal strains. Sales and cash flow enabled this company to survive almost in spite of its management as much as because of it.

It should be noted that the basic integrity of an individual who is willing to commit not only his total material resources but his full personal efforts and the exceptional contribution of a few loyal employees may be worth more than the seeming security of collateral. Material and equipment values can change drastically from those of a going business to those at a liquidation sale. The financier can and, indeed, must force management reforms at times in order to protect himself as well as his client. Such forced discipline has been constructive in this case. At the time it was imposed it was resented and resisted. Had some outside balance not been provided, this story might not have had the more hopeful ending—or rather new beginning.

This case also illustrates the critical importance of pricing—not only as to product but in trade discounts. Had the Better Mouse Trap Company not enjoyed an exceptional innovator profit, strengthened by production margins and comfortable trade discounts, it could not have survived the split and shocks. There is little doubt that the company could be better managed and more profitable. But then it would not be the inventor's company as he has the right, if not responsibility, to run it.

Any company takes a considerable risk when it switches to a computerized data processing system without maintaining its old method until it has been run and re-run more than several times. It is also well to tie down the programming performance as a part of a purchase contract. The negative and costly experiences in this area have been well hidden and minimized. The results justify the investment in most cases, but the conversion risks and start up costs are too often understated. Paying for top talent in this field has been the best safeguard against disastrous loss of data control.

Case 3. Triple Action Company (TAC)

A successful technical sales representative recognized the need for a fast-moving company that could meet the many opportunities afforded by a new family of materials and processes that he was selling for a larger and slower-moving firm. His efforts to spark the giant were met with less than enthusiastic response. Therefore the salesman joined with an engineer and a designer to form their own company to exploit a rapidly expanding market. The three men combined the talents that could take newly developed material and processes such as sintered metals and not only mold and machine components and products but apply other existing skills, such as extrusion and casting, to a rapidly expanding technology.

Personal financial resources constituted the initial—and inadequate —capital. By working night and day and combining the talents of the three founders, the business grew along with the use of the new materials and processes. Much of the early business was of prototype or small runs; it often involved engineering rework and production experimentation. Conversion of the raw material to finished product merited a very high markup, so this engineering and production development work could be absorbed in the price of the final product. The values and results of the new material products merited higher prices and resultant profits. As the market grew, however, and competition among other new small and larger suppliers was felt, price pressures developed. The company did not fully utilize its earlier advantage by charging a research and development or setup fee. As a result, after the first few years of rapid growth and expansion of personnel from a few to fifty and then a hundred, financial as well as management pressures were felt.

About this time, the chief engineer, a founding partner, started another small company with someone else to whom he had originally acted as a consultant in a noncompeting field. The other two partners felt that their company needed more of his time and attention but he was giving less of it. An occasional evening and Saturday commitment began to increase into frequent days away from the plant. It was not surprising, then, that higher engineering costs were identified as a major concern in the profit planning for this company. Again, adequate cost and control data was nonexistant, through the failure of a large accounting consulting firm to meet this need.

One profit solution suggested by an outside consultant was to concentrate on charging setup or tooling fees as well as straight research and development costs where appropriate. It was decided that if these could not be obtained, such business should be bypassed. It was further decided that the company would shift its emphasis to some of the newly developed product lines where an increased margin could be realized as opposed to the standard supplies and materials that had become increasingly competitive in price.

Better product and service pricing helped alleviate what had become a critical capital shortage. The major supplier of the company's raw material was persuaded to enter into a long-term financing commitment as a part of an annual material supply contract. Attempts at Small Business Investment Company financing were unfruitful, as was a well-prepared presentation for a loan from the Small Business Administration (after three refusals by the banks, which were easily obtained).

This oversimplification of the company's problems seems to focus on capital requirements, which are often the result rather than the cause of a more basic problem. Businesses can outgrow key personnel as well as original facilities. The clue to the shortcoming of the creative but erratic engineer who helped start and build the company was ignored at first. Increased engineering costs were thought to result from increased market demands and may have been the result of poor pricing that often accompanies the urge to increase business. In fact, this company's profits increased when subsequent price policy changes resulted in less volume at a better margin.

When his physical absence followed the psychological departure or lack of commitment of the key executive, the signals should not have continued to be ignored. As might be expected, efforts to return the prodigal son to the family were less than fruitful and only increased the mounting financial and work load pressures.

It is difficult to recognize when a partnership dissolves in effect rather than in fact. Even when this was recognized, no easy solution was in sight. A buy or sell agreement could not be financed because the previous profits had been drained and the personal credit of the principals subsequently impaired. Therefore, no equity or ownership redistribution was possible at that time.

The solution was the reassignment of management responsibility and the attraction of technically able personnel on an employee rather than owner basis. Interestingly, the first solution of cutting off the errant partner seemed justified at the time. Finally, he was forced to take a leave of absence without pay to "clean up" his own side venture. He failed at that effort and was considering personal bankruptcy. Meanwhile, a corporate form of ownership was developed and the percentages of ownership realized consistent with past performance as well as original capital and effort contributions. This was a critical capital plan in view of cash drains.

Chastised by his failure as his own boss, the engineer was reassigned duties with a reduction in status and salary. He was advised to take a vacation, rest, and get back in shape. He refused and began tackling certain problems with good results. During this period, he evidently came to the conclusion that he would do best to try to capitalize on several years of previous investment. Once again, he became an important creative contributor to the company. He was relieved of certain management and supervisory responsibilities for which he was not suited.

One of the curious features of this case was the fact that each of the partners had been through an executive management training program. In retrospect, the president of the company commented that not only the individuals involved, but the company, thought that being able to talk some of the language of managers automatically made the individuals and the company think that those involved already were managers. The danger of too many chiefs is sometimes aggravated by what should be the broadening stimulus of an executive training program. The engineer later admitted he got the idea that he was capable of being the boss from that exposure to the executive suite.

This review does not fully emphasize the critical condition that capital shortages caused this company. It does, however, suggest the conclusion that the key problems are more often the people involved rather than finances. Analysis and understanding of the most important individuals are as requisite to sound profit planning as the departmental cash flow forecasts and audits.

Many students of small business have stressed the need for an outside board of directors for the small growing firm. The balance afforded by such outsiders on a board might have helped minimize the almost disastrous experience of this and many other companies.

Funding of required and desired research and development by customers rather than by the company is not a new concept. This salient strategy might well have been introduced earlier if broader experience had been brought to bear. Both industry and government buy a lot of R & D. When to absorb such costs for future product profit benefits is a continuing challenge. But charging for effort as well as results proved to be a critical capital decision for TAC.

Conclusions

These true, but disguised, vignettes help put some of the profit-planning problems of small business into clearer perspective. It seems obvious that these run the full gamut of business functions and responsibilities as well as of human personalities. Planning, often informal, and the organization of "scheming and dreaming" often marks the difference in degree of profit, success, and personal satisfaction.

Organization is often more individualized in the smaller company, but again formalized or defined interrelationships have generally yielded more of the desired results.

Control is often lacking and it, or rather the lack of it, appears to be the most frequent cause of failure after undercapitalization.

The highly variable nature of small businesses does not preclude systematic approaches to successful operation; rather, they provide guidelines for it. A smart pilot uses a checklist in a light private plane just as does the captain of the largest airliner. The only difference is in the greater degree of complexity in the latter. The private plane pilot has a little more leeway for intuition, but he would ignore his instruments and control readings only at his peril. How to retain flexibility in a successful small business can be learned from studying the models of dynamic large companies.

Ultimately, the interpersonal relationships developed within the smaller, growing organization probably contribute more to financial success than any other factor. When the business is not formally defined and does not have such recognized tools of management control as forecasts and budgets, individual motivation can make all the difference. To understand small business, we must understand the small businessman.

Part IV

LENDER REQUIREMENTS FOR SMALL BUSINESS FINANCING

9

The Capital Markets
for Small Business

R. Bruce Ricks

The task of analyzing sources and uses of funds for small business may be approached in several ways. One can take a macroeconomic viewpoint and treat data that measure total amounts of loans of various types to small business firms on an aggregate or national basis. He can then set out to measure the amount of equity funds raised through common stock offerings to the public. However, two problems immediately emerge in approaching the subject in this manner. First, data on loans and equity do not distinguish firms by size of business. Secondly, the figures on loans to business under a certain size ignore information on the degree of variability between businesses within an industry and between industries. Further, it is difficult to correlate loans with other factors of importance within the business. Those agencies which collect and publish statistics on loans and equity have not been concerned with the decomposition of data in a useful manner for the study of small business.

197

An alternative approach would focus attention on the availability of funds to a particular small business. The definition of *small business* is not unambiguous, however.

A major share of debt and equity funds is advanced to small business from private sources and is therefore not included in the totals reported by such agencies as the Federal Reserve Banks and State Insurance Commissioners. Therefore, this chapter will review the available statistics and discuss the traditional and nontraditional sources of funds and the attitudes of such suppliers toward small business. It should be noted that by *funds* is meant long-term funds. Therefore, the sources referred to are those for long-term as opposed to working-capital financing.

Traditional Sources of Debt Capital

The most useful classification of small business loans is by purpose rather than by collateral or contract. Confusion is introduced into the statistics by loans with noncorporate collateral being used for corporate purposes and short-term loans being considered long-term sources of funds. The following outline presents a classification of external suppliers of funds to small business in terms of type of collateral and traditional nature, as well as the two chief internal sources of funds:

1. External—Traditional
   a. Banks
   b. Insurance Companies
   c. Leasing Companies
   d. Commercial Finance Companies: Lenders; Factors
   e. Savings and Loan Associations
   f. The Owner, His Friends and Relatives
   g. Small Business Administration
2. External—Nontraditional
   a. Venture Capitalists and SBIC's
   b. Public Equity Market
3. Internal
   a. Depreciation and Retained Earnings
   b. Payables and Salaries

BANKS

The first source of debt capital that comes readily to the mind of the student of small business finance is that of commercial banks. Statistics on direct bank business loans of a small-size classification (if such data were available) would be misleading. Such direct business loans by banks, with maturities in excess of a year, would drastically understate the total extent of bank financing of small business. A substantial segment of longer-term small business debt financing is done through the refinancing of the owner's personal residence or other real estate assets. Thus, what is classified as a real-estate loan on the bank's books and in reporting forms is in actuality a business loan if classified by purpose rather than by collateral. Additionally, a substantial percentage of personal loans made on an unsecured basis in excess of a year are for business purposes.

Inventory and accounts-receivable loans are difficult to classify as to term, because the contract maturity may be a year or less and the understanding between the bank and the borrower may be that the loans will be automatically renewed, so that in the mind of the banker and the businessman these loans are long term in fact but short term by contract. Banks make both secured and unsecured loans to small businesses, looking typically toward a combination of liquida-table asset collateral in the form of buildings, inventory, and accounts receivable and to the anticipated ability of the corporation to generate, through its cash flow cycle, sufficient funds for repayment. If sufficient funds can be generated for repayment, the bank typically will permit a renewal of such loans. It should be emphasized that the option to renew lies with the bank. It may well be that the cash flow drain that causes the corporation to rely upon this source of external financing is the same drain that causes the bank to decide not to renew the loan at maturity.

INSURANCE COMPANIES

The life insurance industry is a supplier of many billions of dollars of investment funds. This discussion will center on life insurance companies, as opposed to casualty and other insurance carriers, because it is primarily the former whose investment policies permit lending for which a small business might qualify.

Life insurance company assets at the end of 1965 were $158.8 billion. There is almost a total absence of data on life insurance loans to small business. Some idea of the relationships may be obtained by reference to a 1957 special study by the Life Insurance Association of America for the Select Committee on Small Business of the House of Representatives. At that time 67 of the larger insurance companies whose combined assets were $74 billion (slightly less than half of the 1965 year-end figure) were included in the survey. As of the end of 1965, $5.1 billion, or 6.9 per cent of these insurance company assets were invested in commercial, industrial, and public utility loans. When one performs some transposition of that data it is apparent that total life insurance funds invested in small business are very small. Using an arbitrary cut-off of $250,000 as a loan presumably for small business, only 6.1 per cent of the total were in the class of $250,000 and under. This means that .004 per cent (6.9 per cent × 6.1 per cent) of the $74 billion in assets was in this classification. An extremely high percentage of these loans were secured by mortgages—the figure being 97 per cent. Thus, the 3 per cent of these loans to business not secured by mortgages is only .00012 per cent of such assets. If we transpose that relationship without change to the 1965 year-end asset figure of $158.8 billion we see that only $20 million would thereby be life insurance commercial, industrial, and public utilities loans of $250,000 or less, not secured by mortgages. Assuming the relationships still hold, it is obvious that relatively little of the vast reservoir of savings managed within the life insurance industry goes to the general business financing of corporations. Such loans as are made go to those corporations with mortgagable assets.

The reasons for this avoidance of small business loans included the following: (1) Many state laws prohibit life insurance company loans to unincorporated businesses except where secured by real property, and most small businesses in number are unincorporated; (2) such lending is usually housed in either the bond or the mortgage and real estate investment department of life insurance companies and does not receive the primary attention of such departments; (3) the smaller the borrower the less attractive an unsecured loan would be to the lender. It would seem worthwhile for those concerned with, and responsible for, the flow of funds to small business to seek ways of freeing insurance companies from restrictive legal requirements. It could be argued that such institutions with their vast assets and risk experience would be ideal places for diversifying the risk among a group of small business loans. From our standpoint of reviewing the sources of funds, however, the insurance companies provide relatively little in the way of capital to businesses other than mortgage capital. It should be observed that the loan-to-value ratio of such insurance companies indicates that only some 70 per cent of the value of mortgagable assets would be advanced by an insurance company. Thus, rather than deriving funds from pledging of fixed assets, it is probably the case that small businesses who borrow from insurance companies are faced with putting out some 30 per cent of the cost of such assets in cash equity. This immediately leads small businesses to consider the leasing of assets.

LEASING COMPANIES

From the above comments concerning bank and insurance companies lending on a collateral and a general credit basis, it can be seen that a wide gap is left for leasing companies to fill in supplying small businesses with the use of assets without committing equity capital. Leasing companies and bank leasing departments have taken advantage of this lack of competition, particularly in the supplying of those assets that (1) are quite standardized and therefore have a resale market beyond the borrower in question, (2) are easily repossessable in the sense that they are portable and relatively difficult for the lessee company to damage, (3) are less subject to rapid obsolescence, and/or (4) are used in longer term contracts with the government or major companies wherein the contract assures the lessee of sufficient revenue generated from the use of such assets to amortize the lease over the term secured by the contract.

Small businessmen find that leasing companies specialize in dealing with small businesses and are relatively unconcerned with restrictions on the general operations of their lessees. Beyond restrictions on inappropriate use of the specific assets, if the assets are nonstandard, or if the anticipated revenue from the use of the leased assets will be short, periodic amortization payments required by the leasing company will be quite high. The renter is not building up an equity in the assets unless he is able to negotiate a reasonable purchase option as part of the leasing contract. The primary advantage is that he gets

100 per cent financing of the asset as opposed to a mortgage loan with a smaller loan-to-value ratio. Evidence of this is the fact that banks and insurance companies have begun to enter the field and, typically, have more lenient renewal options and repurchase contracts than do the leasing companies.

COMMERCIAL FINANCIAL COMPANIES

Another traditional source of external funds, where corporate collateral is pledged, is the commercial finance industry. Here, as with the bank's short-term loans, the commercial finance industry is normally considered to supply short-term funds. However, to the extent that a minimum balance of borrowing may be kept with the commercial finance company, and to the extent that it is not necessary to pay off loans over a period of less than a year, they do provide a relatively constant source of long-term money.

The commercial finance companies are usually divided into two categories. The first includes companies such as James C. Talcott and Walter Heller that primarily loan funds secured by the pledging of accounts receivable. Upon payment of the loan title to the accounts receivable is then returned to the borrowing corporation. The second are factoring companies that purchase accounts receivable. With the exception of nonrecourse factoring where the company simply buys accounts receivable at so many cents on the dollar, there is little difference between a company that loans money secured by accounts receivable and a company that purchases accounts receivable with recourse, since a fractional percentage of the funds represented by the accounts receivable will be advanced in either case. Often the full value of the accounts receivable will only be advanced as collections are made by or for the factoring company on an average maturity basis.

Factoring has been traditionally restricted to the apparel industry, but there are indications that these lenders are attempting to diversify their customer mix. Commercial finance companies are beginning to offer a package of services to the small business which includes an accounting system for accounts receivable, credit cards and billing forms, credit evaluation of customers, and an assumption of the collection process if desired. Such financing, essentially, takes over the entire credit sales procedure of the participating company. The charge for this may be included in the interest rate. Small businesses would be well advised to cost out such services compared with their own operations, which may be understaffed and inefficient.

Savings and Loan Associations

The savings and loan industry provides funds to small businesses through mortgage loans. These lending institutions are relatively unconcerned with the use of the funds by the small business but, rather, look to the real estate collateral as their source of security. Unintentionally, they provide funds whose use is for small business financing. There has been much discussion of the possibility of broadening the outlets for savings and loan funds. However, little progress has been made in permitting savings and loan associations to lend directly to small business where either the loan is on an unsecured basis or real estate security is a relatively minor part of the collateral for the loan.

The Owner, His Friends and Relatives

The owner, his friends, relatives, and other individuals whom he can convince to become involved in the project are an important traditional source of funds. In this category, the primary instrument may be debt or equity but the ranking of the security, if debt, is junior to bank loans and, of course, if preferred or common stock, is junior to debt financing. The decision whether to call this layer of financing junior subordinated debt or equity financing is primarily a matter left to the tax accountants who advise the owner and his friends as to the amount of such money that can be classified as debt thereby making the interest payments deductible to the corporation. We know little, quantitatively, about the supply of these funds from what might be called the private equity market, except that the evaluation of the integrity and optimism of the owner may be at least as great as any formal financial evaluation of the probability of success of the firm. The owner is thus, in effect, selling himself and faith in his entrepreneurial ability as much as he is convincing friends and relatives of the basic financial strength of the corporation under more typical management.

SMALL BUSINESS ADMINISTRATION

The Small Business Administration has for many years conducted programs designed to bring what might be called sympathetic money to small business. A major contribution of the SBA is counsel and management consultation. Regardless of whether the small business actually gets a loan, the owner is able to avail himself of counsel and guidance that is backed by the advantage of the SBA officials' knowledge of the records of numerous small businesses. This advice is free to the small business applicant and can be an important contribution to his financial management.

Nontraditional External Sources of Funds

VENTURE CAPITALISTS AND SBIC's

Under the classification nontraditional sources of funds fall the venture capitalists and Small Business Investment Companies (SBIC's). This is not because such sources of funds are new or unique. Rather it is to indicate, particularly in the case of venture capitalists, that this source is often overlooked in discussions of institutional lenders. Venture capitalists do not operate as an industry. They do not have an industry association, nor are they required to report to a state or federal agency. Venture capitalists are made considerably more effective by their lack of public exposure and their ability to work as intermediaries between those seeking money and those with money.

The institutionalization of such a group in the form of a Small Business Investment Company imposes certain requirements in the name of protection of investors and borrowers which make it undesirable for successful venture capitalists to convert to the SBIC form. A definition of *venture capitalists* is in order. By this is meant an individual, or perhaps a small group of individuals, loosely organized, placing capital into risky business situations where the profit pay-off if successful, is extremely attractive. We are referring to a small probability of a large gain combined with a large probability of a small loss—such loss being all or substantially all of the money that the venture capitalist marshalls to the particular small business.

Most venture capitalists are housed in law firms—particularly in those which specialize in tax, corporation, or SEC matters. Another place where venture capitalists are often found is in the investment banking and brokerage business. Such firms have found that they are often approached by a small business well before the time that it is appropriate to go to the public equity market. Such small businesses may appear to have excellent growth prospects. To the extent that the venture capitalists in the brokerage firm can provide interim financing for the corporation it also has prospects of a payoff including the underwriting profits when the firm is, in fact, ready to go public. A third area is the investment counseling industry. Numerous investment counselors combine conservative long-term investment advice in stable securities for wealthy clients who have large cash positions with recommendations for acquisition of investment positions in small business ventures.

It should be stressed that each of these types of venture capitalists —the lawyer, the stockbroker, and the investment counselor—has as part of its reward the business that is associated with such financing. The lawyer gets incorporation fees, filing fees, perhaps a retainer from the small business, and perhaps one from the investors whose funds he places with the small business. He probably also is acting as tax or legal counsel to these individuals. The stockbroker obtains a potential future source of underwriting and trading business in the small business, as well, perhaps, as options in the stock when the company goes public. He also provides clients with the service of monitoring the future market for them. The investment counselor is paid a management fee for supervising the entire portfolio of his investor group and is able to offer them high-risk, potentially high-return securities with which to diversify their portfolios of conservative investments. Occasionally, a group of such intermediaries will organize itself to the point of offering to provide management services on a fee or partial equity basis to small business.

Most venture capitalists do not make themselves available to any small business that walks in the door. They must protect the limited time that they have available for this work, since such an activity is typically subordinate to their regular profession. Also, they wish to protect the anonymity and availability of funds on the part of their investors. The advantages arising from the lack of structure, the lack of reporting requirements, and the ability to serve the small business, the investor, and the intermediary's own affairs so that the cost of this activity could be spread, were not given sufficient attention in the development of the Small Business Investment Act. The author submits that many successful venture capitalists reviewed the SBIC Act and said something like the following: "We have a very successful activity that is generating certain losses but is generating sufficient very large profits to more than offset these. We have access to all the funds we are able to process. We do not need the Government's source of funds. If we were to have to comply with the Government's reporting requirements and submission of loans to them for review we'd have to add staff and increase our direct overhead. We couldn't conduct such a business on a 'whenever we want to' basis. If we add overhead, we are firmly committed to such business and have to do a sufficient amount of advancing of funds to cover the overhead and still secure the profits we have been getting so far. We can take capital gains on our profits. Therefore, the SBIC Act only permits the advantage of taking ordinary losses instead of capital losses on our unsuccessful investments. This is not the problem. If they were to reduce the capital gains on the profit we might be interested. In any case the SBIC Act puts too many restrictions on dual charging; they seem to feel we're dishonest. They want to protect somebody against us rather than recognizing the fact that we are providing a smooth-functioning, though small, flow of funds to the most deserving small businesses."

To summarize, the author contends that the SBIC movement is not appealing to many of the most efficient venture capitalists.

The final nontraditional source of funds to small business is the Small Business Investment Company. The SBA set up an institution coming between the exhaustion of the owner's equity capacity and the point in time when the small business was ready for a public equity offering that was itself subject to conditions in the public equity market. Many firms which rushed to become SBIC's then entered the public equity market and raised many millions of dollars with inadequate outlets for proper investment of the proceeds. Thus, even if limited investments turned out to be successful, the sterilization of substantial uninvested portions of their portfolios in treasury bills meant that their over-all yields were unattractive.

At the other end of the total assets spectrum is the group of SBIC's who contribute the statutory minimum in outside equity and then apply for the SBA contribution, trying to take advantage of what appears to be cheap public money. The distribution of SBIC's by asset size shows many firms at the minimum statutory level of outside equity and numerous firms of large size, having raised $10 million and more from the public market. What is desirable to the SBA, to small business, and to the efficient flow of funds, however, is the SBIC that begins small and is able to raise additional investment money as it is able to find attractive small business investments. This is what venture capitalists did prior to the SBIC legislation but the function was not effectively transferred to the SBIC industry.

Finally, it may be said of the external sources of funds, that many major financial institutions place extremely small portions of their portfolios into loans for small business. Such institutions have not been free to make many small business loans. The Small Business Investment Act was an attempt to organize and to increase the effectiveness of venture capitalists. For the reasons previously given, such legislation was unappealing to many extremely effective venture capitalists who continue to supply funds on an *ad hoc*, no publicity basis to what they consider to be the most attractive small businesses.

PUBLIC EQUITY MARKET

The public equity market is treated here as a nontraditional source of funds because it is not generally available as a source of funds for small business. By the time the business gets to the point where it can economically justify a public offering, it is undoubtably beyond our classification of a small business. The factor that keeps this statement from being one that is accurate over time is the variability in receptiveness of the new issue market to small underwritings. In the time of a "hot new issue" market when the public is willing to invest funds based mainly on the name of the corporation, and when it has "-onics," "-tronics," or "electronics" in its title, the standards of minimum size and demonstrated profitability are drastically relaxed. The small business owner is tempted to cash in on this period and recoup his own investment and substantial profits. From the standpoint of the corporation, however, the "hot new issue" market may in retrospect prove a very poor time to market a new issue if the stock drops substantially from the offering price and develops a poor trading record in the after-market. This makes successive offerings more difficult when new equity capital needs to be raised.

On the other hand, the corporation may be successful in finding interim financing following the exhaustion of the owner's equity and produce the type of earnings, assets, and sales growth that brings it up to an appropriate public offering level, only to find that the public market is at the bottom of the cycle for new issues. Regardless of its record, it cannot market its stock. The public market, therefore, becomes an extremely undependable source of funds to the corporation. Not only must the firm establish a record of performance that would entitle it to a reasonable new-issue price, but the record must bring it to the point of a new-equity issue at a time when the market is not highly unfavorable to small offerings. Table 9-1 indicates the number

Table 9-1—Public Stock Offerings Under Regulation A (By Number)

Size	1964	1963	1962	1961	1960	1959	1958	1957	1956	1955
$100,000 or less	126	143	160	165	220	222	231	307	481	544
Over $100,000 but not over $200,000	96	104	208	201	216	162	165	163	246	312
Over $200,000 but not over $300,000	240	270	697	691	613	470	336	449	736	772
Offerors										
Issuing companies	418	476	1000	1006	1021	797	704	865	1389	1517
Stockholders	39	34	24	28	27	31	28	52	62	109
Issuers and stockholders jointly	5	7	41	23	1	26	0	2	12	2

Source: Annual Reports of Securities and Exchange Commission (Washington, D.C.)

and dollar amount of new issues marketed under $300,000 between 1955 and 1964. This table indicates the build-up of new issues to 1962 and then an immediate fall-off as the bloom came off the new-issue market prior to the bear market in stocks in general in 1962. The new-issue market does not provide the dependable source of capital to small business that has been the objective of the SBA and other proponents of small business finance.

Internal Sources of Funds

DEPRECIATION AND RETAINED EARNINGS

The problem of sources of funds would of course be simplified if the corporation was able to generate, internally, funds sufficient to meet its expansion needs. With established corporations, retained earnings and the noncash charge of depreciation provide considerably more funds than external sources. This is possible in a firm where new investment is a relatively small portion of assets and therefore small in relation to earnings on total assets. With the small business on the other hand, expansion capabilities are severely limited if the corporation is unable to build up the owned asset base necessary to generate a return and depreciation. This, therefore, requires it to adopt an extremely short-term viewpoint with regard to investment projects, one that in the long run may prove highly costly to the corporation. Depreciation is a major source of funds to major corporations. Table 9-2

Table 9-2—Internal Sources of Funds: Manufacturing Corporations ($ Billions)

Year	Corporate Profits	Depreciation	Depreciation as % of Total
1955	23.0	15.7	40.6
1956	23.5	17.3	42.4
1957	22.3	19.1	46.1
1958	18.8	20.3	51.9
1959	24.5	21.6	46.9
1960	22.0	22.9	51.0
1961	21.9	24.1	52.4
1962	25.0	27.5	52.4
1963	26.7	28.8	51.9
1964	31.6	30.5	49.1

Source: Economic Reports of the President (Washington, D.C.)

indicates the relationships between retained earnings and depreciation. But the relationship exhibited by a major corporation having substantial fixed depreciable assets is not valid for a small business. It was previously indicated that the small business may be well advised to lease assets rather than commit its limited equity by borrowing only some 70 per cent of them from lending institutions. In the case of the leased assets, of course, depreciation charges are not available as a deduction from earnings.

PAYABLES AND SALARIES

In the absence of hard data it must be assumed that the major sources of funds generated internally by the small business are expansion and lengthening of the accounts and notes payable items and the understatement of the appropriate salaries that should be taken by key officer and owner personnel. The owner is making new capital commitments to the corporation to the extent that he takes a salary less than warranted. In terms of the appearance of his balance sheet when coming to a public offering or to a lender, he may make his statement look more attractive by understating salaries and thereby overstating corporate earnings. This, however, may have the effect of freezing the owner's equity in the corporation, making it difficult to raise salaries when the corporation is borrowing from a financial institution.

This brief sketch of the major sources of capital for small business is not meant to be definitive but rather to provide a review of certain major suppliers and their attitudes toward small business loans or equity commitments.

10

Analyzing the Financing Potential of a Business

Royce Diener

Many seekers of business credit—and doubtless all individuals connected with the sources of such credit—will agree that a
successful financing program can be achieved only if the applicant has
made a prior determination of his exact needs, and if he understands
in realistic terms the availability of the type of financing he is seeking.
Unfortunately, these understandings are not widely held. In these days
of consistently improving technical and marketing proficiencies, it is
paradoxical that the means of tapping various capital sources are not
generally known. As a result, a businessman whose knowledge of his
own industry is far advanced, compared with that of a predecessor a
decade ago, may have little more financial know-how than his earlier
counterpart. The knowledge gap seems to exist primarily in the realm
of recognizing the financing potential of a particular business.

During the past quarter century substantial progressive changes
have occurred in the methods of business finance. This evolution, in
both domestic and international spheres of trade, derived its basic
momentum from the steady growth of our economy. Further impetus

came from activation of new government programs, and—surprising for some people to learn—from the development of keen competition among lending institutions to devise new financing applications in an effort to put more of their money to work. The result has been the creation of a broad spectrum of business finance, whose analysis is a prerequisite for every seeker of capital.

Basically, the analysis of the financing potential of a business should be made in a context of the following two criteria: (1) the specific type or types of capital needed for the business, and (2) the eligibility for the types of capital required.

The analytical procedure normally followed to arrive at a determination of financing potential can be simply stated thus: *The measurement of the financial picture of a business against the yardstick of the requirements of each of several specific types of capital.* We must, therefore, initially understand the nature of these types of capital.

In financial circles, capital is usually categorized by referring to its source and to its function. In its simplest form, the categorization stems from two questions: Where is the money to come from? What is it to be used for? We should begin by differentiating between the two generic sources of capital—public and institutional financing.

Public financing is obtained by the issuance of securities to more than a very small group of investors and requires registration with the Securities and Exchange Commission (with the exception of intrastate issues). Public financing almost always involves the services of stock brokerage firms (who refer to this function as investment banking), and it is usually applicable only to experienced businesses that have already traveled the other routes of financing.

Institutional financing encompasses the greatest range of borrowing variations that business firms utilize. These are the types of institutions that may serve as sources: commercial banks, insurance companies, commercial finance companies, pension and welfare funds, Small Business Investment Companies, factors, Small Business Administration, industrial loan banks, and investment bankers (for private placements).

The size of this list presents some idea of the wide variety of institutional funding available. However, we should recognize that all lending institutions stand on one side of a definite boundary line. This line is drawn somewhat short of what we might term "hundred per cent financing."

Functional Types of Capital

Some businessmen have the erroneous idea that financial institutions may occasionally provide, on a loan basis, *all* the money required to finance growth or the undertaking of a new operational direction. This is not so, although they may advance as much as 90 per cent of the required capital. Of course, reference here is only to the limitations of the lending institutions. Total financing requirements can be obtained on a permanent or semipermanent basis from private sources or public issues. It is this type of financing that leads us into the first functional category of capital—equity.

Equity is usually represented by the original investment in a business plus retained earnings—plus financing later obtained on a permanent investment basis in anticipation of a dividend or capital gain possibility. In the analysis of financing potential, equity is significant because it represents the total value of a business, since all other financing (with the exception of publicly issued equity securities) amounts to some form of borrowing, which must ultimately be repaid. The ratio of these amounts that must be repaid—in other words, the debt—to the net worth, or equity, is a limiting factor on the financing potential of a business. Even then, there are shadings to this definition when it is applied to certain financing arrangements. For example, funds obtained through the issuance of subordinated debentures or notes are usually also considered as equity by lending institutions. This viewpoint can be extremely helpful to any efforts made to pyramid the borrowing abilities of a business.

Equity capital can be more clearly understood if a distinction is made among the following three functionally different types of funding: equity capital; working capital; and growth capital.

Equity capital is not generally obtainable from institutions—at least not during the early stages of the growth of a business. Working and growth capital, on the other hand, can be obtained in a number of ways. Both become necessary when equity capital has been used to the limit of its availability. They extend the effectiveness of equity by providing the leverage on investment present in the financial picture of every successful business.

Working capital needs arise from the generation of activity in a going business. For example, as sales increase, accounts receivable increase and funds are required to carry these. Concurrently, inventories enlarge and payroll costs mount; these, too, require additional money. It is to satisfy such needs that working capital is required. Although borrowed funds may be used for working capital over fairly long periods of time, the amount used fluctuates, depending on the cyclical aspects of a particular business. In fact, it is the varying use of greater or lesser amounts of money over a single year that most quickly identifies the funds used on such a fluctuating basis as working capital. It provides the money to carry a business through its annual period of greatest cash need.

Growth capital, although frequently grouped with working capital by many financiers, is different because it is not directly related to the cyclical aspects of a business. Instead, growth capital is usually involved with a planned program of expansion through purchase of better production or handling facilities, or through increased promotional expenditures. If, based on activating such a program, a projection of greater profits can reasonably be demonstrated, various types of financing can be arranged. Rather than looking toward seasonal liquidity for reducing this type of borrowing, institutions that make growth capital available will rely on the creation of future profits to provide for orderly repayment of such loans over a longer period.

We have reached the point where we can use one-word descriptions in analyzing a need into the three functional types of capital:

1. Fluctuating (working capital)
2. Amortizing (growth capital)
3. Permanent (equity capital)

The differentiation between equity, growth, and working capital which exists in the mind of a lending officer should now be plain. If you are asking for a working capital loan, you will be expected to demonstrate how the loan can be reduced or repaid during your firm's period of greatest liquidity in a cycle of one year. If you are asking for a growth capital loan, you will be expected to demonstrate how the purchase of additional fixed assets, or an increase in funds spent for promotional activities, will yield cash flow enabling you to repay the loan over several years.

If you are not clearly asking for either working or growth capital, an institutional lender will say to you, "We would like to accommodate you, but we cannot *invest* in a business—that is the role of equity capital; we only make loans." Specifically, the lender will explain that the loans he can make are only temporary and that the institution cannot be "locked in" with its money, as would be the case with a stockholder or an investing institution that invests in a private corporation for a dividend return, an advantageous conversion, and/or, a future capital gain.

Actually, working capital loans can be arranged which in practice almost entirely serve equity capital functions and purposes; the differentiation can be very subtle and can depend entirely on the availability of, and the eligibility for, a particular type of institutional financing.

Beginning with an understanding of the three basic types of capital, a business should be analyzed into its financing potential for each of these categories. After a determination of the amount of funding that will be required, we then have a goal for the size and required term of the financing to be sought. Practically every analyst who deals in the broad spectrum of available financing will follow a procedure of sifting the possibilities according to a descending order of desirability. Obviously, each business should analyze its position in an attempt to obtain the best financing available to it on the most attractive terms. Failing that, the other orders of financing are considered, based on the qualifications as revealed by analysis.

Analyzing for Equity Financing

First in order of desirability is undoubtedly a public equity financing. In modern business, this view is held almost universally by sophisticated financial executives. Particularly since the shake-out of the new issue market in the spring of 1962, a well-conceived public issue has almost always been the most beneficial financing step that any company can undertake. Of course, there have been exceptions; however, these do not usually appear in a well-conceived underwriting sponsored by a responsible investment banking syndicate. In earlier days when analysis was less stringent and criteria less well-defined, there could be debate about the relative merits of a public financing. Within the scope of today's refined practices by responsible financiers, if a business qualifies for a public underwriting, this is the route usually most beneficial for it to follow in its financing aspirations. In other words, the requirements of responsible underwriting syndicates today are such that, if these are satisfied, the negative arguments that can be raised against public financing are not valid. Obviously, a public issue should not be entertained prematurely until other forms of financing are used to obtain proper leverage and to build the company to a point where the owners realize their best potential capitalization of earnings by the establishment of a valuation on the business based on an earnings multiplier. Most small businesses, within the federal government's official definition, are not yet ready for a proper public financing. The analyst can quickly make a superficial determination by reviewing the profit-and-loss statement to determine if after-tax earnings are substantial—are growing on a steady curve—and that there are indications from the nature of the business that this growth will be sustained in the future. The role of earnings is preeminent in making this determination, almost to the exclusion of the normal criteria considered in other forms of financing. Regardless of the type of security package ultimately decided upon—common stock, preferred, convertible debentures, or some unitized combination—the present and past earnings (usually for a minimum of five years), plus future increased earnings potential, determine the eligibility for, and the size of, a public issue financing.

Using an oversimplified example, let us assume that a business reflects an after-tax profit of $300,000. It has increased its profits 25 per cent each year for the past five years. It is indicated that, with additional capital, the growth rate will not only be sustained but will accelerate. The company operates within an industry, or a marketing field, that has excellent future prospects. Such a firm might easily be evaluated at a worth of $3 million (almost regardless of its book value) on a ten-times earnings-multiplier basis. An investment banking syndicate might underwrite common stock to provide $1.5 million to the company through issuance of 50 per cent of its shares to the public.

Obviously, only relatively few firms qualify for public equity financing. Many hundreds of companies can be analyzed for their financing potential before one encounters a firm that is eligible. Therefore the analyst usually moves on to the next order of desirability.

Analyzing for Unsecured Working Capital and Growth Capital Loans

The simplest means of obtaining working and growth capital financing is by borrowing on an unsecured basis. The mechanics are the least cumbersome; loan-handling requirements are minimal and therefore the cost is low. For this reason we find that commercial banks—the largest source of this type of financing—prefer to make unsecured loans to operating businesses whenever they can. Analysis for the eligibility of a business to qualify for unsecured financing centers first on the balance sheet of that business. Since unsecured lenders do not enjoy a priority position among creditors, they must place more emphasis on general liquidity, over-all financial strength relative to the size of credit, and present indicated ability to repay. This does not mean that the possibility of obtaining small initial unsecured credit is precluded; it is merely a matter of proportion to the size of credit sought.

A simple approach to the analysis of unsecured borrowing eligibility is found in the net current asset position on the balance sheet. Net current assets are obtained by subtracting the current liabilities from the current assets; the resultant figure is sometimes also called the working capital of a business. Banks normally limit their unsecured lines of credit to 40 per cent or 50 per cent of working capital, sometimes going a little higher to allow for seasonal peaks. Therefore, a business which shows $200,000 in current assets (cash, inventory, and accounts receivable) and $100,000 in current liabilities (accounts payable, current accrued expenses, and taxes payable) would qualify for approximately $50,000 unsecured credit. This same guideline will apply on much larger amounts; however, consideration must then be given to the current ratio and to the debt-to-worth ratio of the business.

The ratio of current assets to current liabilities is useful primarily as a quick appraisal of the liquidity of a business and its eligibility for unsecured borrowing. Although the ideal current ratios are from two to one and upward, this is not necessarily a minimum requirement for unsecured borrowing. As long as the total amount of unsecured credit is in the neighborhood of 50 per cent of the working capital, a current ratio of as low as 1.25 to 1.0 may be tolerated. Obviously, if the current ratio is much lower than that, there will be practically no working capital; thus the possibility of obtaining unsecured loans will disappear on both counts.

As larger unsecured credits are sought for working capital, our analysis will have to take into consideration the debt-to-worth ratio. Here we are referring to total debt, which includes everything but capital and surplus on the liability side of the balance sheet, including all current obligations such as trade accounts payable. There are many mitigating factors in determining the effect of the debt-to-worth ratio as a limitation on unsecured borrowing; however, most companies that qualify for unsecured working capital loans possess debt two to five times the net worth. Since unsecured lenders must look to the general resources of a company for repayment, rather than occupying a secured creditor's prior position, the presence of a higher ratio of debt to worth may preclude unsecured borrowing.

Up to this point, the unsecured borrowing potential we have analyzed has been primarily relative to satisfying working capital requirements. However, we should also analyze for the possibility of unsecured growth capital financing. Here we are talking about a loan which will run for more than one year; in fact the term may vary from two years to more than five years. Many lenders will provide such financing based on the indicated ability to repay—even if the total amount of the financing is in excess of the previously described limitations of unsecured working capital loans in ratio to net current assets. Although there will still be limitations relative to total debt in ratio to worth, here the prime consideration is the annual cash flow. We will define cash flow as the profits plus noncash expenses such as depreciation. Many businesses that have substantial depreciable physical equipment can obtain unsecured financing in excess of the usual net current asset limitations because the depreciation adds such a material factor to their total cash flow. For example, a company that has $25,000 annual profits and $50,000 depreciation creates $75,000 per year cash flow. If, after deducting all other debt servicing obligations such as mortgage payments and conditional sales contracts for equipment, there is still available $25,000 per year over and above any increased needs for operating capital, such a company might qualify for a three-year unsecured growth capital loan of as much as $75,000. In practice, the determination is not usually set so finely; normally, the "debt coverage" should be at least one and one-half times the annual repayment requirement on the loan.

In more substantial financings, debt coverage can run from three to six or seven times the annual repayment requirement. This is particularly true in the case of private placements of substantial amounts with institutions such as insurance companies, trust funds, and investment companies. These placements—ranging in size from several hundred thousand to millions of dollars—are usually made in the form of debentures or notes. Although some placements are for terms as short as five years, present practice is for terms of twelve to fifteen years with interest-only payments the first several years to help provide the sinking fund.

To qualify for an unsecured debt placement, a company must have a substantial history of earnings for several years—sometimes a minimum of five years or more. Debt coverage—the cash flow available to service the loan—should be from three to six times the required amount. A beginning private placement may be equal to, or greater than, the net worth junior to it, in the case of higher risk placements that include "kickers" of conversion rights or warrants. However, the usual institutional placement rarely exceeds an amount equal to the junior capital and, in first placements, can be limited to half that.

For example, a company that qualifies on various criteria, including a history of earnings, may have capital and surplus of $1 million. Such a company should qualify for a private placement of at least $0.5 million if the cash flow available to service the placement provides a good cover. Level principal and interest payments on a 6 per cent ten-year placement of $0.5 million would be approximately $65,000 per annum; debt coverage should therefore be at least $200,000 out of the available cash flow.

Actually, the financing potential in a funded debt placement of the type described above is not limited to the amounts of the placement itself. This is because such placements are, in one way or another, usually subordinated to current bank borrowings; therefore a leverage is provided. Debentures are normally subordinated on their face. Senior note placements may not be specifically subordinated; however, because they are long term—and current bank borrowings are usually structured on 90-day notes—they are, from a practical viewpoint, subordinated to the bank's position by term. In general, each dollar of subordinated debt that is matched by at least one dollar of equity (capital and surplus) can create one dollar of unsecured bank credit. If, for example, the net worth of a company is 1.5 million and a $1 million placement is obtained, the company should qualify for $1 million in unsecured short-term bank credit. The $1.5 million net worth is therefore leveraged with $2 million in growth and working capital.

To complete the analysis of the unsecured borrowing potential, it should be realized that both working and growth capital financing programs can be combined on a smaller scale with only bank financing. For example, a company with $100,000 net current assets might qualify for a working capital loan of $40,000 that can be repaid during the annual slow season of its operations. At the same time, if its annual cash flow amounted to $40,000, an additional growth capital unsecured loan might be added to the package covering an initial advance of $75,000 to be repaid in equal annual installments of $25,000 over a three-year term. Obviously, at the peak season during the first year, the total financing might amount to nearly $100,000.

These combinations of short-term working capital, plus longer term growth capital on an unsecured basis, will still be subject to the debt-to-worth limitations earlier described. However, here again the financing source will give credit toward the total worth for all subordinated liabilities such as principals' advances to the corporation and other subordinated liabilities from other sources.

Analyzing for Secured Financing

If the use of the various forms of unsecured borrowing heretofore described will not provide sufficient capital, we must then determine the secured borrowing potential. Here we have a drastically different set of criteria because the lender is indeed a preferred creditor on the basis of a statutory lien and he can look to certain assets being allocated strictly to liquidation of his lending exposure. Since he is not on a par with the other creditors of the company, the secured lender does not place as much emphasis on the debt-to-worth ratio. On a secured lending basis, the following assets are analyzed for their financing potential: (1) fixtures, machinery, and equipment; (2) inventories; and (3) accounts receivable.

Among these three categories of collateral, the simplest form of financing can be obtained by a chattel mortgage on the fixtures or equipment. Loans can be arranged that require merely monthly or quarterly payments over a term, which may run from two to five years. The financing potential will be determined by the liquidation value of the collateral and the indicated ability to repay.

If the collateral is standard equipment, a quick estimate of its liquidation value is that—after about five years' depreciation has been subtracted from the original cost—the net book value is roughly equivalent to the liquidation value. Depending on the rate of depreciation, the net book value will be between 40 per cent and 60 per cent of the original cost value. At such depreciated book values, we can expect a loan availability of between 100 per cent and 125 per cent of the liquidation value. This is because the lender feels he knows enough about the present condition of the company to postulate repayment for at least the first year and that thereafter his advance will be below liquidation value. However, the borrower must still demonstrate his ability to repay, based on past or projected cash flow as previously described.

With an understanding of the foregoing information, it is fairly simple to estimate financing potential on furniture, fixtures, and equipment. Let us assume that a manufacturing business has equipment at original cost value of $250,000. The balance sheet indicates that a total of $125,000 depreciation has been taken. Further, from the profit and loss statement we see that the yearly depreciation cost has been $25,000; therefore, the total asset in this category has been depreciated an average of five years. Although an appraisal may be required by the lender, for analysis purposes we can assume that the remaining $125,000 net depreciated asset approximates liquidation value. The collateral consists of punch presses, drills, press brakes, materials handling equipment, and office furniture and machines. (If this total should include some special equipment built by the manufacturer for his own use which would have no ready market and whose liquidation value could not be established, this increment would be ineligible as collateral.) Assuming all collateral to fall into standard equipment categories, however, the manufacturer should be eligible for a secured loan of between $100,000 and $150,000—provided that adequate cash flow was demonstrated. If we assume a maximum loan of $150,000 to be obtained over a three-year term with equal monthly amortizations, the manufacturer would obviously have to demonstrate that he has available yearly cash flow of at least $50,000 after all other debt servicing requirements are met.

Another source of secured financing uses inventory as collateral. In this type of financing, there are several different forms of liens that can be granted to the secured lender; namely, public warehousing, field warehousing, and inventory liens. Each of these arrangements insures a priority creditor position to the lender; however, by their nature they can create differing financing potentials. Public warehousing and field warehousing are known as "ostensible" liens, they are readily apparent to trade creditors and to the general public, and they are more stringently controlled. Therefore, under warehousing arrangements, a higher percentage of loan against collateral may be obtained. The reporting and control of collateral under inventory liens is much simpler and less stringent; therefore, the lender will tend to advance a lower percentage of funds against the cost value of the inventory. The entrepreneur of a business seeking such financing will have to weigh the advantages and disadvantages of these types of lending arrangements in making his choice—a higher loan under more strictly controlled arrangements versus a lower loan under a looser, more flexible arrangement.

The financing potential inherent in an inventory depends on the processing status of the inventory, the commodity nature of the inventory, and the inventory turnover.

The processing status of the inventory is analyzed into three classifications; namely, raw materials, goods in process, and finished goods. If the finished goods are manufactured to fill orders and represent standard marketable products, the percentage of advance over cost can be fairly high, ranging from 65 per cent to 85 per cent. Advances against raw materials can also be substantial, running from 40 per cent to 70 per cent. This will depend on the nature of the raw material— whether it consists of basic raw materials for which there is a daily trading market, whether these materials have been specifically produced for special needs of the particular company involved, and whether there is any obsolescence or stale factor in the raw materials.

The lowest eligibility for advance will be found in the category of goods in process. Here the raw material has been altered so that it probably can only be sold for scrap value unless money is provided by the lender to complete the productive process. Therefore, goods in process may have a loan potential of only 25 per cent of cost value. Retailers or distributors will not be required to make such an analysis because they are almost exclusively handling finished goods for which there is an established wholesale price, which is their basis of cost. Since the wholesale price is above the cost value of a manufacturer, the percentage of advance against a distributor's inventory of finished goods for resale may be lower than that which can be granted to a manufacturer. If the manufacturer has, for example, $300,000 of inventory broken into three $100,000 increments of raw materials, finished goods, and work in process, an analysis is fairly simple. His advance on $100,000 of finished goods might be 75 per cent, or $75,000. His advance on $100,000 of goods in process might be 25 per cent, or $25,000. His advance against $100,000 of raw materials might be 60 per cent, or $60,000. Therefore, this manufacturer would qualify for a total inventory loan of $160,000 on his total inventory at cost of $300,000.

The commodity rating of an inventory is very significant. We will define a commodity as a material that is very basic, possessing standard qualifications as to size, and quality grading, and immediately saleable on a day-to-day basis. Usual commodities are lumber, metals, grains, cotton, wool, coffee, and so on. There is an active daily market for each of these commodities, according to grade and quantity, and they may be disposed of by a few telephone calls to active dealers or traders in these commodities. Percentage of loan against these commodities can be quite high, varying according to potential price fluctuations. Coffee, for example, can serve as collateral for a loan up to 95 per cent of cost. Graded lumber can qualify for 70 per cent to 80 per cent advance against cost, because price fluctuations over a reasonably short period of time are not very severe.

Except in cases of basic commodities, as described above, the inventory has in the annual turnover its third limitation on financing potential. An inventory that is unusually high in proportion to the sales volume of the company cannot qualify for an otherwise maximum loan. In making this evaluation, the normal inventory turnover for the industry involved is used as a guideline. Whereas some retail and wholesale distribution operations may have an inventory turnover of as high as 10 to 12 times per year, the normal manufacturing company is doing well if it has a turnover of five times per year in its inventory. Let us assume that a company doing $1 million in sales has an inventory cost, including burden, of 75 per cent. To create $1 million in sales, $750,000 of inventory would have to be consumed. If a company reported a $150,000 inventory, it would be demonstrating a five times inventory turnover. Depending on the industry, an inventory of up to $250,000 might be acceptable. Anything beyond that figure, however, would probably be disqualified as a basis for additional inventory financing.

The third and certainly one of the most prevalent forms of secured financing is accounts receivable financing. Here the prior lien of the lender is evidenced by the filing of an intention to assign accounts receivable. Accounts receivable, in general, can provide very high percentages of advance because of their liquidity and because of the presence of a third party debtor—the ultimate customer whose receivable is assigned to the lender. The analysis of the financing potential of accounts receivable is dependent upon the credit-worthiness of the debtors (the customers of the borrower), the absence of single debtor concentrations, the prevalence of offsets or claims for faulty materials, and the aging of the total accounts receivable.

The credit-worthiness of the customers of the borrower is certainly an obvious requirement for this type of financing. In fact, unless he follows general credit precaution, the borrower simply will not qualify because the lender will feel that he is not exercising common business prudence for his own protection, as well as for the protection of the lender.

Debtor concentrations provide a different sort of problem. The reason that accounts receivable financing can go as high as a 90 per cent loan against collateral is that there are a great number of debtors from whom repayment will come. A distributor or manufacturer selling a volume of $200,000 per month may have 2,000 customers or more, the risk to the lender is therefore spread among 2,000 different business firms as debtors. On the other hand, there are some companies doing $200,000 per month who may have only 20 customers on their books at any one time. Taken on the average, such a company would have accounts receivable of $10,000 from each customer. This situation, in itself, may not be too much of a problem because accounts receivable financing will generally allow concentrations as high as 10 per cent of the total outstanding accounts receivable to be owed by one debtor— and, in some cases as high as 20 per cent to a single debtor (provided that there are no other debtors who account for this high a percentage of the outstanding receivables). In most cases, heavily concentrated debtors may have AAA-1 credit standings, but it is not their credit-worthiness that creates the problem. Rather, when a large increment of the accounts receivable is concentrated with one debtor, substantial values are at stake if a dispute arises between that single customer and the borrower.

Accounts receivable must also be evaluated with reference to possible offsets and claims for faulty merchandise. Offsets arise normally when a business sells its goods or services to a customer from whom it also purchases. Since the customer can offset his sales against his purchases, the account receivable that has been financed may not be repaid in cash, which will leave the loan made against it unpaid even when the debtor obligation has been satisfied. Therefore, all possible contra accounts (in dealing with which offsets can arise) are considered ineligible for receivables financing. A study is also made of the history of rejections, returns for reworking, and so on. An average is taken to establish a safety factor for the dilution of the accounts receivable arising from this possibility.

The most general yardstick for evaluation of receivables is in the monthly aging. Normally, accounts receivable less than 90 days old are eligible for advance; thereafter, they are ineligible if no special dating arrangements have been made at the outset.

Taking all of the foregoing factors into consideration, we can quickly arrive at the financing potential to be obtained from assignment of accounts receivable. Let us assume that the balance sheet reflects $300,000 as the total accounts receivable outstanding. Normally, after allowing for considerations stated above, an 80 per cent advance against *eligible* collateral might be available. As a quick guide, 10 per cent of the total accounts receivable can be assumed to be ineligible for one of the reasons stated above. This would bring the total to about $270,000 in the example we are using, and 80 per cent of this eligible collateral figure would be $216,000, which is the figure we might assume to be available at a quick determination. Going into the matter a little more in detail, we will assume that there are practically no offsets (which is usually the case), that no single debtor accounts for more than 20 per cent of the total receivables, and that no group of the three or four largest debtors accounts for more than 30 per cent of the total receivables.

We will assume that the claims for faulty merchandise run only 1 per cent or 2 per cent of the annual sales. Further, we will assume that the aging reflects that about 75 per cent of the total receivables are current or no more than 30 days past due, and that not more than 5 per cent to 10 per cent of the total receivables are more than 90 days old. Since an 80 per cent advance against the total accounts receivable shown on the balance sheet includes a 20 per cent reserve for the lender, the example we have used above will probably provide the lender ample protection. In other words, after deducting 10 per cent from the total accounts receivable on the balance sheet for the various types of ineligibilities, 80 per cent of the remainder can be borrowed on a revolving basis with no requirements for amortization during the time that the accounts receivable financing arrangement is in effect.

Summary

We have seen that, after checking for the possibility of a public financing based on sustained and growing earnings, one should analyze the unsecured and secured borrowing potentials of a business.

If unsecured borrowing can satisfy the financing needs of the business, management should go no further.

If funds greater than those that will be available with unsecured financing are required, then secured financing potential should be analyzed. Here is an example:

ASSETS		
Cash	$ 25,000	
Accounts receivable	225,000	
Inventory	300,000	
Total current assets		$550,000
Machinery & equipment	300,000	
Less depreciation	(150,000)	150,000
Real property, net		150,000
Goodwill and prepaid expense		25,000
Total assets		875,000

LIABILITIES

Accounts payable	200,000	
Current portion, long-term debt	50,000	
Taxes payable	50,000	
Other accruals	50,000	
Total current liabilities		350,000
R.E. mortgage payable	100,000	
Subordinated notes payable	100,000	
Contracts payable	50,000	
	250,000	
Less current portion	(50,000)	
Total long-term liabilities		200,000
Total liabilities		550,000
Capital & surplus (net worth)		325,000
Total liabilities & capital		875,000

Earnings are $80,000 plus $30,000 depreciation; therefore, cash flow is $110,000.

Following are the potential financing alternatives:

1. An unsecured working capital loan equal to 50 per cent of net current assets of $200,000. Potential: $100,000
2. An unsecured growth capital loan. The cash flow of $110,000 less $50,000 required for existing debt service results in available debt coverage of $60,000. Maximum growth loan potential for three years: $180,000
3. Secured financing based on the following:
   a. Accounts receivable total of $225,000—less 10 per cent for ineligibilities—total eligible is $202,500. Potential at 80 per cent advance: $162,000
   b. Chattel loan on equipment at 125 per cent of liquidation value with $60,000 available cash flow. Potential, 3 or more years term: $187,778
   c. Inventory loan at average of 60 per cent on cost of $300,000. Potential: $180,000

   Total secured financing potential $529,778

The secured financing can obviously reach a total in excess of the net worth of the company—if this entire amount is needed. In practice, if such a maximum loan is made, provision for additional interest must be equated against the total loan amount in the event that it cannot be immediately postulated that the additional profits to be developed from the borrowing will absorb the extra cost of money. And here we have the *raison d'être* for maximum financing; namely, that it must create rewards in excess of its cost. Money cost in terms of stated interest is not definitive; for some business situations 5 per cent interest may be too high, whereas for others a 10 per cent rate can be a bargain. The significant criterion is the total dollar cost versus the additional dollar profits that the money can create by utilizing maximum financing potentials.

11

Long-Term Senior
Financing for Small Business

Greene F. Johnson

The United States is fortunate in having a very broad capital market where sufficient funds are usually available to finance any
sound business, be it large or small. The present time is an exceptional
period of tightness in the money market, but despite this tightness
there has been a tremendous volume of financing.

The fundamental principles underlying the financing of small firms
are not different from those that are basic to the financing of large
ones. The trouble lies in the application of these principles to small
businesses. Because of the personal nature of the operations of many
small businesses, the management sometimes pays very little attention
to sound financial principles until outside financing is needed.

Small Business Loan Problems

There are various reasons why small businesses have difficulty in
borrowing on a long-term basis. One of the usual difficulties is lack of
an appropriate equity base. Many people start a small business with

little, if any, equity and want to borrow funds for expansion before an equity base has been created sufficient to support the desired loan. In other words, the prospective lender is asked to put up most of the money and take most of the risk, while the owner reaps the profits, if any, and saddles the loss on the lender if the business fails. There are, however, no set rules for determining the appropriate equity base, which varies greatly from business to business. For the average industrial business, a lender would require that the equity base be substantially in excess of the capitalization represented by debt financing. As a rule of thumb, maximum debt should not exceed 30 to 40 per cent of the total capitalization; in other words, there should be at least $6,000 invested as equity for each $4,000 of debt. If a small business does not have a satisfactory equity base along with a good earnings record, it should not be surprised when any potential lender might request some equity participation in consideration of his taking the greater risk involved. However, if the equity base is adequate and the earnings record is good, there is no logical reason for the small business to grant an equity participation.

Another common problem with small business financing is depth of management. A small business often has one capable man running it but may have no one capable of taking his place. This is a situation where quite frequently life insurance in an amount sufficient to pay off the loan furnishes adequate protection to the lender.

In making a loan the lender naturally looks at the historical record of the business and relies largely on this record, rather than on future projections. If the cash flow from the business in the past would not have been sufficient to service the loan, a lender is hesitant in making a loan which, in such a case, would be based largely on future projections. However, if some other well-established company underwrites the future projections, such as by a long-term contract to purchase the goods being manufactured, then the lender, relying in whole or in part on the credit of this other company, may very well be willing to go ahead and make the desired loan.

Frequently, much more time is spent on small loans than on large ones; consequently they are more expensive to consummate. The out-of-pocket expenses, such as printing and legal fees, plus the time required to consummate the loan make the relative expense of a small loan, both from the borrower's and the lender's viewpoint, greater than for a large loan.

Finally, it is a well-known fact that the mortality rate of small businesses is higher than that for large businesses. This added risk tends to increase the risk factor in the interest rate that a small business loan carries.

In summary, therefore, the five most common problems with small business loans are (1) insufficient equity, (2) quality and depth of management, (3) poor historical earnings record, (4) time and expense involved, and (5) high mortality rate of small businesses.

Long-Term Loan Decisions

The subject of long-term loans to small businesses is as broad as the variety of small businesses themselves. The United States Government and also some states have played an important part in subsidizing or encouraging loans to small businesses. Many small firms go to finance or factoring companies, or to their local banker and borrow either on a term loan or on a current basis. However, if the business needs permanent capital, it is more conservative to borrow on a long-term basis rather than on a current basis. Many small business loans are made through the operation of the real estate mortgage route. These loans are generally known as income loans and are usually made to finance such ventures as apartments, hotels, warehouses, and shopping centers. Finally, the sale and leaseback route, or some variation thereof, is often used by small businesses. The interest factor calculated into the rental obligation is higher than the corresponding interest rate in debt financing. Often this type of financing is a sign of weakness and is used only because the small business cannot obtain the necessary financing in any other way. In considering whether or not a loan should be made to a particular corporation, an investor will normally consider any long-term lease obligation as a part of the debt structure. If the main plant of the corporation is leased, this may, in effect, result in the plant being beyond the reach of general creditors in times of trouble and, to some extent, the rental payments may constitute a prior charge ahead of any loan that might be made. In the event of trouble, if the business is to continue, pending reorganization, the creditors (or the reorganization trustees) will feel it necessary to pay the rental if the use of the building is to continue. Leasehold financing, therefore, eliminates the real estate backlog that a company would normally have if it owned its property outright and thus may possibly increase the risk of any ordinary business loan. In most instances, it is better to borrow the money and buy the plant than to rent it, assuming that the borrower has any choice in the matter.

A small business has a number of different potential sources of funds to explore together with a variety of financial plans to consider. Emphasis will be given here to long-term loans to industrial companies that might be made by an institutional investor, such as an insurance company. In dealing with financial subjects, it is conservative to recognize that there are exceptions to most financial generalizations and that the word "never" is a dangerous one to use. There are, therefore, exceptions in one way or another, depending upon the particular business, to the various generalizations contained in this chapter.

Many small business executives have had very little experience with long-term debt financing and, naturally, turn to their local banker for help in formulating a financing program. If further help is needed, the executive might well consider consulting an investment banker. Insurance companies welcome investment bankers, who act as agent for the borrower, in making any particular financing presentation, particularly if the financing transaction is at all complicated. A small borrower, however, may approach the proposed lender directly should it decide that it does not need the help of an investment banker, or should the borrower be unable to interest an investment banker because of the size of the loan, or for any other reason.

Lender Requirements

At this point the borrower will find it advisable to investigate the proposed lender to determine whether or not the policies of the particular institution are satisfactory. The borrower and the lender are establishing a long-term relationship and the borrower needs to be reasonably confident that its relations over the years with the lender will be satisfactory.

Thorough preparation for the initial contact with the proposed lender is very important. It is helpful to present a well-thought-out financial plan, rather than merely asking for a certain amount of money; otherwise the lender may obtain a bad first impression as to the capabilities of the financial management. To give the proposed lender a reasonably complete picture of the entire proposal, the borrower might prepare a memorandum setting forth in some detail the following points:

1. A general description of the business now conducted and proposed to be conducted.

2. Amount of the loan desired.

3. A proposed schedule of repayments, which should be spaced over a period of from ten to fifteen years.

4. Purpose of the loan.

5. Audited financial statements for the past five years.

6. Cash flow statements for the past five years, and projections for the next five years.

7. Breakdown of sales by products, showing the profitability of each item.

8. List of important customers along with bank and other references.

9. Names, ages, educational background, and business experience of executive officers.

To expedite the initial conference, the supporting information should preferably be sent to the proposed lender ahead of the first meeting. The lender is then in a position to give the proposed transaction a preliminary examination to determine whether or not the proposed loan fits the lender's current investment program. The lender will carefully check into the proposed borrower and will want confidential information concerning its operation. It is essential for the borrower to disclose fully its situation, which should include a discussion of any potential trouble situations, such as antitrust, income tax, or litigation.

If the borrower decides to request a loan from an insurance company, the loan must first meet the requirements of the insurance law of the state under which the insurance company is incorporated. Usually if the requirements of the New York Insurance Law are met, the proposed loan will also be eligible under the laws of the other states. Section 81.2(a) of the New York Insurance Law permits adequately secured loans wherein the speculative element is not predominant. Since the provision is expressed very flexibly, the question of whether or not there is adequate security is largely a matter of

financial judgment. If the loan is to be secured, there should be sufficient margin of security so that in the financial judgment of the
lender it meets the test of adequacy. Section 81.2(b) permits an insurance company to make unsecured loans based on an earnings test
requiring that the net earnings of the borrower for fixed charges (including rentals) for the period of the five immediately preceding
years must, on the average, have covered fixed charges by one and
one-half times and must, in either one of the last two years, have
covered such fixed charges one and one-half times. This is purely a
historical test, and for all practical purposes, the earnings requirements
are such that usually an insurance company would not, in any event,
want to make an unsecured loan unless these minimum tests were met.
In addition to these specific standards, insurance companies in New
York (as well as in many other states) are permitted by statute to
make loans that do not meet these standards, provided that the aggregate amount of all such loans made under this so-called "basket"
provision do not exceed 3.5 per cent of the admitted assets of the
insurance company. A loan only has to meet these eligibility requirements at the time it is made; once a loan is eligible, it is always
eligible, although the amount at which it is carried on the books of
the insurance company is subject to change.

Interest Rates

One question that arises usually very soon in the negotiations is
that of interest rate. It is difficult for an insurance company to express
an opinion as to interest rate until a study of the borrower has been
made. Before approaching the insurance company, however, many
borrowers feel it desirable to make an independent examination of the
interest situation to have some idea concerning an acceptable rate.
One place to start might be with the company's commercial banker,
keeping in mind that in normal times long-term money is more expensive than short-term money. A small company should expect to pay
an interest rate somewhere from 0.5 per cent to 1 per cent above the
rate that his local bank would charge him for a current loan. If an
investment banker is involved, he would advise the company regarding an appropriate interest rate. In any event, a small business must

expect to pay a higher rate than a well-established large business. The matter of the exact interest rate is a question of judgment, and it may be better to pay a slightly higher interest rate to a lender in whom the borrower has confidence than to borrow at a lower rate from an uncertain lender. If the lender is persuaded to accept a rate considered to be on the low side, it may very well feel that the loan restrictions should be tighter than would otherwise have been the case. On the other hand, if the lender feels that the rate is favorable, it may be inclined to be more flexible so far as restrictions are concerned. It follows, therefore, that the interest rate is not the only factor to be considered when a borrower is selecting a lender, keeping in mind always that the Government usually pays almost one-half of the interest rate. If the company and the lender can agree on a rate that both consider fair, the transaction should then be agreed upon immediately. If the interest rate as suggested by the lender is considered too high, the company should be frank about it. The company would not be wise to attempt to hold the proposed lender's rate while it shopped around to see if a lower rate could be obtained. If the company cannot accept the rate, the loan proposal should be rejected and the funds should be sought elsewhere.

The matter of whether or not the loan is to be secured will usually be considered in setting the interest rate. Because of the various problems associated with small business loans, the usual pattern is to have a mortgage on the property of the borrower. This is not burdensome to the average small business, since it does not have property widely scattered and since a mortgage is relatively easy to place on the real estate. A number of small business loans, however, are made without any specific security. A secured loan will usually, at least in theory, bear a slightly lower interest rate than an unsecured one.

Except in unusual situations, insurance companies are not interested in making short-term loans. The obligations of life insurance companies are long term in nature and the projected cash requirements are based on actuarial calculations over the years. After the amount of cash needed for current purposes has been determined, the balance can be invested on a long-term basis, keeping in mind that even the long-term loans are usually paid back on a regular basis each year of their duration. Short-term loans would add greatly to the work involved in keeping the available funds fully invested. The final maturity of any loan, however, should be related to the particular purpose of the financing being consummated and the projected cash flow of the company over the years. For example, if a new plant is being financed, the mandatory loan repayments would reasonably be based to some extent on the depreciation available from the plant. Most small business loans made by an insurance company are repayable in equal installments over a ten to fifteen year period. It is also customary to permit optional prepayments of the loan at a premium, which for the first year usually equals the interest rate and is scaled down each year in approximately equal amounts to zero during the last year of the loan. The only restriction on these optional prepayments is that the loan may not be prepaid for a stated period of years out of funds borrowed, directly or indirectly, at a lower interest rate. From the standpoint of the lender, it does not seem fair that the borrower should take advantage of declining interest rates until such time as the loan has been outstanding for a reasonable period of time. The lender, of course, has no option, in the case of rising interest rates, to take advantage of the situation by calling the loan prior to its stated maturity. However, because equity financing is so desirable from a sound financial standpoint, many lenders permit a loan to be prepaid at the stated premium with the proceeds from the sale of common stock.

Covenants and Restrictions

There are many covenants and restrictions necessary in the negotiation of a small business loan, although all of the covenants have, or should have, a logical reason for their inclusion in the loan agreement. The various covenants and restrictions require careful consideration by the borrower to determine whether they are unduly restrictive and whether they fit the particular business being financed. Because in many cases small business loans are considered marginal, the covenants will be more restrictive than would otherwise have been the case. The over-all purpose is not to attempt to tell the borrower how to run its business but merely to set up broad guidelines, which experience has taught are necessary or desirable for the protection of the lender.

In general, the covenants are loosely classified as positive and negative covenants. The positive covenants are relatively routine and usually reflect the policies that any well-managed corporation would follow. Sometimes the inclusion of such provisions is questioned largely because of their routine nature. On the other hand, there usually are no fundamental objections to the principles involved. Because the loan will exist over a long period of time, these covenants do furnish some protection against the possibility of future irresponsible management. Rarely are these covenants used to precipitate acceleration of the debt, but the threat of such potential use in extraordinary circumstances furnishes some protection. It is generally customary to include such covenants in public bond issues, and the failure to include them in any loan might be used as the basis for claiming that the intent was to give management full leeway in these matters without any restrictions whatsoever so far as the lender is concerned. These positive covenants cover maintenance of the existence of the borrower and its subsidiaries, payments of taxes and other obligations, compliance with all applicable laws, maintenance of properties, adequate insurance against customary risks, setting up of appropriate reserves, and keeping records in accordance with sound accounting principles. The lawyers sometimes spend an inordinate amount of time agreeing on the wording of these provisions. In drafting the exact language, reference should be made to the Model Debenture Indenture provisions of the American Bar Foundation. This Model does not contain wording for all of the covenants but does contain the best thinking of a group of eminent lawyers on the provisions included.

Far more important are those restrictive covenants usually called negative covenants because they prohibit the borrower from certain actions or from exceeding or failing to meet certain goals. These are the important covenants that must be lived with over the years and that should be tailormade to fit the particular business involved.

NEGATIVE PLEDGE COVENANT

One of the most important covenants is the so-called negative pledge. This provision is almost universally found in unsecured loan issues and is a common provision in secured loans. It prohibits all types of liens securing indebtedness that would result in the particular creditor having priority over the specific loan being considered. The obvious purpose, where the loan is unsecured, is to prevent any other lender from having priority over the loan being made. There are certain routine exceptions, such as statutory liens, landlord liens, and normal tax liens. In addition, it is usual to grant a limited exception should the borrower desire to purchase property with a mortgage already on it; such a mortgage is often called a purchase money mortgage. This exception is usually of a limited nature and the principal amount secured by such mortgages is usually limited to an aggregate dollar amount not to exceed 5 or 10 per cent of the unsecured debt. This purchase money exception is not intended to be used as a major financing vehicle; it is merely inserted to give some flexibility in the case of after-acquired property that might carry with it a mortgage not subject to redemption or which has an interest rate so favorable that it would be economically unsound to insist on its retirement. If there were no limitations on the amount of purchase money mortgages, a company could finance a new plant through this route. In the event of financial trouble, the new plant would probably be the most efficient one the company had; thus, to effect a reorganization, purchase money debt on the plant would of necessity be given priority over the other creditors. Finally, in considering the general theory underlying the negative pledge clause, it should be kept in mind that under the Federal bankruptcy laws any debts to the United States Government have priority over the claims of other unsecured creditors; hence, it is logical to prohibit the company from borrowing from anyone who, by statute or otherwise, would have priority over unsecured creditors. Sometimes in connection with a secured loan, the necessity for the negative pledge clause is questioned because the original loan would have a prior position. One reason why the negative pledge clause is usually advisable is that if the credit of the borrower has become so poor that the proposed lender would insist on a second lien position, then it very likely is dangerous to add to the debt a burden that the borrower might be unable to carry.

DEBT RESTRICTIONS

Tied in closely with the negative pledge provision is the covenant restricting the amount and type of indebtedness. Usually this covenant is drafted so as to prohibit all types of indebtedness except as specifically set forth in the covenant. For the purposes of this restriction and the loan agreement generally, indebtedness is defined very broadly to include all direct and indirect debt, contracts which directly or indirectly support or provide for the purchase of indebtedness of others, and indebtedness secured by any liens on the property of the company, whether or not the company has assumed the debt. Some loan agreements absolutely prohibit debt arising from supporting contracts or guarantees. Direct or indirect guarantees have an impact on the guarantor different from direct debt. If everything goes smoothly, there is no problem. However, if the guarantor is called on to make good on its commitment, usually the holders of the guaranteed debt have first to realize on the assets of their direct obligor and then, to the extent that their debt is unpaid, seek to share with other creditors of the guarantor in the guarantor's assets. Where a company guarantees the debt of another and is required to meet an asset test, there is, in effect, a double penalty because the guaranteed debt is added to the liabilities but in the absence of specific provisions to the contrary, nothing is added to the asset side of the picture. In small loans it is quite customary to prohibit any additional funded debt and to limit current debt to unsecured indebtedness incurred in the ordinary course of business, provided that, with respect to current indebtedness for money borrowed, the borrower shall have a period of at least sixty days in each calendar year when it is free from such borrowings. If the borrower is unable to clean up such debt for a reasonable period each year, then more equity is needed or more funded debt to avoid the uncertainty of its renewal from time to time and the dangers inherent in such a situation.

Funded Debt

If the borrower is to be permitted to have additional funded debt, such debt may be limited to 40 per cent of net tangible assets, which are defined as equal to (a) net current assets and (b) net depreciated value of fixed assets, minus (c) all intangible assets, (d) all liabilities (other than funded debt) not otherwise deducted, and (e) any deferred income tax reserves. Some companies prefer to have the debt limitation based on net worth. The same result is accomplished, as would be the case if the net tangible assets concept had been followed, by subtracting from net worth any tangible assets that otherwise would have been subtracted from gross assets to arrive at net tangible assets. Assuming the 40 per cent standard referred to above, debt limited to 66 per cent of adjusted net worth would arrive at about the same amount of permitted debt.

In many loans, besides the formula restricting the aggregate amount of funded debt, there is also a debt service test that must be met before additional funded debt may be incurred. This is in some ways a more realistic test because, no matter what the balance sheet looks like, if the borrower is not generating enough cash to cover its debt service requirements any loan would be at best speculative. This additional requirement might be set forth as a condition that the earnings available for interest for the last three years immediately preceding the loan must have averaged at least four or five times the pro forma interest charges (including the interest charges on the requested loans), and that the earnings available for interest (net income before income taxes and interest) plus depreciation for these years must have been at least equal to two or three times the entire pro forma debt service (interest plus required principal payments). There can be many variations of these requirements, and with respect to any particular loan, the specific requirements should be based on the type of company, its balance sheet, its historical record, and its current condition.

Subordinate Debt

Subordinated debt has been used frequently as a method of financing. In many cases the subordinated debt is convertible into common stock at a price from 10 to 15 per cent above the market price at the time of issuance of the debt. The issuing company hopes that it will become profitable for the debt holder to exercise the conversion option because of an increase in the market value of the stock, thus resulting in the retirement of the debt and a sale of stock at a higher price than could have been realized at the time of issuance of the debt. In the meantime the company has obtained the money at an interest cost lower than would have been obtained without the conversion feature. Such debt, whether or not it is convertible, represents a cushion for senior debt resembling equity and, at least to a substantial extent, is therefore favorable from the standpoint of the senior debt. A default under subordinated debt can cause a company the same sort of trouble as a default under senior debt. If it is desired to complicate a small loan with this feature, the borrower might expect an over-all debt limitation that would cover both senior and subordinated debt. Assuming senior debt limited to 40 per cent of net tangible assets, the over-all limitation for both senior and subordinated debt might be 50 per cent.

SUBSIDIARIES

Appropriate provisions regarding subsidiary companies must also be included among the covenants where subsidiary companies are involved. The first general principle is that the borrower should not be able to do indirectly through subsidiaries what it is not permitted to do directly itself. It is generally assumed that the parent company will do all of the financing and that subsidiaries will not themselves borrow money except from the parent. A large part of the parent company's business might very well be done through subsidiaries, and if these subsidiaries were permitted to borrow freely, the result would be to place a claim upon the subsidiary's earnings and assets ahead of the parent company's stock ownership. Since preferred stock of a subsidiary outstanding in the hands of the public constitutes a claim on the business and assets of the subsidiary ahead of the common stock, all such preferred stock is treated as debt of the subsidiary for the purposes of this kind of restriction. Where a company is doing a foreign business through subsidiaries, it will often wish to finance as much of this business as possible in the countries where the business is being done; therefore, exceptions will be made so that foreign subsidiaries may borrow on the basis of their own business and assets, and such assets will not be included in the borrowing base of the company.

LONG-TERM RENTALS

Closely allied to the debt limitation is the limitation on long-term rentals. Lenders recognize that rental obligations represent another method of financing a given transaction. Long-term rentals of fixed property are, therefore, restricted to a relatively nominal amount or are capitalized as debt and included as such in any appropriate calculation.

SALE OF PROPERTY

Many loan agreements will contain a provision prohibiting the sale of a substantial part of the property or business. One objective of this restriction is to require a company to consult the lender on any such major transaction so that he can assess the situation and share in the proceeds of any such sale by reduction in the outstanding loan, if this is deemed appropriate. Usually, the sale of subsidiary companies is prohibited, except as a whole and for either fair value in cash or purchase money obligations. Such a sale would be prohibited if it represented a substantial part of the over-all business.

INVESTMENT RESTRICTIONS

A loan to a company is usually made on the basis of the business then being conducted and the lender may want to confine the company's activities to its present business. If the loan is being made largely on the basis of domestic business, then it may be appropriate to limit foreign investments and extraneous domestic investments. However, to the extent that the dividend payments are permitted, there is no reason why investments otherwise restricted should not be made out of funds otherwise available for the payment of dividends.

DIVIDEND RESTRICTIONS

The main purpose of the dividend covenant is to prohibit dividend payments (other than stock dividends) and any retirements of stock to the extent that such transactions would reduce the net worth below an amount agreed on. Where the equity base is thin, aggregate stock payments might be limited to 50 per cent (or less) of net income from the end of the fiscal year immediately preceding the making of the loan to the date of payment. Assuming continuing earnings, such a provision would, over the years, build up the equity behind the loan. Any stock retirement would be treated the same as the payment of dividends, except that any future sales of stock for cash would be an offset against any stock retirements.

In many small businesses, the owners of the stock have a choice as to whether or not they wish to be compensated by salaries or through dividends. To prevent the payment of salaries not commensurate with services rendered, any salaries over a stated amount paid to stockholders could be subtracted from net income otherwise available for the payment of dividends. Another refinement in the dividend restriction is to permit regular dividends on preferred stock issued subsequent to making the loan. This provision encourages the issuance of preferred stock, which in turn increases the safety of the loan. However, in determining whether or not the borrower may pay cash dividends on common stock or retire stock, the amount of preferred stock dividends is deducted from the amount otherwise available. Sometimes when companies have established a regular dividend policy that they want to preserve, provision is made to a limited extent for regular dividends by adding an amount equal to one year's dividends to the formula. The result of this would be that the borrower could have a loss year or two at the beginning of the period or at some subsequent time, without necessarily having to stop the payment of regular dividends. The usual dividend formula goes back to a specified date and is cumulative from that date. In other words, the formula is not calculated for each year but is calculated for the entire period that has elapsed subsequent to the beginning date. Even though the net income might be sufficient for the payment of dividends, such payments would not be wise if the net working capital of the company were reduced below a stated amount. The net working capital requirement here would be an amount higher than that which might be found in an absolute maintenance covenant. The penalty for not being able to meet this requirement would be only the discontinuance of the payment of dividends, whereas the failure to meet the maintenance covenant might result in bankruptcy.

MAINTENANCE OF WORKING CAPITAL

A provision requiring the maintenance of net working capital (the excess of current assets over current liabilities) is quite common in bank loans. Sometimes such a provision is called the "sudden death" provision because a company, for reasons entirely beyond its control, may be unable to meet the requirements of such a provision. However, in cases where a company does not have a great amount of fixed assets and is borrowing to support its working capital position, such a maintenance provision would appear to be necessary. In examining the working capital position of any company, particular attention must be given to the accounts receivable and to the inventory. Only good and collectible accounts receivable should be included in the current assets, and inventory should be conservatively valued at its estimated liquidation value in order for this covenant to furnish the protection contemplated. Such conservative valuation practices, however, would suggest a relatively low maintenance figure, the exact amount depending on the margin over the outstanding loan which would give reasonable protection to the lender.

DEFINITIONS

The effect of many of the covenants depends directly upon the definitions. It is always important to read them carefully in order to understand the exact nature of the restrictions. Many people prefer to draft definitions which closely follow the ordinary meaning of the term. Artificial definitions should be avoided as much as possible. For example, purchase money obligations would normally be considered indebtedness, but if the definition of indebtedness excluded purchase money obligations it would, to that extent, be artificial. If it is desired that leeway be given for indebtedness represented by purchase money mortgages, the definition should include such purchase money obligations as debt and then make the necessary exception in the covenant restricting indebtedness. An exception made in a definition for one particular purpose may be discovered later to be entirely inappropriate in another covenant incorporating the same definition.

REMEDIES

After all the covenants and definitions have been placed in final form, it is always necessary to consider what remedies a lender may have in case of a default in any of the covenants. The remedy for the positive covenants is usually acceleration of the maturity of the debt after the borrower has been given a chance, by notice, to cure a particular default. Many of the negative covenants, however, are of such importance that the lender is not required to give any notice of their violation. Sometimes the violation of such covenants—for example, the negative pledge or the dividend covenants—gives the lender an immediate right to accelerate the debt. On the other hand, many borrowers feel that this right to accelerate should not accrue until a reasonable period of time has elapsed after the particular violation. For example, the right of acceleration might be limited to ten days after the violation of any of those important restrictions that are specifically within the knowledge of the borrower and could hardly be violated accidentally. The failure of the borrower to meet any of its other debt obligations, the filing of any bankruptcy or reorganization proceedings, or the permitting of any substantial judgment to remain unpaid, would also give the lender the right of acceleration. One main objective of the default provisions is to try to prevent any other creditor from getting preferred treatment over the lender. To carry out this objective, the provision regarding interest after a default should be worded so that the accrual of interest of any other creditor does not occur faster than the accrual on the debt in question. This is not too important if early liquidation is assumed, but in connection with reorganizations, which extend over a period of years, the claim of each creditor is substantially increased by the amount of interest accruals.

Loan Documentation

After the basic terms have been agreed on, a memorandum is usually prepared setting forth these terms and the drafting of the necessary loan documents, which is handled by legal counsel, is begun. To save expense in many small loans, legal counsel of the lending institution (regular counsel) will draft the first proof of the loan agreement and debt obligation before it is submitted to the lender's special counsel, which is customarily an outside firm. The necessity of special counsel is sometimes questioned. Although there is some duplication of the work of regular counsel by special counsel, the extent of this duplication is not nearly so great as it may appear to be and varies greatly from lender to lender, and from institutional lender to institutional lender, depending upon the policy of the lender and the organization and size of its legal department.

Special counsel's organization is usually flexible enough to assign one or more men to give full time to a transaction if this is necessary; rarely, if ever, can regular counsel for the lender enjoy such a luxury. The combination of special counsel and regular counsel seems to be an ideal one, with regular counsel bringing into the picture his experience with many different loan transactions involving different special counsel, and with special counsel bringing a broad legal background, a flexible organization, and specialists who can be called in to meet any emergency. There are other reasons for the desirability of having special counsel. When an insurance company makes a loan, it does not contemplate selling the security; however, circumstances in the future may require such a sale. Investors have become accustomed over the years to receiving opinions of independent counsel with respect to any security they may purchase. Therefore, the sale of any security acquired is facilitated if the lender or inventor can furnish an opinion as to the validity of a particular security from an independent firm whose existence can reasonably be expected to continue over the years.

Although having several participants in small loans is unusual, it is quite customary in large ones. In such a situation it is not desirable for the legal department of a particular investor to assume the responsibility for legal matters that might affect the other investors. All investors, therefore, can rely on special counsel's opinion without recourse to any investigation of work done by any of the regular counsel of any of the participating investors. The negotiation of the principal terms of a loan is not the duty of a special counsel or regular counsel for a lender. However, the line between financial matters and legal matters is often very difficult to draw, so that some negotiation is of necessity carried out by counsel, especially concerning formal matters and the exact phrasing of the substantive terms of the loan.

Special counsel usually undertakes the many details necessary for the closing of a loan. This is very important since any fumbling or inefficiency here would result in a delay of the closing beyond the original contemplated date. Although it is customary in Canada for special counsel to pass upon the legality of a particular loan from the lender's standpoint, this practice is not customary in the United States. Special counsel, however, is always aware of the problem and points out any aspects of a particular loan that might possibly affect the legality of the loan as an investment. In an unusual situation, special counsel may be called on to render an opinion on the legal authority of the investor to make a particular loan.

The borrower enters customarily into a loan agreement that would put into exact language the principal terms agreed upon. In transactions that are not unusually complicated, the short form of loan agreement with the long form of note or obligation may be used. If so, the note or obligation appears lengthy but it is complete on its face and contains all of the substantive terms normally found in a formal loan indenture. In more complicated situations, however, there are advantages to using the long form of loan agreement, containing most of the substantive terms, and the short form of note, which refers to the provisions of the loan agreement.

In a loan agreement the borrower is expected to represent and warrant all of the basic facts, including its financial statements and the nature of the business conducted and proposed to be conducted. Warranties covering pertinent situations—such as any litigation in existence, income tax problems, and the status of pension liabilities— are also included.

In addition, the loan agreement would spell out the conditions under which the loan is to be closed. When a company is anticipating a capital expenditure program extending over a long period, it is often desirable to have more than one closing, thus saving interest charges on the unused funds. In such cases the lender usually charges a stand-by fee, ranging from .025 per cent to 1 per cent per annum, on the funds committed for but not taken down from time to time. The loan must be a legal investment on each closing date and usually the representations and warranties are brought up to date. Special counsel will furnish a complete opinion on the first closing date; on each subsequent closing date the validity of the loan then being made will be covered, as will other pertinent matters that have come up since the first, or any preceding, closing date. The exact provisions would be set forth in the loan agreement.

The loan agreement would also require the borrower to furnish periodic annual audited financial statements and unaudited quarterly statements and to furnish the lender with additional financial information, including the right to inspect the books and properties of the company and its subsidiaries. Finally, the borrowing company would agree to pay all out-of-pocket expenses incurred in connection with the loan.

Proofs of the loan agreement and note are customarily submitted to the interested parties. At this time, the borrowing company should examine carefully the exact language to determine whether or not the company can reasonably live within the various provisions. It is impossible to cover every imaginable situation, but any foreseeable or likely problem should be covered.

After the proof of the loan agreement and note, or other obligation, has been cleared, careful preparations must be made for the agenda of the actual closing, on which date the money will be paid and the obligation delivered. A well-prepared closing usually takes only a few minutes, unless there are documents to be recorded simultaneously with the closing. The borrowing company should expect the lawyers for the lender to examine carefully their corporate proceedings, corporate charters, and by-laws to be certain, among other things, that the borrowing company has the power to incur the proposed obligation, whether any stockholders' approval is necessary, and whether there are any other loans or contracts that would be violated by the proposed loan. The borrowing company would be expected to adopt a resolution of its Board of Directors authorizing the consummation of the loan. There are usually two general types of resolutions—a long type that goes into considerable detail as to the transaction, and a short type that authorizes the transaction and usually incorporates the basic documents by reference. The short type of resolution has certain advantages in that one does not have to be sure that the terms have been correctly set forth since the basic documents constitute a part of it.

Borrower-Lender Relations

After the loan has been consummated, financial statements are received from time to time. These statements are examined to discover whether or not there has been any sudden or unusual change in the borrower's earnings, working capital position, or the like. It is a sound policy for the borrower to discuss with the lender any material transactions or changes before they become public or before they are reflected in the financial statements. This gives the lender a feeling of confidence about the whole situation. Once a year the borrower is asked to furnish what some people call a "Good Conscience Certificate," to the effect that an adequate examination has been made and no defaults have been found. It is expected that the independent auditor will inform the lender of any defaults that come to their attention during their examination of the company's records.

Despite every effort to avoid any situation where the covenants will unduly restrict the borrowing company, sometimes over the course of the years some such situation does develop in connection with a transaction obviously favorable to all parties concerned. Under such circumstances the borrower customarily presents the entire matter to the lender and gets a waiver of the particular covenant that affects the transaction in question. These consents, or waivers, are usually given without any trouble. This flexibility is one of the major advantages of direct loans as contrasted with public loans where there are scattered holders of the security, thus making it difficult, if not impossible, to obtain any amendments or consents.

Part V

LEGAL AND TAX ASPECTS
OF SMALL BUSINESS
FINANCING

12

Legal Aspects of Small Business Finance

Bertram K. Massing

Although it is difficult to imagine any small business finance transaction that does not have legal aspects, this chapter will concentrate primarily on the legal problems under state and federal law which the small business encounters in attempting to obtain equity financing and problems which result from its having obtained such financing.

The former involves the laws generally known as blue-sky, or securities, laws; the latter may be loosely characterized as corporation law.[1] The term *investors* will be used to signify the persons who supply funds to the business but do not participate in managing it. The persons who operate the business will be referred to collectively as *management* except where a more specific term is required for clarity of meaning.

Federal Securities Laws

The Securities and Exchange Commission acts under seven federal statutes,[2] comprising in the aggregate the federal scheme for regulating the distribution and trading of securities, the securities business, and some aspects of management (investor relations). The most significant federal statutes for our purposes are the Securities Act of 1933, which regulates the distribution of securities, and the Securities Exchange Act of 1934, which regulates securities markets and trading and also contains report and disclosure requirements applicable to some corporations.[3]

Although Congress conceivably could have pre-empted the states from regulating securities when it enacted the federal securities laws, it chose not to, and most of the states have their own blue-sky laws.[4] Moreover, the general law involving the formation and operation of corporations and their relations with shareowners and others is found primarily in the statutes, regulations, and common law of the states.

Conflict of Laws

The United States Constitution resolves conflicts between state and federal laws in favor of the federal;[5] to the extent that they do not conflict, federal law and state law may both apply to the same transaction unless Congress has pre-empted the states.

With the improvement in transportation and communication facilities in our society there are few businesses that do not have at least an occasional interstate transaction, and sometimes the several states in which a transaction partly takes place or whose residents are involved will have different or conflicting laws applicable to such transactions.

If a dispute results from an interstate transaction, a court may ultimately have to decide which state's laws govern the consequences. More importantly, if a lawyer is consulted before the transaction is entered into, he must take into account possible conflicts of law that may arise in unforeseen disputes and advise his clients on the basis of a prediction, which at times will be only an educated guess.

The provisions of the United States Constitution which touch on the subject have been interpreted as imposing only broad standards;[6] in most conflict of laws cases the law of any one of the states having substantial "contact" with the transaction could constitutionally be applied.

To illustrate: Assume that Y, a resident of New York, arranges by mail to borrow money from X, a resident of Illinois, and signs a promissory note in which he promises to repay the money plus interest. When Y defaults, X brings an action in the New York State courts to collect the principal plus interest. No matter how enamored the judge considering the case may be of the laws of, say the State of Kansas (where he grew up, went to law school, and so on) he cannot on these facts constitutionally interject Kansas law into the decision. Assume, however, that the interest specified in Y's promissory note is at a rate that Illinois law permits but that is higher than the maximum rate permitted under New York law and is therefore, if New York law governs, usurious, entitling Y not to pay the interest. The court could decide that the consequences of the transaction are to be decided under either New York law or Illinois law without violating the United States Constitution. Once the decision of the New York court became final, it would be entitled to full faith and credit under the Constitution and would be honored in every State.

If, however, the identical case were presented in the Illinois State courts involving different parties, say A and B, the Illinois court could constitutionally decide the case of A vs. B exactly opposite to the decision of New York in X vs. Y, and when the decision became final, it too would be entitled to full faith and credit, even in New York whose courts would have decided the case differently.[7] If the action were brought in a federal court—where jurisdiction would be based on "diversity of citizenship," one of the bases for using the federal courts—the court would be required to apply the law that would have been applied had the case been brought in the courts of the state where the federal court is located.[8] Thus, conflict of laws problems are not avoided by using the federal courts.

Conflict of laws cases are generally decided along the following lines of reasoning:

1. *Procedural matters.* Matters classified as procedural are decided according to the law of "the forum"—that is, the state in whose courts the action is brought—for the reason that it would be

inconvenient for the courts and enforcement officers of one state to
learn and apply the procedures of the other states. Ideally a procedural rule should not be the deciding factor in a case; unfortunately
this is not always true.[9]

2. *Substantive matters.* Substantive matters are defined as those
that have a determinative effect on the result in a case, although some
procedural matters also can have such an effect. Although the law of
the forum qua forum governs procedural matters, to arbitrarily apply
forum law to substantive matters would invite "forum-shopping"—that
is, selection by the plaintiff of the forum (among those whose laws
could be constitutionally applied) whose laws are most favorable to
his position; this would be unfair. Therefore the courts traditionally
attempt to apply rational principles to the "choice-of-law" decision.
Earlier this attempt led courts to adopt more or less arbitrary choice
of law formulas. For example, questions concerning validity of a
contract might be determined according to the law of the state where
the "last act" in the alleged creation of the contract took place;
questions of performance and breach of contract might be determined
according to the law of the state where performance was to be
made; and so on. Under these choice of law formulas the decision
in a case might depend on fortuitous events having little relation to
the real transaction, to say nothing of the "characterization" problem
—the difficulty of deciding which category best fits the case.

More recently courts have sought to make choice-of-law decisions
by carefully weighing and balancing the "interests" of the states having
"contact" with the transaction in having their laws applied. Deciding
to uphold one state's policy at the expense of another's is a tricky
business at best, and perhaps arbitrary formulas would be better. An
ameliorating factor—but probably not a cure—is the effort of such
groups as the American Law Institute and the American Bar Association to promote the adoption by various states of uniform laws on a
variety of subjects.

A different aspect of the conflict of laws problem is presented to
the practicing lawyer when his client proposes to enter into a transaction that requires affirmative compliance, such as, the obtaining of
a special license or the filing of documents, and the client must be
advised which states' statutes to comply with.

Relevant to the discussion of corporate finance, many of the blue-
sky laws require affirmative compliance (principally filing of docu-

ments) by the issuing company, or a broker acting on its behalf, or both. A corporation organized by filing a charter in compliance with the laws of Delaware, and whose factories and employees are located in California, may sell its securities through underwriters licensed in several states to persons whose homes and families are located in various states. Failure to comply with the laws of any state having sufficient "contact" with the transaction may result in civil liability to purchasers of the securities, administrative action by the local blue-sky law Commissioner, and even criminal sanctions.

To restate these last two sentences: "A corporation *domiciled* in Delaware, *doing business* in California, may sell its securities through underwriters *doing business* in several states to *residents* of various states. Failure to *qualify* under the laws of any state having *jurisdiction* . . . , and so on." Each italicized word represents a legal conclusion substituted for a more descriptive term. In context they are valid substitutes, but it should not be assumed that the deleted material is the *definition* of the substituted material; nor are any definitions suggested. Suffice it to say that the term *jurisdiction,* in a variety of contexts, usually refers to some aspect of a particular official's lawful power to deal with and affect the right of others, and that terms like *doing business, domicile* and *residence* usually refer to attributes that make particular persons subject to the power. Legal conclusions made in one context cannot be safely carried over into other contexts. Thus, a corporation *domiciled* (incorporated) in Delaware but having its *principal place of business* in New York may not be able to invoke the jurisdiction of the federal courts on the basis of diversity of *citizenship* to sue an individual who is domiciled in New York; the Delaware corporation may be considered a New York corporation in this context.

Securities Regulation

TYPES OF SECURITIES LAWS

Three general types of regulatory provisions are found in the various state and federal securities laws.[10] Most of the states have at least two of them and many, like the federal regulatory scheme, have all three. They are as follows:

1. Antifraud provisions, imposing both civil and criminal sanctions prohibiting fraudulent statements and practices in connection with the sale of securities.

2. Dealer registration provisions, which may include some or all of the following: (a) requirements that, subject to certain exceptions, securities be offered only through licensed persons in various classifications, such as brokers, dealers, and agents; (b) establishment of standards for obtaining licenses, including, for example, minimum capital and education requirements; and (c) establishment of rules and standards regulating the conduct of licensed persons.

3. Securities registration provisions whereby, subject to certain exceptions, securities may not be offered unless and until affirmative action has been taken to clear them.

Antifraud Provisions. Even before the first blue-sky law, fraud was actionable at common law or under specific statutes in all states, and an aggrieved plaintiff could obtain various remedies in civil courts; moreover, fraudulent conduct could also be punished by criminal sanctions. Common law fraud, however, is narrowly defined and subject to many subtle exceptions. Blue-sky law antifraud provisions generally relax the common law definition and impose greater responsibility in persons who make representations that others may rely on. Another advantage of blue-sky law antifraud provisions is that the blue-sky laws generally establish an administrative mechanism at the expense of the state (rather than private litigants) with the power and duty to investigate, stop, and prosecute fraudulent practices. Although there are various exemptions from other blue-sky law provisions, typically there are no exemptions from the antifraud provisions.

Securities Registration Provisions. Although securities registration provisions found in the state and federal law all require some form of affirmative action before securities can be offered or sold, subject to specified exemptions, there is considerable variation in the extent of affirmative compliance required and in the standards by which qualification is judged.

Thus in some states, securities may be sold and offered immediately after the issuing company or a broker-dealer participating in the offering files a notice containing the required information, unless and until the regulatory authority takes action to stop the offering. This will only be done if the administrator finds that the securities themselves are fraudulent or that they are being offered in a fraudulent manner.

More commonly, however, securities may not be sold or offered until the regulatory authority takes affirmative action. Perhaps the most stringent requirements are found in the State of California. A corporation desiring to sell its securities in California must first file an Application for Permit with the Commissioner of Corporations of the State of California, and offerings may not be made until the Commissioner grants a permit, which may contain a number of conditions. The California Corporate Securities Law requires that, before granting a permit, the Commissioner must find "that the proposed plan of business of the applicant and the proposed issuance of securities are fair, just, and equitable, and that the applicant intends to transact its business fairly and honestly, and that the securities that it proposes to issue and the method to be used by it in issuing or disposing of them are not such as, in his opinion, will work a fraud upon the purchaser thereof."

Many states provide a simplified procedure without reducing their qualitative standards when a registration statement has been filed under the Securities Act of 1933 with respect to the same issue of securities.

There are also numerous exemptions and exceptions to the application of the various registration provisions.

The Securities Act of 1933, which we will consider next, is almost unique among registration provisions in that it contains no qualitative standards for the securities proposed to be offered. It is merely concerned that there has been a full and adequate disclosure.

THE SECURITIES ACT OF 1933

The Securities Act of 1933 is a combination of antifraud provisions and registration provisions. Its constitutional basis is the "commerce clause,"[11] and it applies generally to sales and offers (broadly defined) made, directly or indirectly, by the use of any means or instrumentality of interstate commerce, or of the mails.[12]

The requirement of "full and adequate disclosure" is the underlying philosophy of the Act in both its antifraud and its registration provisions. Thus, both Section 17(a), which is the general antifraud provision, and Section 8(d), which empowers the Securities and Exchange Commission to issue an order suspending the effectiveness of a registration statement, refer to "any untrue statement of a material fact or (omission) to state a material fact necessary to make the statements made, in the light of the circumstances under which they were made, not misleading."

Registration Provisions. Unless a specific exemption applies, it is unlawful to sell a security subject to the jurisdiction of the Securities Act of 1933 (that is, involving any instrument of transportation or communication in interstate commerce or the mails) unless and until a registration statement containing the information required by the Act with respect to the sale has become effective, and delivery of the security sold must be accompanied or preceded by a prospectus meeting the requirements of the Act. During the waiting period (that is, after a registration statement has been filed but before it has become effective), certain kinds of offers (but no sales) are permitted; part of the purpose of the waiting period is to give the investment community an opportunity to familiarize itself with a proposed offering.[13] Unless an exemption applies no offers may be made before a registration statement has been filed.

During the waiting period the staff of the Securities and Exchange Commission reviews the registration statement and proposed prospectus for the purpose of advising the Commision whether the disclosure standards of the Act have been met. If the disclosure is inadequate, the Commission can issue a stop order to prevent the registration statement from becoming effective; this is rarely done. In practice, the staff sends the issuer and its counsel a "memorandum of comments" on the deficiencies it has found. The registration statement can be amended one or more times and ultimately, with diligent application, the registration statement may become effective. The fact that the S.E.C. has declared or permitted a registration statement to become effective does not prevent purchasers from bringing private actions on the grounds that the registration statement and prospectus actually contained untrue statements of material fact or omitted to state necessary facts.[14] The S.E.C. itself can issue a stop order even after the registration statement has become effective.

It should be obvious from the foregoing discussion that the registration procedure is time-consuming and expensive. Audited financial statements conforming to requirements established by the S.E.C. must be included in the registration statement; there will be legal fees, printing expense, and the like. The amount of time to be spent in preparing and processing the registration statement may discourage the small business from making a registered offering; it may need its funds faster. Some of the more important exemptions from the registration provisions of the Act are presented below.[15]

The Private Offering Exemption. Section 4(2) of the Act exempts "transactions by an issuer not involving any public offering." The availability of this exemption is a question of fact depending on a number of factors, such as the number of offerees, their relationship to the issuer, and the size and manner of the proposed offering. The fact that a limited number of offerees is involved or that all of them are employees does not necessarily preclude a public offering.

The Supreme Court has stated that the proper test should be whether the offerees need the disclosure protections of the Act.[16] Thus the exemption would appear to be available if all of the offerees had a sufficiently close relationship with the issuer or a sufficient bargaining position to have access to the same kind of information that they would get under a registration statement.

The fact that they can freely contribute additional capital or raise money from key employees will usually be of little comfort to the management of a small business. They will want to use the private offering exemption, if at all, to raise money from an outside source which, in keeping with the foregoing, must usually be limited to a small number of institutions or individual sophisticated investors.

This brings into play other factors that management will want to consider carefully before proceeding. An investor group being asked to make a sizable investment may be in a position to negotiate quite a different bargain than an underwriter undertaking a public offering would even attempt. Private investors may ask for control of the business or at least for a direct voice in its management which the public, even with its rights as shareholders, could not muster.

Assuming that a satisfactory business bargain can be made with an investor group, it will also be necessary if the transaction is to be exempt to determine that sale to the investors is not just a step in a contemplated wider distribution of the securities, for then the issuance transaction could not be considered as one not involving a public offering, and the purchasers would be considered underwriters, requiring a registration statement for their subsequent resales.

The exemption is available only if the purchasers take "for investment," again a question of fact and a difficult one because no matter how diligently the issuer inquires into and investigates a purchaser's intentions, a subsequent resale to the public by a purchaser, under circumstances apparently inconsistent with his announced investment intention (for example, a resale promptly after the purchase), may lead a court to conclude that he never had an investment intention, thereby making the sale to the public "through" him a violation of the Act. The issuer should investigate to the extent practicable and, for maximum protection, it should (1) require the purchaser to express his investment intention in writing by signing an investment letter, (2) type or print on the certificate evidencing the security a restrictive legend that will inform prospective subpurchasers that the security was sold under an exemption from the registration provisions of the Securities Act of 1933 and that the issuer will not recognize any subsequent transfer unless it receives a satisfactory opinion of counsel that the transfer will not violate the Securities Act of 1933, and (3) instruct its transfer agent not to process any transfer and to immediately notify the issuer when a certificate bearing such a legend is presented for transfer.

Having taken these safeguards, the issuer will want to know when, if ever, it may permit an investor who purchased in a private offering to resell his stock to the public. The answer is that an investor who purchased securities for investment under the private offering exemption is free to resell his securities—even to the public—at such time and under such circumstances that the resale will not be inconsistent with his asserted investment intention. It is clear that a resale shortly after purchase would be inconsistent with the original intention unless there were a strong showing of changed circumstances not in contemplation at the time of the purchase; however, there is no time period the passage of which automatically exempts the subsequent resale. The question; "Can I now resell?" can rarely be answered with certainty, and even a "no action" letter from the S.E.C. does not prevent a subpurchaser from alleging a violation.[17] Because of this uncertainty, investors purchasing securities in a private offering frequently require the issuer to agree that it will, upon request in the future, file a registration statement to permit them to resell their securities without fear that they are violating the Act. Whether the issuer or the investors bear the expenses of preparing and filing such registration statement is normally a point of negotiation at the time of the original issuance.

Thus, not infrequently, the expenditures of time and money necessary to the filing of a registration statement are not avoided but are merely postponed by making a private offering. However, postponement alone may be a sufficient advantage to the issuer; the subsequent offering may come at a time when the issuer is better able to afford the expense, and moreover the issuer may use the opportunity to register a sale of additional securities on its own behalf, thereby avoiding the expenses of at least one registration statement.[18]

The Intrastate Offering Exemption.   Under Section 3(a)(11) the mails and other instrumentalities of interstate commerce may be used in connection with an offering—even a public offering—if the entire issue is offered and sold only to persons who are residents of a single state, which is also the state in which the issuer was incorporated and is substantially engaged in business. If any portion of the issue—even a single share—is *offered* to a nonresident, the exemption is lost. This raises at least two types of problems.

First, if the issuer has recently sold or offered securities to nonresidents, and if the securities were sold or offered for the same purposes as the contemplated offering, the two offerings may be integrated so as to constitute a single issue.

Secondly, assuming no prior sales to nonresidents, it is the ultimate purchasers who must be residents. Thus, while the distribution is in progress, if one of the purchasers resells to a nonresident, this resale may be considered part of the original distribution, again making the exemption unavailable for all securities offered in that issue. The question of who the ultimate purchasers are and when a resale may be considered not part of the original distribution are questions of fact similar to those raised in connection with the private offering exemption. Not surprisingly, counsel frequently advise their clients who rely on the intrastate exemption to type or print on certificates representing the security a legend to the effect that they may not be resold to nonresidents. This is not necessarily effective, since a mere offer (not necessarily a sale) to a nonresident is sufficient to disqualify the entire offering from the exemption.

Thus, the exemption is best confined to "issues which in reality represent local financing by local industries, carried out purely through local purchasing."[19] Carefully used, the intrastate offering exemption can be of considerable advantage to corporations meeting the above description. Of course, the exemption will be more useful to western corporations—because they are not located in a multi-state urban area—than to corporations organized in the eastern or midwestern states.

The Small Issue Exemption (Regulation A). Section 3(b) of the Securities Act of 1933 empowers the S.E.C. to exempt additional small issues of securities whose aggregate offering price to the public does not exceed $300,000, if it finds that registration is not necessary in the public interest. Under this authority the Commission has promulgated Regulation A, consisting of its rules 251 through 263.[20] The Regulation A procedure is, in effect, a simplified registration. A notification is filed with the regional office of the Commission in which the issuer has its principal business operations. The notification must contain certain required information and is a matter of public record. There must be filed as an exhibit to the notification a form of offering circular which is proposed to be used in connection with the offering. There is even an exemption from the offering circular requirement for offerings by certain issuers limited to $50,000 or less. Unlike other exemptions that are automatically applicable if appropriate facts are present, exemptions under Section 3(b), including Regulation A, must be qualified for. When the regional office has finished its review, and when the proposed offering circular has been amended in accordance with its comments, securities may be offered provided that copies of the offering circular are furnished to offerees and purchasers.

In practice Regulation A may be as difficult to use as a registration statement, and indeed Regulation A is not available to every issuer.[21] However, it is generally less expensive and less time consuming. For example, although great care must be used in preparing financial statements, audited statements are not necessary.

Consistent with the statutory purpose, the registration provisions of the Act are broad, and the exemptions are narrow; nevertheless, if they suit the company's purposes, the exemptions should be used when available.

Business Combinations

The possibility that a combination with another corporation will simplify its financing problems, and possibly solve them, should not be neglected by a small business corporation. Of course, the management of many small business companies—who are usually the substantial owners—may be dedicated to "being their own boss." Nevertheless, the right business combination or merger situation might be worth looking into.

STATE LAW ASPECTS

A *merger* is generally defined as a combination of two or more corporations into one of the corporations. A *consolidation* is a combination of two or more existing corporations into a newly formed corporation. State law governs the formalities necessary to consummate mergers and consolidations. If corporations that are incorporated in more than one state are involved, there may be conflict of laws problems. Normally the approval of holders of a specified percentage of the outstanding stock of each corporation involved is required. Some states permit shareholders who vote against the merger or consolidation to insist upon being paid in cash the appraised value of their shares. Sometimes a transaction cannot be accomplished as a straight merger, but it may nevertheless be possible to achieve the same result—that is, two or more companies are combined and the stockholders of all companies end up as stockholders of a single company—without going through the statutory formalities. This is called a de facto merger; it is generally believed that, although it may be possible to avoid using the statutory merger or consolidation formalities, most state courts will, if called upon, protect the rights and remedies of creditors and stockholders to the same extent as if a formal merger or consolidation were involved.

SECURITIES LAW ASPECTS

In those states that require shareholder vote to approve a merger or similar transaction, the affirmative vote of the holders of the requisite percentage of outstanding stock binds all of the shareholders to the action, including those who voted against the merger and whose remedy is to insist upon their appraisal rights in those states where appraisal rights exist, or otherwise to go along with the transaction grudgingly. The S.E.C. has ruled in its Rule 133 that in those cases the issuance of shares of the surviving corporation and their distribution to the shareholders of the corporations going out of existence are not a sale of securities (because of the absence of individual free choice) and therefore need not be registered under the Act.[22] The rule also permits subsequent resales by such shareholders, except those who are classified as affiliates (persons in control of any one or more of the constituent corporations); the rule also has some provisions for the benefit of those persons. This is a very useful rule, and where it applies it facilitates many business combinations. Some state securities laws also exempt such transactions.

TAX ASPECTS OF MERGERS

Section 354 of the Internal Revenue Code permits shareholders of a corporation that is a party to a reorganization to exchange their shares for shares in another corporation that is also party to the reorganization without recognizing gain or loss. Their tax basis for the stock surrendered is transferred to the stock acquired, and gain or loss is recognized only when and if the stock acquired is disposed of. Section 361 permits a corporation that is a party to a reorganization to transfer property to another corporation in exchange for stock or securities without recognizing gain on the transfer of properties. Section 368(a)(1) defines *reorganization* as including the statutory mergers and consolidations referred to above, and various other types of transactions having the same or similar effects. Great care and diligence are required in reorganization transactions; however, the advantage of tax deferral is worth working hard for.

Corporate-Shareholder Relationships

The principal (and often only) shareholders of most small business corporations are also its managing officers and directors, and such corporations are usually operated informally, often to the dismay of their lawyers, who would prefer greater adherence to corporate formality. (I cannot recount how many times I have shuddered on hearing such officer-director-shareholders refer to each other as "my partner.")

The corporation contemplating bringing in investors should consider in advance the new relationships that management will have with these outsiders. We will consider some aspects of such relationships in this section.

Standards Governing Conduct of Directors

Corporate powers are ordinarily exercised by the board of directors elected by the shareholders. Directors must use reasonable care and diligence in exercising corporate powers and should be familiar with the corporate business, its programs and its policies. They are not mere figureheads and they may be held liable for their negligence. In general, however, directors are less likely to err in business judgment if they exercise the same care and diligence that an ordinarily prudent man would exercise in the management of his own affairs.

Each director is a fiduciary owing his complete and undivided loyalty to his corporation. He must exercise his duties in good faith and for the best interests of the corporation. As a fiduciary, he is held to the highest standard of fairdealing: "Not honesty alone, but the punctilio of an honor of the most sensitive." He must place the corporate interest before his own. Accordingly, if a business opportunity is presented which the corporation might reasonably be expected to undertake, the law prohibits the director from seizing the opportunity for himself; he is prohibited from competing with the corporation.

Directors, as fiduciaries, are not allowed to retain any personal profit or advantage from their official action. England and some American states absolutely prohibited directors from entering into any contracts with their corporations in which they had a personal interest that might conflict with their duty of utmost loyalty. The modern view, however, permits a contract between a director and the corporation if it is fair, if there has been a full disclosure, and if the contract has been approved by a disinterested voting majority of the board of directors.

Transactions in Shares of the Corporation by Directors and Controlling Shareholders

Transfers of Control. A seller of stock will receive more per share for stock that transfers control of the corporation to the buyer than for shares not giving control; ordinarily the seller will be able to keep the premium received. However, there are several theories by which minority shareholders have successfully compelled majority shareholders to pay the control premium over to their corporation. In one case, for example, majority shareholders were required to account for the premium received where they were paid more than twice the value of their stock for a sale of control to persons whom they had reason to believe would loot the corporation, And in *Perlman vs. Feldman,* during a favorable market for sellers of steel, the controlling shareholders of Newport, a steel manufacturer, received a premium for selling control to a company that needed steel and would operate Newport as a captive supplier.[23] In effect, the sale of control was accompanied by a loss of corporate opportunity and the selling shareholders were accountable for the premium. It has also been argued that control is a "corporate asset" and that therefore any premium paid for control belongs to the corporation.[24]

Directors' Purchases of Shares. Although a director owes a fiduciary duty to his corporation, most of the older cases held that in his personal dealings in the corporation's stock he owed no duty to disclose facts learned in his official position. On the other hand, a few courts held that a director could not buy stock from a shareholder unless he discloses all known material facts. A middle position adopted by many courts in recent cases holds that, if no special facts exist, a director could buy shares without disclosing any information to the selling shareholder. Special facts creating a duty of disclosure may consist of knowledge of a pending merger, sale of corporate assets, or declarations of unusual dividends. In these cases, although the director-buyer may be liable to the selling shareholder, he will not ordinarily be accountable to the corporation.

Insiders' Liability Under Rule 10b-5. Section 10 of the Securities and Exchange Act of 1934 and its Rule 10b-5 were adopted to prohibit fraud in connection with the purchase or sale of securities. Rule 10b-5 makes it unlawful for any person, by the use of any instrumentality of interstate commerce, or of the mails, or of any facility of any national securities exchange in connection with the purchase or sale of any security:

1. To employ any device, scheme, or artifice to defraud;
2. To make any untrue statement of a material fact or to omit a material fact necessary to make the statements made, in the light of the circumstances under which they were made, not misleading;
3. To engage in any act, practice, or course of business that operates or would operate as a fraud or deceit upon any person.

The scope of Rule 10b-5 is broad. It applies to any person and to any security whether or not traded on an exchange or over the counter. It prohibits deceptive activities whether or not they constitute common law fraud and deceit. Most importantly, Rule 10b-5 requires insiders to disclose material facts known to them by virtue of their position but not known to the persons with whom they are dealing. Furthermore, since many transactions utilize the mails, a stock exchange, or an instrumentality of interstate commerce, Rule 10b-5 will frequently apply in addition to the "special facts" doctrine or whatever standard is applied by the state in which the transaction took place or the lawsuit was brought.

Short Swing Profits Under Section 16(b). Section 16 of the Securities Exchange Act of 1934 provides that every officer, director, or owner of more than 10 per cent of any equity security of certain corporations, shall be liable to the corporation for any profits resulting from a purchase and sale, or a sale and purchase, within less than six months, of any of the corporation's equity securities.

In determining the profits realized from insider transactions, the lowest purchases are matched against the highest sales within six months before or after, without regard to the order in which they were made.

SHAREHOLDERS MEETINGS AND VOTING RIGHTS

The primary right of a shareholder as such is to vote for the election of directors and to vote on certain types of transactions not in the ordinary course of business, such as mergers, consolidations, and sales of substantially all of the assets of their corporation. Most corporate charters and the laws of many states require an annual meeting for election of directors.

A meeting of shareholders must be attended by shareholders or agents (proxies) acting for shareholders sufficient to constitute a quorum, which is usually present if a majority of the voting power is present or represented. Once a quorum is present, the vote of persons holding a majority of the votes present is sufficient to elect directors, or to decide any question, unless there is some express provision to the contrary. Furthermore, once a quorum is present it cannot be broken by the withdrawal of a part of the stockholders.

Each owner of shares in a corporation has the right to vote the shares at all corporate meetings. Difficult problems sometimes arise as to who should vote certain stock, for example, as between a pledgor and pledgee, but ordinarily the problem is resolved in favor of the person appearing on the corporation's books as the owner of the stock.

The vote of the individual shareholder in any large corporation whose stock is widely distributed is generally insignificant in determining the composition of the board of directors. However, in close corporations the individual shareholder's vote is important and even in large corporations may be sought after by those seeking control or representation on the board of directors.

In most corporations, a bare majority of the voting shares elects the entire board of directors and can control the corporation without any minority representation. To enable minority shareholders to obtain representation on the board, approximately twenty states require cumulative voting and a substantial group of other states permits, but does not compel, corporations to provide for cumulative voting in their charters.

Under cumulative voting each shareholder is entitled to votes equal to the number of his shares multiplied by the number of directors to be elected, and he may cast all of his votes for one or more nominees rather than distribute them evenly. The minimum number of shares properly cumulated needed to elect N directors is determined by the following formula:

$$\frac{NY}{X+1} + 1$$

Y is equal to the total number of shares to be voted at the meeting, and X is equal to the number of directors to be elected. Thus the minimum number of shares properly cumulated that can elect two directors to a five-man board where 600 total shares will be voted is 201.

Proxy Solicitation and Reports—Unregulated. At common law shareholders were required to vote in person at shareholders' meetings. With the advent of the modern business corporation and its numerous and geographically dispersed shareholders, it became impossible for shareholders to personally attend meetings. The proxy system thus became a practical necessity. A proxy is the authority given by a stockholder to another to vote for him at a shareholders' meeting. The term is also used to describe the document that evidences the authority of the agent—the proxy holder—to vote the shares. Ordinarily the proxy is revocable, even if stated to be otherwise. Revocation of the proxy may be accomplished orally, by the grant of a subsequent proxy to another, or by the shareholder's attending and voting at the meeting in person.

Many corporations do not solicit proxies; they merely notify the shareholders of the time and place of the meeting. Shareholders who do not attend or send a proxy to the meeting are disenfranchised and the management in power is perpetuated. Other corporations send proxies but do not fairly describe the business to be accomplished.

Some corporations also send inadequate and sometimes misleading reports to their shareholders; the fact that state law may permit them to inspect the corporation's records on their own is of small comfort to most shareholders.

Effect of Securities Exchange Act. The Securities Exchange Act of 1934 contains a number of sections which are aimed at these problems. Section 14 makes it unlawful for any person to use the mails or interstate commerce or any facility of any national securities exchange to solicit any proxy or authorization in respect to any security subject to its provisions in contravention of the Commission's rules.

The rules adopted by the Commission set forth a four-way approach to problems posed by the use of the proxy.[25] First, management is required to disclose all facts pertinent to the proposals submitted to the shareholders through the corporate machinery in a proxy statement. Second, fraud in the solicitation of proxies is made unlawful. Third, stockholders are given the opportunity to compel management to include proposals for action in management's proxy statement.

Fourth, opportunity is given shareholders to solicit proxies from other shareholders, but a disclosure is required as in the case of management's solicitation. Companies covered by the proxy rules by reason of the 1964 amendments referred to below, must send substantially the same information to shareholders whether they solicit proxies or not.[26]

Prior to 1964 only securities listed on a national exchange and those of some corporations who had filed a registration statement under the Securities Act of 1933 were subject to the reporting and disclosure requirements of the Securities Exchange Act of 1934. Amendments enacted in 1964, however, extended the periodic reporting requirements, the proxy solicitation requirements, and the insider reporting and trading requirements described earlier to securities of all companies engaged in interstate commerce or in a business affecting interstate commerce, or whose securities are traded by use of the mails or of interstate commerce if they have total assets in excess of $1,000,000 and a class of equity security held of record by a specified minimum number of persons or more (500 or more for fiscal years ending after July 1, 1966). Since the asset requirement refers to total assets and not to net assets, many small businesses will be subject to the requirements.

Each solicitation of a proxy covered by the rules must be accompanied by a proxy statement that sets forth the matters to be acted upon and gives financial information about the company and the persons seeking to be elected directors, including their salary arrangements with the company. The proxy must make provision for the person solicited to indicate approval or disapproval of all referred matters except the election of directors. Any solicitation relating to a meeting must be accompanied or preceded by the company's annual financial report. The form of proxy must indicate whether it is solicited on behalf of management and must clearly identify each group of related matters to be acted upon and whether proposed by management or by a security holder. Finally, proxy statements and all written proxy soliciting material must be filed with the Commission in advance of distribution. The Commission will then process the documents and determine whether they comply with the disclosure standards of the rule. If not, revisions will be requested which, if not made, can provide the basis for an action to enjoin the solicitation or restrain the voting of proxies.

SHAREHOLDERS' ACTIONS

As a general rule injuries to a corporation, even though they may impair the value of each shareholder's interest, must be remedied by an action brought by the corporation. The separate entity of the corporation is thus recognized, the rights of creditors are protected, and all of the shareholders are protected by a recovery that benefits all equally. Conversely, to permit shareholders to sue separately for wrongs to the corporation would, among other things, negate the corporation's existence, lead to a multiplicity of suits, and endanger the interest of creditors.

Injuries to corporations may be inflicted by the very officers and directors entrusted with the corporate assets and with the corporate management. In such cases, the corporation probably will not institute an action to redress its wrongs. This is especially true where the majority shareholders benefit from the directors' breach of duty and continue to elect the same directors to office. Where the injury is to the corporation but the directors refuse to sue, the minority shareholders are permitted on behalf of the corporation to assert the right and bring the lawsuit joining the corporation as a nominal defendant. This action is called a derivative action because the wrong was not done personally to the complaining stockholder but was inflicted on the corporation from whom the action is derived. The derivative action is the principal remedy by which defrauded minority shareholders may hold directors, officers, and controlling shareholders responsible for the diversion of corporate assets and the theft of corporate opportunities.

The derivative action presents an entirely different situation from that which arises when a third party—or perhaps even the corporation, or its officers and directors—is charged with invading the stockholder's independent rights. If, for example, a shareholder has been induced to sell his shares at a loss because of the fraudulent conduct of a director he will be given a personal right of action for damages for the fraud. A shareholder may have the personal right to bring an action to enjoin an invalid amendment of the corporate charter or to prohibit any attempt to change his voting rights.

The need for determining whether a shareholder's action is personal or derivative is readily apparent. If derivative, the action cannot be brought unless certain procedures have first been followed. Therefore a shareholder who sues individually only to have a court determine that the wrong was to the corporation and that the suit should have been brought derivatively, if at all, is out of court and out a great deal of time, energy and money.

The authority to sue for corporate injuries is in the board of directors. Before a shareholder may sue on behalf of the corporation he must either demand that the directors sue or have facts showing that it would have been useless to make such a demand as, for example, when the acts complained of were committed by a majority of the directors. Furthermore, an independent board of directors' good-faith business decision not to sue may bar a derivative action. In addition to making demand on the directors to institute suit, a substantial number of courts hold that the complaining shareholder must also seek relief through a shareholders' meeting or have an adequate reason for having failed to do so.

To bring a derivative suit the plaintiff must be an owner of shares when the suit is brought and while the action is pending. Furthermore, in Federal courts and in many states a shareholder cannot bring a derivative suit unless he was a shareholder at the time of the transactions complained of. As a general rule, courts will not consider the motive of the plaintiff in suing as a possible defense to his action. However, some states such as New York have attempted to control potential abuses of derivative suits by legislation requiring the complaining shareholder, under certain circumstances, to post security for the litigation expenses of the defendants.

These and other complexities make it difficult to bring a derivative action.

13

Tax Incentives
for Small Business

Neil R. Bersch

The essence of a successful profit plan is an accurate advance determination of income and expense. Few of the income and expense items involved in a projection of estimated profit and loss are so susceptible to accurate forecasting as is the federal income tax expense. On the basis of a given set of financial data, one should be in a position to determine accurately the amount of federal income tax which will ultimately be applied to his net earnings. However, like any other type of projection, a forecast based on incomplete information, unreliable facts, or less than accurate knowledge of the pressures that affect the determination of federal income tax could cause a gross discrepancy between projected figures and actual results. It is the purpose of this chapter to explore some of the general and specific tax decisions that must be made by management prior to or in the course of running a successful business operation.

Since most items of income and expense are considered in computing one's federal income tax liability, it is clear that such amounts cannot be considered in terms of one-hundred-cent dollars, but should be thought of in terms of fractions of a dollar, depending on the rate at which the net income may be taxed. The principal true expenditure of a one-hundred-cent dollar is the federal income tax. Thus, the elimination of one dollar of federal income tax may often have the same effect on net profit as the elimination of two or more dollars of other expense.

The purpose here is not to overemphasize the importance of tax considerations but it should be noted that good business judgment generally initiates good tax planning.

Any sound tax program should be evaluated not only with regard to its current application but also to its future effect. Many of the tax decisions made today are final and thus actions taken today will somewhat predetermine future planning. It is important to look several years ahead. Today is never too early to plan for the next few years.

Forms of Tax Incentives or Opportunities

The Vast Jungle of Alternatives

The Internal Revenue Code and its Regulations offer many opportunities for decision-making at the earliest stages of a business venture. Also, in many instances during the life cycle of the business the Code offers the taxpayer the opportunity of a choice among various alternatives. One's method of accounting, fiscal year, or form of operation is left to the discretion of the individual businessman. These preliminary decisions should not be based solely on the immediate facts at hand but generally should take into consideration the projected future operations of the business.

Special Tax Incentives

The Legislature has at various times enacted both long- and short-term special tax incentives. Many of these incentives are motivated by specific pressure groups in the economy and bear little or no general interest to business as a whole. Others, however, are of general importance and include such things as the investment credit, the creation of pension or profit sharing plans, and the willingness of the Internal Revenue Service to agree in advance on the tax effect of a particular transaction entered into by the taxpayer prior to the time that it is consummated.

The latter item is extremely helpful to businessmen all over the country, in that it adds a note of finality and assurance to an income tax law that at best is often mysterious and difficult to interpret.

THE DEFERRAL OF INCOME TAXES— AN IMPORTANT FINANCING TOOL

Most businesses at one time or another find it necessary to borrow money from financial or other institutions. There is one source of funds, however, that has often been overlooked, and it is the least expensive source available.

There are many provisions of the Internal Revenue Code which allow a company to defer part of the profit on its business operations for tax purposes. This deferred tax, in effect, becomes an interest-free loan from the government until such time as the tax is required to be paid. In many instances the deferral may almost be permanent in nature, only becoming due if and when the business is terminated or when the volume of business shrinks from its normal level. The long-term or permanent deferral of income tax is an important financing tool and is probably the only instance where the government will provide interest-free capital to business.

The balance of this chapter will be devoted to the exploration in depth of some of the above concepts. Many of these ideas are applicable to business as a whole and are not necessarily the sole domain of the small business. However, many of the provisions in the Code were enacted specifically to provide opportunity or incentive for small business.

Preliminary Decisions and Their Effect on the Future Tax Structure of the Business

THE FORM OF OPERATION

One of the first decisions that must be made is the organizational form under which the business will operate. A business organization may choose either the corporate form or the proprietorship or partnership form.

Most businessmen are familiar with the benefits of limited liability, continuity of management, and the differential between corporate rates, which have a current ceiling of 48 per cent, and individual rates, which apply to both proprietorships and partnerships and rise as high as 70 per cent. The corporate rate of 48 per cent, however, does not apply until the corporate net profits have reached $25,000. Profits over that level are taxed at the full 48 per cent. Profits earned between zero and $25,000 are normally taxed at the rate of 22 per cent. The individual income tax rates, on the other hand, vary from a low of 14 per cent to a high of 70 per cent.

There are also tax benefits derived by dividing a corporate business into several separate legal entities—that is, multiple corporations. The taxation of income at the lower rates offers important incentives.

The corporate form has many advantages:

1. It divides the business into a number of tangible shares that may be easily transferred among different parties. This may be very helpful where it is one's desire to transfer part of the ownership of the business to one's family or appropriately to provide an estate plan to minimize future inheritance taxes.

2. Many fringe benefit programs, such as pension plans, profit sharing and deferred compensation plans, stock option plans, insurance programs, and medical expense plans are available only to corporations.

3. If multiple corporations are utilized, several additional benefits may be available, such as more than one accumulated earnings credit and more than one surtax exemption, even though under the provisions of the 1964 Code a penalty tax of 6 per cent must be paid on the first $25,000 of taxable income if multiple surtax exemptions are elected.[1] Even with this 6 per cent penalty tax, however, the rate for affiliated corporations on the first $25,000 of profit is only 28 per cent, as opposed to the top corporate rate of 48 per cent.

4. It may also be possible to receive an exemption from the payment of estimated federal income tax due to the use of multiple corporations, since such taxes do not become due and payable unless the estimated tax of each corporation is in excess of $100,000.

One must realize, however, that there are certain risks involved in dealing with multiple corporations. The government has many methods of attacking the use of such corporations. Section 1551 of the Code provides for the elimination of the $100,000 accumulated earnings credit and the $25,000 surtax exemption when it can be proven that a major purpose of the multiple corporation arrangement was the derivation of these tax benefits.

In addition, the government may reallocate income between related corporations where this is required, in order to clearly reflect taxable income or to prevent evasion of taxes.[2]

Still another Section of the Code dealing with the determination of gross income gives the Commissioner of Internal Revenue the right to attribute gross income to the corporation that earned such income as opposed to another corporation that reported the income.[3]

In some extreme instances, the Commissioner may actually disregard the corporate entity entirely and tax the net income directly to the shareholders. It is unusual, however, that such extreme action is taken.

The use of multiple corporations can create certain problems, such as the cash flow between related companies, potentially greater administrative expenses, which include both legal and accounting costs, and the inability to offset profits and losses of various corporations against each other, unless the companies are affiliated in a parent-subsidiary relationship and a consolidated return is filed.

Multiple corporations may best be defended in situations where there are sound business reasons for divorcing the various aspects of a corporation's operation—that is, the manufacturing operation and the ownership of real property.

A partnership, on the other hand, may have several advantages over the corporate form of doing business:

1. It offers a greater ease of movement of capital between the owners of the business and the business itself.

2. It offers the owners of the business an opportunity to offset any business losses directly against the personal income of the partners. In the corporate form, of course, under normal circumstances, the losses of the corporation remain in the company and cannot be availed of by the shareholders.

3. A return of the initial investment to the participants in the form of a distribution is not subject to a double tax in the partnership form, whereas such distribution would normally be considered

a dividend in the corporate form and, therefore, subject to tax both at the corporate level (as earned) and by the recipient (when received).

There is a middle ground between the legal insulation afforded by the corporation and the flow-through of profits and losses to the participants afforded by the partnership form. This is the general concept of the tax option or "Subchapter S" corporation.[4]

In a Subchapter S corporation no corporate tax is assessed against the company, but the shareholders are taxed individually on their pro rata share of the corporate profit. In the alternative, any losses incurred by the corporation are deductible by the shareholders with some limitations.

An election to be taxed under Subchapter S of the Internal Revenue Code must be made by the end of the first month of the taxable year for which it is to be effective.[5] The election of this Subchapter S status is not available to any corporation, but is only allowed where the corporation has ten or less shareholders (none of whom is a corporation) and not more than one class of issued stock.[6] There are other qualifications that a corporation must meet in order to qualify for the election.[7] These must be studied carefully.

In some cases, the existence of long-term debt in a corporation has been held to be a second class of stock.[8]

As indicated earlier, any losses incurred by a Subchapter S corporation are deductible by its shareholders. In this connection it should be noted that losses are deductible only to the extent that the shareholder has basis for his investment in the corporation.[9] Basis may be determined by adding not only one's contribution to capital and paid-in surplus, but also considering the amount of loans he has made to the corporation.

If a loss cannot be used by a shareholder because of lack of sufficient basis, this loss is forever forfeited and cannot be used at any later date by either the corporation or the shareholder. This differs significantly from the treatment in a partnership where any losses not currently utilizable by the partners owing to lack of sufficient basis, can be used at any later date when the deficiency in partner's capital is repaid to the partnership.[10]

A recent revenue ruling held that where losses were incurred by the corporation and passed on to the shareholders, thereby reducing the basis of the shareholder's stock and notes to zero, the eventual repayment of the stockholder's note resulted in the realization of a capital gain.[11] One may observe, therefore, the potential tax benefits to be derived from the possible exchange of an ordinary loss for a capital gain, even though economically no gain or loss has been recognized.

Many business enterprises have used the opportunity for election under Subchapter S in the earlier years of the corporate existence when losses may be incurred. At a later date, when the operation of the business enterprise becomes profitable, the Subchapter S election is terminated or revoked and the future profits of the corporation are taxed at the corporate rate as opposed to the higher individual rates. The decision to be taxed under Subchapter S should constantly be rechallenged. The operations of a business have a habit of changing and whereas Subchapter S might not be a proper vehicle for taxation this year, a changed operation next year may provide the ideal situation for its election.

One of the most interesting, but least publicized provisions of the Internal Revenue Code is Section 1244. Prior to the enactment of this Section, the businessman who decided to operate in corporate form and was unsuccessful in his venture found himself faced with a capital loss rather than an ordinary loss deduction for both his investment and any loans he had made to the corporation. One can contrast this with the businessman who operated in an unincorporated form and received an ordinary deduction for any losses. The purpose of Section 1244 was to provide a partial cure for this discrepancy between the treatment of losses sustained by a business conducted in corporate form and those sustained by an unincorporated venture.

Needless to say, if one expected to lose money a business venture would not be started. On the other hand, it is wise to plan in advance for the obscure possibility that the venture will not become profitable. Section 1244 provides that vehicle. It is a one-way street. There is absolutely nothing to lose by electing Section 1244. Any gain on the disposition of Section 1244 stock or on the liquidation of a corporation qualifying under this Section would create a capital gain, assuming, of course, that the corporation is not collapsible and that the stockholder is not a securities dealer.[12] However, any loss arising on the sale or liquidation of a Section 1244 corporation by a qualified share-holder will be considered an ordinary deduction and not a capital loss.

The benefits of Section 1244 are only available to individual share-holders who purchased stock directly from the corporation.[13] These benefits, therefore, are not available to anyone who received stock in any kind of a transfer, be that transfer a sale, gift, or inheritance. It should also be noted that the provisions of this Section apply only to small business corporations (as defined in the Statute) and then only to the first $500,000 of issued qualified stock.[14] There is also an annual limitation as to the amount of loss that may be taken under this Sec-tion. This amount is $25,000 annually if a separate return is filed or $50,000 annually if a joint return is filed.[15] Any excess loss during the year will be a capital loss.

A discrepancy between an unincorporated business and an in-corporated venture which Section 1244 generally does not reconcile is that losses in an unincorporated business may be deducted as incurred (by the partners) whereas losses in a corporate venture can only be deducted (by the shareholders) when the corporate business is sold or liquidated.

One should not overlook, however, the possibility of the combina-tion of qualification under Section 1244 and the election by the corpo-ration to be taxed under Subchapter S. In this circumstance any losses incurred by the corporation can be deducted currently by the share-holder. In addition, any further loss incurred on the eventual disposi-tion or worthlessness of the stock upon liquidation can be deducted as an ordinary loss under Section 1244. This appears to be an ideal combination.

In summary, then, the choice of the form best suited for a business depends on a multitude of tax factors. When all of these are consid-ered and the future operations of the company are projected, one is in a position to make a decision as to the proper form of organization for a particular venture.

THE ELECTION OF A FISCAL YEAR

Another critical election to be made at the corporate level is the determination of a proper fiscal year. At the proprietorship or partner-ship level there is substantially less latitude available, since the partnership or proprietorship is required to use the same fiscal year as its principal partners, unless permission is received from the Commissioner to use another period.[16]

The following factors should be considered in the determination of the proper corporate fiscal year:

1. The end of the natural business year or "slack season" should be considered, since at that time it is easiest to close the books of the corporation and accumulate the accounting data for the year.

2. It is ideal under some circumstances to terminate the corporation's first fiscal year when its taxable income amounts to $25,000. In this respect, the income for the first year will be taxed at the lower rate and a new surtax exemption will be available for the following year.

3. If the corporation incurs an operating loss in the first year and it is expected that the losses will continue for an extended period into the future, it may be beneficial to let the corporation's fiscal year run a full 12 months from the organization of the company. In this respect, it will give the company the longest period over which to apply the operating losses to future profits.

It should be noted that a corporation's first fiscal year or any fiscal year may not exceed a period of 12 calendar months.[17]

CHOICE OF AN OVER-ALL METHOD OF ACCOUNTING

Before choosing a method of accounting it is important to have positive knowledge of what the Treasury Regulations consider a method of accounting to be. Two points in the Regulations should be emphasized: the application of sound accounting principles of the particular trade or business, and consistency.

The Regulations under Section 446 provide that the method of accounting chosen by the taxpayer must "reflect the consistent application of generally accepted accounting principles in a particular trade or business in accordance with accepted conditions or practices in that trade or business."[18] The Regulations further indicate that the method "will ordinarily be regarded as clearly reflecting income providing all items of gross income and expense are treated consistently from year to year."[19]

The Regulations impose one additional requirement: "Taxable income shall be computed under the method of accounting on the basis of which the taxpayer regularly computes his income in keeping his books."[20]

A businessman generally has the choice of one of two methods of accounting: the cash receipts and disbursements method (cash basis), or the accrual method.

The cash basis of accounting in most instances will provide the maximum flexibility in achieving a minimization of tax. On the other hand, if inventories are a substantial income-producing factor, the use of the cash basis will not be allowed (with respect to the inventory) and the company will be required to use the accrual method of accounting.[21] In some cases, however, a hybrid method of accounting is possible.

As far as the accrual basis is concerned, the only time this basis may have a detrimental temporary effect on an operating business is when the company's accounts receivable and accrued income are far in excess of the company's payables and accrued expenses. In this instance, the company will be required to pay a tax on the difference between these two, even though the net income has not actually been collected.

Once the general method of accounting has been selected, the businessman has a choice of specific accounting practices to apply to segments of the company's business. A brief discussion of a few of these areas follows. It should be noted, however, that in each of the following instances the company can make an election to treat these items in such a manner as to reduce the current income of the corporation subject to tax. This has the effect of deferring the payment of tax (through the acceleration of deductions) into future years, and, thereby, increasing the current cash available to the corporation for operating purposes. On the other hand, many of these items which are reflected on the tax return are also required to be reflected in the same manner on the books. Thus, while the income for tax purposes is reduced, the income is also reduced for financial reporting purposes. The current income tax payment is down, but so is profit, and this may not create a favorable atmosphere in dealing with a lending institution which relies in part upon the earnings of the corporation in determining whether or not a loan should be made to the company.

Thus, in making a decision to accelerate deductions for tax purposes one must also consider the profit effect on the enterprise and on the borrowing capabilities of the company as a whole.

INVENTORY

Many methods of valuing the inventory are available. The most prominent in current use is the "lower of cost or market" basis. The value of the inventory can be further reduced for tax purposes by electing the LIFO (last-in, first-out) method. This method has the practical effect of valuing inventory at the level of the oldest items in the inventory. Thus, cost of sales is charged at the price level of the latest items to be purchased by the company. This has the effect, in times of rising prices, of understating the value of the inventory and effectively overstating the charge against profit and loss. Needless to say, from a purely tax standpoint this may be an advantage, since the lowest profit is consistently reported as long as prices are rising. However, if prices begin to decline, the advantage begins to dissipate and higher taxes are paid than would have been paid if LIFO had not been elected.

The Regulations are specific with regard to the method of electing LIFO.[22] They also specify that the LIFO inventory method be used on all reports issued by the corporation and on all financial statements, with the exception of interim financial statements used for management purposes.[23] As indicated earlier, the lower taxable income will also create a lower financial income.

DEPRECIATION AND AMORTIZATION

The Income Tax Regulations under Section 167 allow various methods of depreciation and amortization for tax purposes. The most commonly used are the straight-line method, the declining balance method, and the sum-of-the-year's-digits method. The latter two methods are a form of accelerated depreciation and succeed in writing off the major cost of any asset in its earlier years. Again, the purpose of the election to use accelerated depreciation is to defer as long as possible the payment of income taxes by accelerating deductions. Obviously, in a company that is expanding at a rapid rate and continuing to acquire new properties over a long period of time, accelerated depreciation will continue for many years to exceed that which would have been taken had the company initially elected the straight-line method.

The election of an accelerated method of depreciation is limited to those assets which have a useful life in excess of three years.[24] A new election is available each year on any particular segment of the company's fixed properties for the additions of property during that year. Many companies have used accelerated methods of depreciation for the earlier years of an asset and then have switched to the straight-line method of depreciation at the point at which the normal straight-line depreciation would be in excess of the accelerated depreciation.

As a special incentive to smaller corporations Congress enacted Section 179, which allows a special "bonus" depreciation of up to $2,000 on the first $10,000 of property acquired by a corporation in any one particular year.[25] This is an annual election and may be made by a company each year on any $10,000 of property acquired. In order to qualify under this special section, the property must have a useful life of six years or more.[26] The property must be specifically noted as Section 179 property on the tax return of the company. The remaining basis of the asset after deducting the 20 per cent bonus depreciation is then available for normal depreciation under either the straight-line or accelerated method.

RESEARCH AND DEVELOPMENT EXPENSES

The company may expense research and development expenditures as incurred or may elect to capitalize such expenditures and amortize them over a period of not less than 60 months.[27] From a purely tax standpoint, to expense these costs as incurred appears to give the tax advantage of the expense immediately against the profitable operations of the company. However, the future operations of the business should be considered. If the expensing of current research and development costs will cause the operations of the company to reflect an operating loss, the future utilization of this loss should be considered prior to the time the election is made.

There are special provisions under this Section which allow for a separate election on a project-by-project basis.[28] It may be advantageous to elect to expense research and development costs on one project but not on another.

ORGANIZATION EXPENSE

Under Section 248, a corporation may elect in its first return to amortize its organization expenses over a five-year period.[29] If this election is not timely and properly made, the corporation cannot deduct such expense until the corporation ceases its existence.

RECOGNITION OF BAD-DEBT EXPENSE

In the first year in which an accrual-basis company incurs a bad debt, an election must be made as to the method of deducting bad debts—either the specific charge-off method or the reserve method.[30] Under the general provisions of the Internal Revenue Code, any losses sustained by a corporation in its business operations are not deductible on an "estimated" basis but are only deducted when the loss is actually sustained; however, bad debts are the one specific exception to this general rule. The Code and the Regulations provide that a taxpayer may elect the reserve method of deducting bad debts, in which case he will provide a reserve based on estimated losses on his accounts and notes receivable. The reserve must take into consideration the age of the receivables, the credit rating of the company to whom credit is granted, the general economic conditions, the past history of the company, and various other factors. On examination, the adequacy of the bad-debt reserve for tax purposes may be challenged by the Internal Revenue Service. In an old but still potent case, the Court established a formula which the Service has continued to use up to the present time to determine whether a reserve is adequate, inadequate, or excessive.[31] On the basis of this formula, which relates the company's reserve to its average charges-offs over the five previous years, revenue agents will often propose an adjustment to a company's bad-debt reserve.

The treatment of the above items and, indeed, the general accounting method employed by the business, will, in part, determine the amount of current federal income taxes to be paid. The above specific items, however, are merely indications of the tools and alternatives which a taxpayer has at his fingertips. By proper utilization of these tools, the current income taxes of the corporation can be kept at a minimum, even though the economic profit of the concern remains at a high level.

Special Tax Incentives

All corporations are given a beneficial exclusion from both the higher tax rates and the imposition of tax penalties in certain areas. These exclusions, although not specifically designed to assist the smaller corporation, are certainly more meaningful to small business because of the magnitude of the dollars involved. The annual surtax exemption of $25,000 allows a corporation to recognize up to $25,000 of taxable income at a tax rate of only 22 per cent. In addition, every corporation is entitled to accumulate $100,000 in earnings and profits before they can be attacked by the Internal Revenue Service on a basis of unreasonable accumulation of earnings.[32] This is a critical area in which, if the Service can prove that the earnings of the business are being accumulated unreasonably in lieu of distributing them to the shareholders, they can assess a penalty tax[33] or force the corporation to pay a dividend.

A third area is in the requirement to file a declaration and pay an estimated tax in advance of year-end. In this instance, unless a corporation pays $100,000 or more in annual corporate income taxes, they are relieved from the requirement to file a corporate declaration of estimated tax or make any payment.[34] Therefore, the income taxes payable by a small corporation are due in two equal installments; the first is due two and a half months after the close of the corporation's fiscal year and the balance five and a half months after the close of that year. Larger companies may be required to pay nearly 100 per cent of their estimated tax prior to the end of their fiscal year.

INVESTMENT CREDIT

The investment credit provisions of the Revenue Act of 1962 were designed to stimulate an increase in the amount spent by corporations in the capital goods area. All qualified property which was anticipated to be held a minimum of four years, was available for the investment credit.[35] This covered both new and used property acquired by the corporation, except that only $50,000 of used property annually would qualify for the credit.[36] These provisions allowed a direct credit against the corporation's income tax of between 2⅓ and 7 per cent of the actual cost of the goods.[37]

The total amount of the credit was limited in any one year to the amount of tax paid by the corporation and in addition could not exceed the amount of $25,000, plus 25 per cent of the tax in excess of $25,000.[38] Whether or not the corporation was entitled to the full 7 per cent credit depended on the estimated life of the asset. If more than four years but less than six years, only one-third of the 7 per cent was allowed as a credit; more than six years but less than eight years, two-thirds of the 7 per cent was allowed as a credit. If the life of the asset was in excess of eight years, the full 7 per cent of the credit was allowed.[39] The Code also contains provisions that if the property is sold prematurely, part or all of the investment credit attributable to that property and previously claimed may have to be returned to the government as additional tax in the year of disposition of the asset.[40] There is no penalty, however, for the early disposition of property, and the only effect of claiming the investment credit in an early year and repaying it in a later year is that the corporation has borrowed the money from the government interest-free for that period of time.

Any investment credit which cannot be used by a corporation in the current year can be carried back to previous years (but not before 1962) or carried forward to future years (not to exceed five years from the date the credit was taken).[41]

The Code also provides that the investment credit may be taken on certain leased property.[42] For these provisions to be valid the lessor must provide the lessee with an agreement form indicating either the cost or the fair market value of the lessor's equipment.[43] If both parties agree that the investment credit is to be passed from the lessor to the lessee the forms should be signed and submitted with the tax return of the lessor.[44]

In an attempt to curb some of the inflationary pressures in the economy, the Administration proposed a Bill in 1966 (as part of Public Law 89-800) to temporarily suspend the investment credit for all property acquired or constructed from October 10, 1966, through December 31, 1967.[45] Any property ordered or construction begun before

October 10, 1966, would continue to be eligible for the investment credit. Also, if a construction contract was signed prior to the effective date the property would be eligible for the investment credit even though construction commenced later. A special provision in this Bill exempts the first $20,000 of eligible investments made during the suspension period. This would allow a maximum credit of $1,400 (7 per cent of $20,000). The Bill also limits the use of accelerated depreciation on certain real property acquired during the suspension period.

Medical Plans

Section 105(e) of the Internal Revenue Code provides that an employee need not include in his gross income payments from a corporate medical wage continuation plan. Many of the provisions of the Code regarding pension and profit sharing plans require that these plans be nondiscriminatory in favor of higher salaried employees or controlling shareholders. The corporate medical plans covered by this particular Section, however, have no such restriction. Although the description of a plan under the Regulations is relatively broad—it states that a plan consists of "one or more employees"[46]—from a practical standpoint the plan should include at least one employee who is not a shareholder. This may be helpful in defending any Treasury attack against the payments from the medical plan being tantamount to a preferential dividend to the shareholders.

The benefits of the plan are quite simple. The corporation, by reimbursing the individual plan members for all of their medical expenses (and those of their dependents) receives an income tax deduction for the amount so paid. On the other hand, the recipients of the funds covering personal medical expenses are not required to include such amounts in their gross income.

The expenses subject to reimbursement and the maximum amount, if any, for which the company may be liable should be noted in the plan. The plan also may be insured or noninsured.

This is one of the few provisions of the Code where a corporation is allowed to reimburse certain employees for "personal" expenses and have the amounts deductible to the corporation, but not taxable to the employees. This type of a plan has been very popular in smaller, closely controlled corporations, but has not been nearly so popular in larger companies.

CONTRIBUTION OF INVENTORY TO CHARITABLE, SCIENTIFIC, OR RELIGIOUS ORGANIZATIONS

In many instances, especially where a corporation realizes a high gross profit on the sale of its goods, it may be beneficial to make contributions of inventory to charities in lieu of cash. An example may be helpful in showing the tax benefit of such a move. Assume, for the moment, that the corporation has a 60 per cent gross profit on its manufactured goods. If that same corporation were to contribute $1,000 cash to a charity, the net cost of this contribution (assuming a 48 per cent tax rate) would be $520, since the $1,000 cash contribution would be a reduction of taxable income and, therefore, reduce current corporate taxes by $480.00. If, on the other hand, the corporation contributed $1,000 of inventory to the charity in lieu of cash the same $480 tax savings would result, *but,* the corporation would save an additional $288 (48 per cent of $600—the gross profit), since it would not be required to include the gross profit in taxable income. In this instance, then, the corporation receives a definite advantage by retaining the cash and contributing the merchandise.

Needless to say, this technique is not always as simple as it may sound. One question which will arise is the valuation of the goods being contributed. Should the goods be valued at wholesale, at retail, at a discount, or at some other value? This will depend on many factors, but in any case it is doubtful that where the gross profit percentage is relatively high the contribution of cash can be as beneficial as the contribution of inventory.

PENSION, PROFIT SHARING, AND DEFERRED COMPENSATION PLANS

Many small business corporations have formed either a pension plan or profit sharing plan or a combination of the two. The purpose of these plans is not only to keep key employees with the company, but also to provide currently deductible payments for the benefit of top management, which will be distributed to such management after retirement. Over the period of years between the date of the contribution by the corporation and the date of the ultimate distribution to the beneficiaries, the funds are invested and reinvested by a trustee and allowed to accumulate tax-free for the benefit of the ultimate recipients. Since the corporation receives a current income tax deduction for all contributions to qualified pension or profit sharing plans (within prescribed limits), a good portion of the cost of the program is borne by the federal government. The contributions to these plans in many instances can be keyed to profits, or the corporation can determine actuarially a standard amount of payment required for the funding of the ultimate retirement benefits.

A plan will not be approved by the Internal Revenue Service if it discriminates in favor of highly compensated employees or equity owners. In recent years the Internal Revenue Service has begun to attack previously approved plans that were apparently nondiscriminatory in their early stages but later became discriminatory owing to a reallocation of benefits forfeited by terminated employees. In a recent case, the Treasury raised this issue and disallowed certain pension plan deductions that had been claimed.[47] The case was decided in favor of the taxpayer and was appealed by the Treasury; the Circuit Court of Appeals affirmed the Lower Court's decision. In a recent announcement, the Commissioner of Internal Revenue stated that he would not follow the decision in this case and would continue to attack any plans which became discriminatory in their later stages.[48] It was the Service's interpretation that the Code requires the plan to be nondiscriminatory in all phases of its existence. The Treasury Department is currently re-evaluating the entire area of pension and profit sharing plans. A recent announcement has requested comments by the business community on some of the new Treasury proposals that would make the plans far less advantageous to the higher compensated employees.[49]

Deferred compensation plans are also in use by some corporate entities today. The purpose of this type of a plan is to provide executives with compensation after they retire, when they will be in a lower tax bracket. Therefore, the executives should be able to retain a greater portion of their income. As long as these funds are retained by the corporation and not segregated for the specific use of an employee or group of employees, the eventual recipient is not taxed upon these allocated amounts until such time as they are distributed to him after retirement.[50] On the other hand, the corporation is not allowed to deduct such contributions to the deferred compensation plan until such time as the actual distribution of cash is made to the recipient. There is no requirement that these plans be nondiscriminatory.

Does the Form or the Substance of a Transaction Control Its Tax Consequences?

It has long been a general concept in the tax law that the substance of a particular transaction controls its tax consequences, rather than the form.[51] There are isolated instances where form takes precedence over substance.

There are two situations which occur rather frequently and are the subject of difficult interpretive questions on whether the form or the substance of a transaction controls its tax consequences. One of these concerns a company that intends to borrow money on the strength of its fixed plant and equipment; it can either mortgage such property or sell the property to the "lender" and lease it back for the full extent of its useful life. The placing of the mortgage on the property in itself has no tax consequence. On the other hand, if the "lender" requires title to the property and the transaction, therefore, takes the form of a sale and lease-back, the apparent tax consequence is that the seller has realized a taxable gain on the sale of the property (assuming his basis for the property is less than the ultimate sale price) and the purchaser has the right to depreciate such property over its useful life. As a corollary, the payments made by the seller constitute ordinary and necessary rent deductions and are recorded as rental income by the purchaser.

It may be, however, that the substance of the transaction really is a secured loan in that the only reason for the "sale" was that the purchaser required legal title to the property for his own protection. Under these circumstances, the parties may petition the Internal Revenue Service (in advance of the consummation of the transaction) for a ruling to the effect that the transaction, in substance, constitutes a secured loan and not a sale and lease-back. If all the facts submitted to the Internal Revenue Service indicate that the substance of the transaction is a secured loan, there is an excellent chance that the Service will rule favorably that no gain is to be realized by the seller on the transaction. The seller, therefore, would continue to depreciate the property as before. In addition, of course, the buyer will not be allowed to depreciate the property. The payments made by the seller to the buyer will not constitute rent deductions, but will merely constitute a payment of principal and interest on the total amount of funds "loaned." A segregation of the payments will have to be made, of course, to determine the "principal" and "interest" components.

Another common transaction involves an incorporated municipality which, in an attempt to attract new business to the area, agrees to build a plant and grant land to an enterprise that will operate its business in their community. The form of the transaction is that the land and building are purchased by the municipality and general revenue bonds are issued as the source of the financing. The plant is then leased to the business enterprise. The lease payments are keyed to equal the amortization and interest due on the revenue bonds. Some municipalities have also acquired equipment to be used in the plant under the same set of circumstances.

Although the form of this transaction is clearly a lease, the substance of the transaction is the acquisition of the plant and equipment by the enterprise and the payment for such assets over a period of time. Under these circumstances the taxpayer may again request an advance ruling from the Internal Revenue Service to the effect that the substance of the transaction is an acquisition with deferred payment of the purchase price. Thus, the taxpayer will be entitled to depreciation, investment credit, and all the other tax attributes of owning property. However, he would not be allowed to deduct the "lease" payments except as to that portion of the payment which represented interest on the purchase price.

Interest-Free Borrowing from the Government

Through either the short- or long-term deferral of federal income taxes, a taxpayer may effectively provide himself with an interest-free loan from the government. This additional cash may be used to expand, to replenish working capital, or to repay other existing debt.

The over-all accounting method of the taxpayer and the nature of his business operation in part determine the total amount of deferral of income tax possible. The cash basis, under normal circumstances, presents a better vehicle for tax deferral than the accrual basis. On the cash basis one may control the expenditure of funds at year-end. The prepayment of expenses normally due the next week or month could effectively defer the applicable federal income tax savings for the span of the entire year. It is not as easy, however, to defer the recognition of income even on a cash basis, since the theory of "constructive receipt" applies.[52]

Even under the accrual method of accounting with the use of LIFO inventory in a period of rising prices, the deduction of depreciation and amortization on an accelerated basis, the expensing of research and development costs and organization expense, and the use of the reserve method for computing bad debts will all add to the total amount of tax that can be deferred.

There are two other tools which are statutory provisions and allow for the short-term deferral of federal income tax. Under Section 170 of the Internal Revenue Code contributions may be deducted by an accrual basis corporation in the year in which they are committed or appropriated by the board of directors, even though such contributions are not paid prior to the year-end.[53] The Regulations provide, however, that the actual payment of the contribution must be made within two and one-half months after the end of the corporation's taxable year.[54] Thus, prompt action by the board of directors when they are aware of an impending charitable contribution at year-end could allow the company a tax deduction one year earlier than normal.

Another short-term tax deferral plan exists in the Regulations covering the deduction of pension and profit sharing contributions.[55] Such deductions cannot normally be made on the accrual basis but only on a paid basis. On the other hand, the Regulations do provide that the deduction on the accrual basis is allowable as long as the contribution is paid prior to the time that the company's tax return is filed. Thus, if the maximum extension of time for filing the return is required and granted, the company may have as long as eight and one-half months from the end of its fiscal year to make currently deductible payments to a pension and profit sharing plan. It should be noted, however, that generally no more than 12 month's pension or profit sharing expense can be deducted in any one full taxable year.[56]

Two forms of long-term deferral may be quite prevalent in many businesses. The first is a one-shot sale of a particularly large business asset. In many instances, when a sale of this type is made, the seller will not receive all cash as consideration for the property. He must, in the alternative, take some type of a debt obligation from the purchaser. Under circumstances where the transaction meets the strict requirements of Section 453 of the Code, the installment basis may be elected. The installment basis, of course, is a tax-deferral technique that effectively matches the recognition of cash by the seller with the imposition of the tax liability. The Regulations are quite explicit that to qualify for the installment basis, less than 30 per cent of the purchase price must be received in the year of sale.[57] One must take care that both the down payment and the debt amortization received in the year of sale do not exceed the statutory 30 per cent. If the property sold is a capital asset or otherwise produces capital gain, the taxpayer must make equally sure that the debt obligation provides for an interest rate of at least 4 per cent. If this is not the case, the Internal Revenue Service has the authority to reallocate the total price between amounts attributable to principal and amounts attributable to interest.[58] Under these circumstances the entire purchase price of the transaction may change and consequently the amount which constitutes 30 per cent of the purchase price may also change. If the circumstances are sufficiently adverse the transaction could be disqualified from consideration under the installment basis. The Regulations also provide that the sales contract must allow for at least two payments.[59] There is no requirement in the Regulation that there be more than two payments, but two is an absolute minimum. One can readily see the advantages of electing the installment method when the debt obligation covers ten or fifteen years. It is certainly far better to pay the tax ratably over a ten or fifteen year period as collections are made than to lay out the cash in the earlier year when the actual tax may well be in excess of the down payment.

Perhaps the most intriguing application of the installment method was highlighted in an interesting court decision several years ago.[60] A normal retail or manufacturing company often sells goods on what might be called a modified or simulated installment basis. Perhaps a prime example is in the retail department store trade where most department stores have several types of accounts, a 30-day charge account, a revolving credit account, and a regular traditional installment account that covers a period of 24 or 36 months. It is clear that the traditional 24-to-36-month account would generally qualify for the installment basis. It is equally clear that the 30-day charge account would not qualify, since only one payment is involved. However, in the revolving credit account category recent regulations have indicated that this type of account can qualify in many instances for the installment basis.[61] These regulations, in general, opened up to the retail trade and to many other businesses the possibility of claiming the installment basis on the regular sale of merchandise to their customers.

Take the example of a typical manufacturer whose goods are sold to customers on credit. The terms of the agreement with the customer may indicate that payment is to be remitted within 30 days, but traditionally payments often lag to 35, 40, and even 45 days, especially in times of tight money. A recognition by the manufacturer that he is going to be granting credit over an extended period of time could trigger the possibility of switching to the installment basis. For example, if the manufacturer were to contact his customers and indicate that under a new arrangement they would be required to place 5 per cent down at the time of ordering, with the balance due in 40 days, this type of a contract would generally qualify for the installment basis. Regardless of the tax consequences of the transaction, it must make good business sense to contact one's customers on this basis. In addition, one must project in advance whether this slight change in the cash flow will have any effect on the ability of the corporation to meet its obligations as they mature.

If the above program or some reasonable variation can be worked out, the manufacturer will obtain a distinct tax advantage in that the tax on the gross profit, which is included in the manufacturer's accounts receivable at the end of his fiscal year, will not be payable currently but will be deferred until such time as the accounts receivable are collected. The manufacturer or "dealer" in property who is selling on the installment basis is not required to meet the "30 per cent rule" in qualifying for the installment basis.[62]

A switch from the accrual basis to the installment basis is not a "change of accounting method" under the Internal Revenue Code. However, there are provisions in the Code which effectively tax part of the profits of the corporation twice in the conversion from the accrual to the installment basis.[63] This apparent inequity arises in the last year in which the taxpayer reports on the accrual basis, since all sales constitute taxable income even though they are represented by an account receivable. The collection of these receivables in the subsequent year, the first year in which the taxpayer is on the installment basis (which is essentially a cash basis), requires the inclusion in taxable income of these amounts a second time. The Regulations do provide, however, a partial offset to this double taxation and generally only about 15 per cent of the taxpayer's income will be doubly included.

It is possible, however, to avoid the double tax completely. If a corporation sells all its existing installment accounts receivable on the last day of its fiscal year (its last accrual year) prior to converting to the installment basis, it would recognize both the accrual profit and the cash profit in the same year. Thus, it would start off the new installment basis year without any installment accounts on its books. This technique has been used many times and there is ample precedent for its use. However, an advance ruling should be obtained from the Treasury Department to assure that the sale of the accounts receivable at year-end constitutes a "sale" for tax purposes and not a secured loan. If the Treasury considers the sale to be a secured loan, then the opportunity to avoid the double tax is defeated, since the receivables would remain the property of the taxpayer and the funds received would only be in the form of a loan rather than sale proceeds.

It is worthy of repetition that if an accrual basis taxpayer can convert to the installment basis, he will be able to defer for tax purposes the entire gross profit in his year-end installment accounts receivable balance. If the business of the taxpayer continues to expand and the accounts receivable continue to grow with it, obviously the total amount of tax deferred will also continue to rise. So long as the company's volume of business increases or remains relatively constant, the deferral, in effect, becomes permanent. Thus, in this particular instance one may regard this as a permanent loan from the government without any annual interest cost. The only time at which this "permanent loan" would be repaid (and still without interest) is when the volume of accounts receivable declines or the company goes out of business and liquidates.

There is one other instance, however, that could cause the acceleration of the deferred tax. If the receivables are sold to a third party at any time subsequent to converting to the installment basis, the profit on those receivables would immediately be accelerated into taxable income.[64] It is possible, on the other hand, to pledge these receivables as security for a loan without accelerating the previously deferred tax.

Conclusion

It should be abundantly clear that opportunities for tax savings exist in any type of business through the consideration and election of the proper alternatives and the maximum use of available tax incentives. There is no substitute for advance planning. A reasonable prediction of the future path of the company is most important in any type of tax program. The better the tax planning, the higher the profitability of the company and the easier the realization of the entrepreneur's dream.

Part VI

THE GOVERNMENT'S ROLE IN SMALL BUSINESS FINANCE

14

The Economic Role of SBIC's

Donald H. Woods

Information regarding Small Business Investment Corporations is difficult to obtain. The only comprehensive industry survey,
taking into account both operating statistics and management attitudes
was conducted in 1963 by the author with the cooperation of the Small
Business Committee of the House of Representatives and the *Harvard
Business Review*. Since then the industry has not changed significantly
in terms of total capital, number of firms, or operating performance.

This chapter, building on the 1963 *Harvard Business Review* study,
"Are SBIC's Doing Their Job?", will focus primarily on the analytical
aspects of the economic and operational role of SBIC's as financial
risk-capital intermediaries. The implications of government leverage
incentives for actual financial behavior, as well as the interplay between prevailing interest rates and uncertainty, will be described.

Theoretical Economic Role

SMALL BUSINESS CAPITAL GAP

Is there really a small business capital gap? Two authoritative studies have been made on this topic. The first, conducted in England by a British Parliamentary committee under the chairmanship of Harold Macmillan, concluded that there was a shortage in the flow of long-term capital to small businesses that had surpassed the original founders' resources but were not large enough to attempt public ownership through a public offering of their securities. Subsequently, the economic factors underlying identification of the "Macmillan Gap" in England also were found to exist in the United States. The second study, conducted in 1957 by the Federal Reserve Board under Chairman William McChesney Martin, concluded that a gap exists in the structure of financial institutions which impedes the flow of long-term debt and equity capital to small businesses. The Federal Reserve Board estimated the gap at $500 million annually. This crucial financial estimate became both motivation and justification for Congressional approval of the Small Business Investment Act of 1958.

Improving the comprehensiveness and foundations of the capital gap estimate would be an excellent topic for future research on the availability of long-term capital to small businesses. Future emphasis also should be placed on examining the influence of uncertainty on capital shortages. Financial innovations for reducing those uncertainties which encourage overly conservative behavior on the part of lenders should be suggested and evaluated.

THE RISK RATIONALE OF SBIC's

How can SBIC's fill the small business capital gap? Other things being equal, investors are reluctant to invest in small businesses because it usually involves a small probability of a large gain rather than a large probability of a small gain. This is the essential risk character of small business investment. Unfortunately, most potential investors require a more conservative balance of risk and return than small business opportunities can provide.

Theoretically, capital allocations should be guided by expected rates of return with appropriate discounting for risk. The SBIC form of organization can reduce risk discounts by:

1. Improving information flows regarding available opportunities and relevant uncertainties.
2. Reducing search, selection, and control costs through economies of scale.
3. Minimizing risk by portfolio diversification techniques.

Let me elaborate further on these points. As financial intermediaries, SBIC's provide the classic economic advantages of task specialization and financial diversification. If resources are organized around the single task of generating and ranking small business investment opportunities, then development of expert judgment, accurate information flows regarding investment opportunities, and economies of scale would be theoretically possible. Thus, if the investment manager is able to focus primarily on small business opportunities, especially those near a public offering, he should be able to accumulate a large inventory of accurate investment information and develop a high degree of decision-making expertise.

These advantages will be especially apparent if the SBIC limits its specialization to a few key industries. The investment manager's assessments of risk and return certainly would be considered more accurate than those of a comparable investment banker, whose mental processes have to span both large and small businesses as well as considering both public and prepublic opportunities. As the reputation and public image of the SBIC grows, the time and expenses allocated to searching for opportunities should decline. Eventually, substantial investment information should flow automatically to SBIC's. Of course, one must note that a local venture capitalist could achieve the same outcome, but he would be without benefit of national publicity and strategic financial incentives.

Portfolio diversification is another primary economic advantage of financial intermediaries. As the SBIC grows in size, it will be more willing to assume risk; that is, the risk premiums required to justify a specific investment should decline. This result occurs because (1) the relative size of each new investment decreases as total assets increase, thereby diminishing the threat to over-all profitability of an unfavorable investment, and (2) the probability that any single adverse economic event will produce bankruptcy is reduced if portfolio investments are diversified along offsetting industry and geographical dimensions. Consequently, the over-all risk of investing in small businesses will decline for the SBIC as it grows in size and diversifies its portfolio.

An important financial advantage is produced by portfolio diversification. Since the expected over-all rate of return can be achieved with less uncertainty, the SBIC should be able to increase total profits by adding more debt capital. Thus, growth and diversification produce the potential for increased leverage which, in turn, provides the financing for even more growth and diversification.

Federally Financed Leverage: Potential and Constraints

POTENTIAL

The minimum equity financing permitted by the government for an SBIC is $300,000. Between an equity capital range of $300,000 to $700,000 an SBIC can obtain two-to-one leverage in two stages. First, after approximately 80 per cent of the original equity pool has been depleted, new funds can be obtained under Section 302 of the Small Business Investment Act. These SBA funds are 5 per cent, 20-year, subordinated debentures and can be obtained in an amount equal to the equity investment up to $700,000. The matching debt funds then become part of the SBIC's capital and surplus. After these funds are 75 per cent committed, additional debt capital can be borrowed from the SBA under Section 303 at 5.5 per cent interest for 15 years. These funds can be borrowed in an amount up to 50 per cent of capital and surplus. Thus, an SBIC starting with $700,000 in equity financing can invest a total of $2,100,000 by utilizing $1,400,000 in Federal loans, for a debt to equity ratio of two to one. The maximum amount that can be borrowed under Section 303 is $4,000,000, and for this, an equity base of $7,300,000, not including 302 funds, would be required. Thus, debt capacity, as measured by Federal financing potential actually decreases as equity increases. This apparent conflict with accepted principles of financial and economic theory will be demonstrated geometrically in the following analysis.

CONSTRAINTS

If these complicated legislative lending rules are reduced to a simple mathematical model, the behavior of Federally financed leverage as a function of equity capital can be traced. The model is shown graphically in Figure 14-1. Leverage, defined as the ratio of debt to equity, is a constant at 3.0 for equity financing in the $300,000 to $700,000 range, as shown by line *AB* on the graph. The 2.0 ratio indicates that two dollars of Federally financed debt can be obtained for every dollar of equity capital invested. Beyond $700,000 the debt ratio falls sharply as the total amount of equity increases, passing the 1.0 level at an equity investment of $2,100,000, as indicated by point *C* on the graph. At this point the leverage ratio has declined by 50 per cent even though equity funds have increased by 200 per cent. Logically, this implies a shift to a more conservative policy toward risk taking as SBIC's grow in size. At point *D*, the curve terminates with a leverage ratio of 0.64 because $4,700,000 is the maximum amount of Federal borrowing permitted under the present legislation. Of course, if private debt funds were added, the curve could assume an infinite variety of shapes that would be dependent on the preferences of private lenders.

Since Federal funds are the primary source of leverage for this industry, there is a definite incentive to stagnate and stay small. These incentives are contrary to classic economic logic, which implies that increased return and lower risk are the natural results of economies of scale and portfolio diversification. This incentive structure certainly is the reverse of what would be found in freely competitive capital markets.

Traditionally, the debt capacity of corporations and financial institutions increases proportionately as they grow and mature. As the SBIC program stands now, there is actually an incentive to start several small SBIC's simultaneously to exploit the leverage potential. Subsequently, these small units could be merged into a larger one with higher total leverage than an SBIC of comparable size that had grown by generating equity capital internally in combination with maximum utilization of federal leverage.

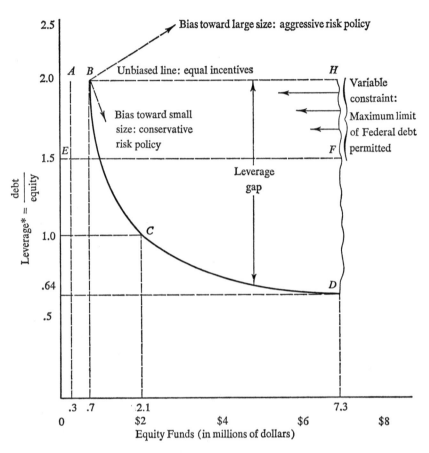

$$\text{*Federal leverage potential} = \begin{cases} 2.0, \text{ if } 0.3 \leq E \leq 0.7 \\ 0.5 + \dfrac{1.05}{E}, \text{ if } 0.7 \leq E \leq 7.3 \end{cases}$$

Figure 14-1—Federally Financed Leverage Potential

The Leverage Gap

Drawing on the previous theory, it seems logical to expect the Government to minimize the risk of exposure of Government funds. Then the question should be asked: Is it better to distribute $100 million in Federal funds to small businesses by utilizing fifty financial intermediaries, with the corresponding compounding of administrative and monitoring costs, or is it preferable to concentrate on five large experienced units that have proven themselves and can be more easily controlled? If we look at other financial intermediaries, such as banks and insurance companies, it is apparent that optimum balances between risk and return are strongly related to size. Thus, for the mutual benefit of all concerned, there should be no incentive to keep the intermediary itself small just because it is in the business of making loans to small businesses. In fact, if the program is going to enter the second growth stage in its development, where it can "cash in" on past accumulated experience and expertise, for which a heavy price was paid, incentives have to be provided for successful SBIC's to grow larger.

Analytically, minimizing the bias regarding size would mean an upward shifting of the leverage line to a more nearly horizontal position as indicated in the exhibit. The area bounded by the horizontal and curvilinear line is referred to as the "leverage gap." The right boundary of the area (constraint HD) would be determined by whatever maximum limits Congress places on the absolute amount of Government funds a single SBIC can borrow. The horizontal line beginning at point A is unbiased relative to size because Federal leverage potential remains constant as additional equity capital is raised. Thus, legislative action to minimize the bias toward small size also would succeed in closing the leverage gap.

Many variations on this theme are possible. For example, the administration may prefer to lower the leverage ratio to a constant 1.5, as shown by line EF. This policy also would close the leverage gap and help to minimize bias. In addition, it would require the inexperienced and risky minimum capital SBIC's to provide more of an equity hedge against unprofitable investments. Since most of the failures occur in the smaller SBICs, this strategy would minimize the risk of government funds while simultaneously increasing the potential for more total leverage financing of the industry itself. The final judgment on the optimal leverage policy should be made by the SBA administrators, who are better able to assess the uncertainties and have to assume ultimate responsibility for program performance.

Interest Rates Under Uncertainty

Interest rates for long-term capital in competitive markets vary with investment risk. According to SBA rules, interest rates paid by SBIC's for long-term debt capital under the Small Business Investment Act are independent of both prevailing market conditions and the risk of default. A former Administrator of the SBIC program has estimated that the government probably will incur losses of approximately $18 million on $300 million in Government funds outstanding. This loss, if it should materialize, represents 6 per cent of the current level of Federal investment. Since the loss estimate is cumulative, the potential default ratio would be much higher because the $300 million was loaned out over a period of approximately six years. Consequently, if we assume linearity in the rate of capital outflow and a normal repayment schedule, then the denominator of the ratio should be $150 million, and this produces a possible loss rate of 12 per cent, or an average of 2 per cent per year over the six-year period.

Under the assumption that the long-term interest rate for riskless capital is 4 per cent, the industry should be charged a 2 per cent risk premium over the riskless rate to compensate for its potential default experience. Thus, the lender should obtain 6 per cent on its money. Of course, these rough calculations assume that historical experience is a valid predictor of future outcomes, and it may be that, in the judgment of the key administrators, the underlying structure of the industry has changed to a less risky position.

From the viewpoint of economic theory, consideration also should be given to multiple interest rates. That is, it seems unreasonable, except for administrative advantages, to charge the large, successful SBIC's the same rate as the small, inexperienced, and highly levered ones. In fact, a higher interest rate for the small equity SBIC's would tend to shift the incentive away from the inexpensive government money to skillful investment techniques and financial sophistication.

This would automatically deter many potentially unstable elements from entering the program at a level where they are too small to be monitored adequately by the relevant agencies.

One alternative would be for Congress to grant *max-min* interest rate authority to the SBA administrator. He then would be able to adjust interest rates according to risk in individual SBIC financing situations and according to prevailing market rates in general.

Implications of Investment Lags for SBIC Stock Repurchases

Venture capital investing, aside from being risky and expensive, is a time-consuming process. Even more time is required for the portfolio to mature and "roll over" after the search, evaluation, and initial investment phases are complete. Investors must be patient and SBIC managers skillful in utilizing uncommitted liquid funds in transitional short-term opportunities. Investors should expect to wait at least five years before the SBIC's initial financing is fully invested. Thus, almost unwittingly, SBIC's can play a unique role in small business financing, for are likely to have a large supply of liquid funds and unused debt capacity when the equity markets (and the money markets, in the case of the real estate and term lending segments of the portfolio) are the least favorable for the small businessman. That is, SBIC's are likely to have liquid investment funds when nobody else does. Given the cyclical and capricious nature of the capital markets, especially the over-the-counter segment, SBICs are bound to be confronted with more and higher quality opportunities when these markets are unfavorable and the cost of small business equity is high, both in terms of the discount public investors apply to future earning streams and investment banking costs.

Since SBIC managers are strongly motivated to invest funds as quickly as possible, they often become frustrated when they find that venture capital investing is a very time-consuming process that involves many rejected opportunities and unpredicted events. At this point, management often considers mergers and stock repurchases. Mergers, of course, will aid in building a strong industry if stable and reasonable exchange prices can be agreed upon. (The *Harvard Busi-*

ness Review mentioned earlier demonstrated that the SBIC's propensity to merger is a U-shaped function of liquidity.) Those who are most actively considering this action are either highly liquid or fully invested. But a word of caution should be directed at those liquid SBIC's who may be considering common stock repurchase, especially during a down turn in the equity markets. The appropriate financial decision guide is to repurchase stock, balanced by an appropriate amount of debt retirement, if the cost of capital exceeds the expected rate of return. With SBIC's the problem of forecasting future rates of return is fraught with uncertainty. SBIC's often have to wait with liquid funds for three, four, or five years before enough appropriate investment opportunities are identified and the deals actually consummated. This waiting could produce the undesirable side effect of leading unsuspecting managers to overdiscount future potential. This pessimistic bias would increase attractiveness of immediate stock repurchase as a way of dispensing idle cash and quelling stockholder disenchantment. It takes cool objectivity to make a repurchase decision under current conditions, and the SBIC usually is acting inefficiently when it does repurchase. An exception of course would be for survival purposes when "raiders" are actively buying up stock in the market place.

Conclusions

For the mutual benefit of Government, the SBIC industry, and small business borrowers, SBIC's should be encouraged to operate as strong banking intermediaries specializing in small business financing. At present their historical image as small, quasi-public venture capital sources acts as a brake on their growth and development.

More research is needed on conceptualizing the SBIC as a mechanism for reducing uncertainty between lenders and borrowers. This represents more of a subjective approach than has been taken in the past. The uncertainty aspects of the capital markets are more relevant than is trying to measure precisely the "$500 million small business capital gap." For example, a range of estimates under varying conditions of uncertainty would be more useful for policy decisions by administrators and legislators than a single number estimate.

Growing SBIC's should be allowed the same leverage benefits as the smaller ones. The leverage incentives provided by current laws are exactly the opposite of those suggested by economic theory. The biases which these constraints imply for growth should be reduced. It is senseless to finance a multitude of small and relatively ineffective SBIC's when the alternative is a reasonable number of large, efficient units. It is illogical to expect SBIC's themselves to be small just because their investment opportunities are in the small business area. In fact, more service can be provided for the small businessman if his banking intermediaries can afford a staff of experts who are specialists in his problems.

Interest rates more consistent with the underlying uncertainty of venture capital investing should be charged for federal financing. A system of realistic risk premiums would have the effect of placing more emphasis on monetary payoffs and less on security: It also would minimize the undesirable side effects caused by the availability of inexpensive Government money. Finally, thought should be given to utilizing multiple interest rates, with lower rates for successful SBIC's with high proportions of equity financing. This need for flexibility might be implemented by granting *max-min* interest rate decision-making authority to the SBA administrator.

15

Small Business Loans from Government Sources

Bernard L. Boutin

The small business community plays an important, indeed vital, role in our national economy. Small businesses by and large are at least as efficient and productive, as imaginative and innovative, as larger enterprises. The small business share of total economic activity has been remarkably stable over many decades.

Why, then, one may ask, is there a need for the Small Business Administration? If small business is holding its own, why did the Congress establish a special advocate for small business in the counsels of Government and special financial and management assistance programs? The basic reason for the existence of the SBA is a widespread recognition that the achievements of small business have been accomplished in the face of heavy odds. There are in the economy many instances of industrial market power, of biases against the financing of small business growth, which operate to reduce the flow of capital into the small business sector below levels that one should logically expect.

Objectives of the SBA

A diverse set of financial institutions exists to serve small as well as large business, running the gamut from commercial banks through mutual banks, savings and loan associations, finance and factoring houses, insurance companies, and investment banks. By far the largest share of small business financing is carried out through such institutions; however, with all this rich variety, the financial needs of the small business are still not adequately covered.

When the SBA commenced its regular business lending program late in 1953, the provision of long-term, fully amortized loans to small businessmen was rare. Thousands of small businessmen with sound collateral and good prospects in need of middle- and long-term financing had to substitute either very short-term financing, high-cost factoring or go without. Too small to float public issues, these firms found, furthermore, a dearth of medium- and long-term credit facilities available to them. Thus, despite the diversity of financial institutions and intermediaries available to American business in general, small business was confronted by a grave shortage of long-term credit, even on a fully secured basis, and an almost complete absence of any organized source of equity capital. Among other things, it was to remedy these discrepancies or gaps in the provision of long-term credit and capital that SBA was created. It was established to provide new avenues of diversified financing for small business, both as a supplement to existing private institutions and as a means of inducing private financing institutions to diversify so as to replace Government credit for small business with private resources.

SBA's fundamental aim is to do its job so effectively and so productively that private financial institutions will move in to occupy the territory pioneered by the SBA. There is no desire either to waste money or to provide unnecessary competition with private institutions. In the future, an increasing share of the financing needs of small business will be shifted to private institutions.

In its regular business lending activities, SBA tends to approach its task in much the same manner as any commercial banker. SBA provides term loans to small businesses for up to ten years where there is need, adequate collateral, and a reasonable chance of repayment through earnings. This is a reasonably low-risk program. Loss rates to date are modest and suggest that this program is run in a very businesslike manner.

However, the financing gaps confronting small business encompass many more dimensions than can be reached by a low-risk, well-collateralized lending program. From the point of view of the economics of the allocation of capital among areas, industries, and firms, it is the rate of return net of risk which should guide the flow of capital. Some may hasten to argue that the financing of risk is the peculiar and specific purpose of equity markets. For large undertakings, this is surely true. But, taking into account the very high cost of floating an issue even as large as a million dollars, it is not appropriate to deny credit to firms where the estimated risk falls in the 2 to 5 per cent area and the total financial requirement is less than say $100,000 to $200,000.

Scope of the SBA

SBA operates its programs through a network of 81 field offices, covering all states plus Puerto Rico, Guam, and the Virgin Islands. In fiscal 1965, SBA had 3,619 employees and it obligated funds totalling $535.5 million. In fiscal 1967, it is anticipated that SBA will employ over 4,300 people with its annual obligations near $621 million.

SBA has $1.414 billion at loan. There are about 83,000 loans outstanding, but this is not a clear picture because half of those loans are disaster loans, and about two-thirds of the disaster loans are for private residences and apartment houses rather than just for small businesses.

SBA is big enough to have a significant impact in the financing of small business, even though a half-billion dollars or so a year can meet only a very small percentage of small business financing needs.

There are three major gaps in the financing of small business: (1) long-term, low-risk, fully collateralized credit; (2) credit where risk is significant but minor; and (3) equity capital in amounts relatively small as compared with typical public flotations.

SBA has moved rather effectively in providing low-risk, long-term credit and has gone a long way in providing credit where risk, while significant, is minor (averaging perhaps less than 6 per cent) through the Small Business Investment Company program. This mechanism also provides a modicum of genuine equity financing but may be only scratching the surface of existing needs. Thus, although SBA programs have added to the diversity of financial institutions and have filled some gaps, it is clear that its programs have a long way to go in meeting the total need.

SBA and the Commercial Banks

At the present time, approximately 58 per cent of all SBA business loans are made through its bank participation program. In this program, the banks participate in extending credit to small business, sharing the risks involved. Under its terms, the bank may charge its own interest rate for its share of the loan, up to a maximum of 8 per cent. Where the bank's share of the loan is 25 per cent or greater, SBA will pay the bank 0.5 per cent on its own share for servicing the loan. This has been a very successful program. Many thousands of banks have participated with SBA. Its benefits are evident: It establishes and maintains a close banking relationship for the borrower; it gives the commercial bank experience in making term loans to small business; and it is a significant and productive form of Government-business collaboration.

SBA also has a guaranteed loan program under which a bank may charge up to 8 per cent on a small business loan of which up to 90 per cent may be guaranteed by SBA. For this guarantee, the bank pays SBA 0.5 per cent. In former years, this program was a very small one but has had vastly increased use in the last year and a half. The reason this program has been so small in comparison with the participation program is that the earnings to the bank tend to be lower in the guarantee program than in the participation situation, while risk levels appear to be comparable. From many points of view, however, it appears desirable to increase the relative importance of the guaranteed loan program. SBA is developing new approaches that will bring this about.

At the present time SBA is engaged in a joint study with the American Bankers Association which is designed to shed light on the degree to which SBA borrowers might have been or could have been adequately financed by commercial banks. The study will explore ways and means by which SBA might induce private banks to experiment further in meeting the long-term credit need of small business.

Through the joint efforts of SBA, the American Bankers Association, and the Association of Independent Bankers a completely new concept of guaranteed loans is being developed; it is being explored with the Bank of America at the present time to measure its productivity and acceptability. The Bank of America is using the program through roughly 50 per cent of its branches, and they are optimistic that this is going to be very successful. In this experiment, the bank does all of the processing as they would on one of their own loans. All that comes to SBA is a single fact sheet, one page, that is processed within 48 hours. SBA also guarantees the bank complete liquidity. If the loan goes into default, within a very few days, as specified in the agreement, SBA has to pick up its portion of that loan, 90 per cent. Later, SBA makes a determination of either trying to save, or reorient, the loan or else liquidate it.

Ideally, all or most of the long-term credit needs of small business will or should in the future be provided by the banks and other private institutions, with increased use of SBA guarantees. SBA can then turn the major part of its efforts to dealing with the gaps in the supply of venture capital and to special problems such as those associated with minority opportunity and stagnant areas in the economy.

The SBIC Program

The Small Business Investment Corporation has been the subject of controversy. There were a number of weaknesses in the program which needed correction.

A study of the 1958 Act shows the clear intent of the Congress that the emphasis should be on equity or equity-type loans rather than the long-term loans under Section 305. However, only 15 per cent of the roughly one billion dollars available from Government and private funds have been of a pure equity variety. The balance has been equity type and it has had every variation that one can imagine, with about 50 per cent, or a little bit better, in long- and short-term loans. The licensing standards were so nebulous and weak that many people got into the program who had no business in it. These are shortcomings, but it is perhaps more important to consider the SBIC program in terms of the positive assistance it has given to small business.

The bank-affiliated SBICs by and large have done a very good job. Many of the public companies have been very successful, although a few of them have had problems. By comparison with the privately owned, closely held companies, the bank affiliated and the publicly held companies have provided the major successes that we have been able to identify. Many small SBIC's have been unsuccessful. They have abused SBA regulations and the rights and privileges granted by the license.

As of today, not one penny of the nearly $300 million of Government money made available has been written off. This does not mean that the program has been without losses. It means that the SBA has not been in sufficient control to make a judgment whether a loan was good or not, whether a company was viable or was in or on the verge of bankruptcy. That has been changed. Many things are being done about it.

Licensing standards have been tightened up so that SBA can be assured that any company in the program is going to have a capable manager. The breakdown in management capability has accounted for many failures in the program. SBA is reviewing every one of these companies and every one of the principal owners. In one instance almost a hundred cross-deals were made; this will not be permitted to recur. Here was a group of men meeting around a table and scratching each other's back: I loan to your company, you loan to mine, then set up a dummy company and recoup, by a loan to that company, the amount of money originally put into the SBIC. Unfortunately, through the publicity that occurred the good companies were hurt, their public image was damaged because of some of the "mugs" who got into the program. This does not mean the program is bad; but it does indicate the need to tighten it up.

SBA examined virtually all 682 of these companies during the past year. The inactive companies, the little companies which have been making short-term loans and are merely personal finance companies, the companies that have used their money not to provide equity capital but to buy out and become operators of firms, are going to be taken out of the program. New legislation will strengthen the hand of SBA in carrying out this function. Annual examinations will give the continuity of information necessary to the administration of the program.

In addition, SBA will insist on the provision of periodic reports audited by independent accountants. When all of this is accomplished SBIC will probably end up with about 250 companies, mostly publicly owned and many of them bank owned or affiliated.

A company with a private capital of $300,000, even with the $600,000 from SBA, can hardly be successful in the long run unless it is going to concentrate on loans, and that is not the primary purpose of the SBIC. The base has to be larger, and SBA has to look to larger companies, much larger companies, who can afford competent management. New business ties, in addition to bank affiliations, must be found so that topnotch management can be provided without the urgent pressure of immediate income from loans. SBA tells a company that they have to make money and provide good management, yet, they must be patient with equity-type financing which is very long term. One set of demands contradicts the other. SBA has got to broaden the base of Section 302 money.

Some of the companies have done an outstanding job. In Boston, one can travel Route 128 and see many companies that have developed through the activities of SBIC's. Chicago has a great many success stories, and there are many in Los Angeles. This program can be made to work and work very well. The SBA intends to develop new legislation that will provide incentives for the efficient companies so that they will stay in the program and, in fact, expand. In the meantime, SBA is eliminating those companies which are hurtful of those who are trying to fulfill the requirements of the law. Also under examination are our regulations to minimize the number of reports required, the paper shuffling, the built-in costs that are punitive to good companies. Once the bad companies are eliminated, there is no reason why SBA cannot cut down substantially on the number of regulations that inhibit the good companies from doing a full-scale job.

Economic Assistance Programs

Other than the "equity gap," there are three special financing problems of small business in our society that require a helping hand from the Federal Government. One is the great need for minority and other disadvantaged groups and individuals to enter into the mainstream of American society. Another set of problems is the economic dislocation caused by urban renewal and highway construction. And, finally, there are the baffling problems of economic development of many depressed counties and communities throughout our land.

Economic Opportunity Loan Program

Title IV of the Economic Opportunity Act of 1964, provides for an assistance program aimed specifically at the disadvantaged. To do the job, SBA has devised a two-part Economic Opportunity Loan program known as EOL (I) and EOL (II).

EOL (I)

Loans of up to $15,000 are available to businessmen and prospective businessmen whose efforts to date have afforded them only a marginal economic existence. Emphasis is placed on existing businesses, but where there is a promising projection and management appears capable, loans will be made to establish new businesses. Special consideration is given to loans that will afford disadvantaged persons, including minority group members, business opportunities traditionally not available to them.

EOL (II)

Loans of up to $25,000 are available to businessmen and prospective businessmen who (1) do not qualify for financial assistance from any other source, including EOL (I) and SBA's regular business loan program, and (2) have suffered from lack of opportunity and thereby have been denied the chance to compete in business on equal terms. As in the case of EOL (I), emphasis is placed on assisting minority group members and other disadvantaged persons. EOL (II) applicants are expected to have a strong management capability. Emphasis is given to those loans to the following:

1. Businesses engaged in manufacturing, research and development, wholesaling, and distribution.

2. Businesses offering opportunities for substantial growth.

3. Firms that strengthen the economy of low-income areas by providing needed services or products.

4. Businesses that employ the unemployed, unskilled, and/or the underemployed, especially when these offer employees the opportunity to upgrade their skills.

EOL (I) and EOL (II) loans can be made for terms of up to 15 years. The interest rate is 5½ per cent, except in EDA-designated communities where it is 4% per cent.

Traditional credit requirements are relaxed for Economic Opportunity Loan applicants and maximum consideration is given to the individual's character, management ability, and other factors which indicate whether there is reasonable assurance that the loan will be repaid.

Management assistance is a vital part of this program. Virtually all Economic Opportunity Loan applicants are in need of management counseling and SBA provides this through its personnel, members of SCORE, and other volunteers from the business and professional community.

In fiscal 1966, the SBA set aside $28 million for people in the low-income areas who fall within the definition of poverty. The agency made only 1,651 loans totaling $17.7 million. During that period the program was limited to low-income persons living in 50 communities. Fifty million dollars is available for EOL (I) and EOL (II) in fiscal 1967, and loans are being made in every one of the 50 states and in SBA offices in the District of Columbia, Guam, the Virgin Islands, and Puerto Rico.

No depressed community in this country will be deprived of this program because it is unaware of its existence or does not know where to find SBA. This is often the case in trying to reach low-income groups and ghetto populations. The directors of our 73 regional and branch offices are working closely with community action agencies, small business development centers, and other organizations representative of the individuals we are assisting. These agencies are helping to bring word of the program to the low-income and disadvantaged communities. SBA loan specialists are setting up shop in the heart of depressed neighborhoods for the purpose of interviewing and assisting loan applicants and seeking out those businesses which provide the greatest stimulus to those neighborhoods.

Successful businessmen are being recruited to provide counseling and training for loan applicants and recipients, and to help them find their way into the economic mainstream.

Local Development Company Programs

Vast shifts in population have changed the economic face of many counties and communities. Too many communities, even in these times of high prosperity, are retrogressing and decaying. The Local Development Company program, or the 502 Program, is designed by SBA to meet this problem head-on. Not merely a lending program, it is an economic development program designed specifically to utilize the growth potential of small firms. The program works exclusively through a community development corporation—local citizens interested in improving the local economy. Community interest, not private gain, is its motivating force. Local citizens put up their own dollars and, as a corporation, assume full liability for any project they sponsor.

Under Section 502 of the Small Business Investment Act of 1958, the SBA may make loans for plant construction, conversion, or expansion, including the acquisition of land, to state and local development companies. These loans may be made either directly or in cooperation with banks or other lending institutions. Loans up to $350,000 for each individual small business may be made under this program.

In fiscal 1966, some 312 local development loans totaling over $50 million were made. This was a record volume. The program will be accelerated in the years ahead, and SBA is currently examining ways to make it even more suitable for the economic development of local communities.

Procurement Assistance Program

One of the key provisions of the Small Business Act is concerned with procurement assistance: "It is the declared policy of the Congress that the Government should aid, counsel, assist, and protect, insofar as it is possible, the interests of small business concerns in order to preserve free competitive enterprise, to insure that a fair proportion of the total purchases and contracts or subcontracts . . . be placed with small business enterprises."

Under the mandate to carry out this program, approximately 20 per cent of the total prime contracts of $26.1 billion awarded by the Department of Defense in fiscal 1965 were awarded to small business. Similarly, 46.4 per cent of the total awards of the civilian agencies of 2.8 billion in fiscal 1965 went to small business. This figure is exclusive of the Atomic Energy Commission and NASA.

SBA is searching for ways to improve this program. The key to its approach lies in a phrase from the Act—"to preserve free competitive enterprise." This is the fundamental purpose of SBA—to help preserve, maintain, and further competition in the American economy.

SCORE Program

SBA is enlarging the SCORE Program, the Service Corps of Retired Executives. There are 164 chapters of SCORE and 2,724 volunteers. SBA is going to be expanding that to roughly the 5,000 level over the next 24 months, and will endeavor to improve the matching up of the type of business with the experience of the volunteer available, thus providing the best information that is available, and from a person who has had a history of success in a business at least reasonably closely identified with the small business that SBA is servicing.

Also, it will cut down substantially on the need for additional SBA personnel.

SCORE is limited to those firms who are incapable of financing a private consultant. This is a completely noncompetitive program. SBA will not go in where it feels that a firm should go to a private consulting firm. The program is confined to businesses of under 50 employees. Much of the growth here will be in the so-called Title IV Program—the very small businessman, many of them in the ghetto areas or rural poverty areas of the country. This program cannot possibly be conducted by running a night school; it is going to take very frequent counseling. As soon as they believe the firm is capable of obtaining help privately, SCORE volunteers must recommend that this be done. SCORE operates on a no-cost basis.

The caseload per volunteer averages about ten on a nation-wide basis. Those who have very few are being weeded out to make this a more productive program. During the last 12 months SBA has handled about 30,000 cases. Some have involved a single visit, others have required a great number of visits.

Information Systems and the Data Bank

At present SBA cannot assess the rate of return or, to put it more broadly, the payoff of its lending programs in terms of their impact on the performance of its borrowers. There is no simple measure of such a rate. Even if a performance index of this nature can be developed, prediction of the probable payoffs from borrower to borrower will not be easy. A great deal of analysis and research work must be done to develop a system for setting loan priorities and criteria. It is equally apparent that, if SBA is successful in developing such norms, formidable information requirements will have to be met.

The SBA is engaged in an operation to generate and organize the information capabilities needed to carry out this difficult task. A data bank is being developed which is capable of sorting and providing access to comprehensive economic and financial statistics on all borrowers. At the same time, the machinery for collecting, verifying, transmitting and storing this information is being overhauled for rapid access and analysis.

In constructing its information system and data bank, SBA is going beyond its own program and management statistics and is bringing into its system other data of relevance to the study of economic and financial conditions. This will be a tool of major significance for research and analysis in the general area of business performance and financing—a tool of use both to the SBA and other Government agencies, as well as to researchers in universities and private business.

The Future of the SBA

SBA has had a rather stormy history. It has been an "on-again, off-again" program because of the funding mechanisms that were available. Recent Congressional action has changed this picture substantially.

First, SBA now has two separate revolving funds—one for disaster loans, and one for business loans of all types. No longer will there be an impact on our business lending programs caused by national disasters. Last year there were 49 declared disasters in the United States, and a total amount of lending of $197.2 million. The two revolving funds have no limitation except for loans outstanding. There is no limitation now on the disaster fund, and the only limitation on the business loan fund is because of the number of dollars in loans outstanding. SBA has a $1.4 billion level for the regular loan, the displaced business, and the EOL programs; $400 million for the Investment Division, the SBIC Program; and $200 million for the state and local development company program.

The SBA, too, has been helped substantially by the participation sales authority granted by Congress. No more does the program have to depend solely upon appropriations. In June 1966, as an example, the SBA sold $350 million in business loans, so that it was able to recoup the funds to keep its program going. SBA is presently authorized for a level of $850 million of sales. Its programs are now well financed and the future, so far as continuity is concerned looks very bright. SBA does not foresee the possibility of having to go into the kind of moratoria that have been damaging to the public image of the agency and destructive of its relationships with the banks.

Until very recently, SBA was a passive agency. People had to seek out SBA. The agency had some so-called "circuit-rider" activity where its loan officers were on the road, but it worked primarily through the vehicle of contact officers. Now, SBA staff members are directed to get out into the field to find borrowers who can benefit best from these programs and the small businessmen who most need management assistance.

The SBA is placing a major emphasis on developing an improved liaison with established banks. It recognizes the importance of having a close relationship between a banker and a small businessman. Hopefully, within the next three years, depending on the availability of money, at least 50 per cent of all SBA loans will be handled through banks, serviced by banks, and made on a guarantee basis. At least another 25 per cent of SBA loans will be participations, with the bank doing the servicing.

Since 1953 SBA has had only $26.1 million in losses. The income—the difference between the interest SBA charges and the interest it pays the Treasury for the money it borrows—has largely made up for this. Thus, outside of administrative costs this had been a very low cost program for the taxpayer.

SBA is taking a harder look at all of the size standards. Most of these were set in 1953, and much has happened to business and to the dollar since that time. SBA is reviewing norms. Some are being adjusted upward, some downward. The measure is being applied to particular industries as well as to whole classes. A new program has been prepared, in keeping with the statute, which provides that the administrator shall take such actions as he shall deem necessary to preserve and enhance competition. For procurement purposes only, new criteria for "smallness" have been set in industries where fewer firms are surviving and which are characterized by economic concentration. The first two were the tire and automobile industries.

SBA is concerned about the management of firms and is placing more emphasis on its evaluation of individual management's capability than on its collateral. The agency is concerned about the individual and his motivation, ability, and experience and is going out of its way to try to match up people with new inventions, new ideas, and new techniques, with those who have management ability. SBA is helping to put together new firms by this device.

The "Mom and Pop" grocery stores are a great tradition in

America—but that is not where we should concentrate our effort. The agency should have a major impact in terms of new job opportunities and new products, in terms of export expansion and export opportunities. The business loan program is budgeted at a level of $428 million for fiscal 1967. A $100 million is estimated for disaster purposes. In five years SBA will probably have a program of about $750 million a year, based on the number of new businesses being established. This anticipates a further growth in two particular areas. First, the Community Development Loan Program, where SBA provides up to 80 per cent of the money in communities of 50,000 and less. Twenty per cent comes from the injection of local capital. This program will probably double from a rate of $50 million to a rate of $100 million in five years. Second, the Displaced Business Loan Program, because of the increased use of urban renewal and the acceleration of the highway program, will double from $25 million to $50 million. There will also be substantial growth in the SBIC program if the forecast is correct, and there are some 200 to 300 solid companies with proper incentives. The 7(a) loan program is also expected to grow significantly.

SBA, until this year, has never had a long-range plan, nor a short-term planning system beyond the current fiscal year. It now has corrected this.

Congress has assigned a great many responsibilities to the agency. The following indicates part of the scope of SBA's mission:

Program	Mission
1. Business Loans (7(a))	". . . encourage and develop small business capacity and opportunity in order to preserve and expand the American system of free, competitive enterprise, thus promoting the national security and strengthening the over-all economy. In specific terms, the mission is two-fold: (1) to educate and encourage private lenders to narrow the credit gap that exists for small businesses because of financing biases which hamper adequate access to credit; and (2) to fill the remaining credit gap, within the circumscription of our resources, through extension of term credit with emphasis, in descending order of

Program	*Mission*
	priority (to comply with our legislation and minimize the involvement of federal funds) on loan guarantees, immediate participations and direct loans."
2. Disaster Loans —Physical Type	". . . provide financial assistance on favorable terms and as expeditiously as possible to victims of natural disasters for rehabilitation of property damaged or destroyed."
3. Displaced Business Loans	". . . re-establish small businesses which have been physically displaced by urban renewal or highway construction programs."
4. Economic Injury Disaster Loans	". . . provide relief from economic injury sustained by small business concerns as a result of disasters declared by the President or the Secretary of Agriculture for the areas in which such concerns are located."
5. Economic Opportunity Loans	". . . provide meaningful business opportunity to those among the culturally disadvantaged who have genuine entrepreneurial capability."
6. Loan Administration (Servicing)	". . . maximize intended assistance and improvement in borrowers' financial position and probability of success by counselling and enforcement of appropriate loan conditions with equitable consideration of borrowers' and Government's interest."
7. Loan Administration (Liquidation)	". . . maximize and expedite protection of Government's interest and recovery to revolving fund from loan security if borrower cannot or will not repay the loan according to its terms or in a reasonable period."
8. Loan Appraisal	". . . provide the Agency with expert valuation advice pertaining to collateral offered to secure an indebtedness or held by the Agency for liquidation purposes."

Program	*Mission*
9. Investment (Excluding Development Companies)	". . . stimulate and supplement the flow of private equity capital and long-term loan funds needed by small concerns for the sound financing of their operations, and for their growth, expansion and modernization. This is to be done by establishing, regulating, and making loans to a small business investment industry which will supply such funds to small concerns, while encouraging the maximum participation of private financing. The mission differs from that of the business loan program, in that SBICs are not arms of the Government, and this financing generally goes to less credit-worthy, higher-risk small concerns in a mix of equity, equity type securities, and straight loans."
10. The State Development Company (501)	". . . assist the growth of small business and private economic growth, through the vehicle of loans to state development companies."
11. The Local Development Company (502)	". . . promote the health and growth of the national economy by marshalling the efforts, thoughts, and dollars of the average citizen for the strengthening and improvement of his own local economy through assistance to small business. Implicit in the above statement is the opportunity that the community's assumption of responsibility provides for 'decision at the local level.' In this way economic development decisions are based on the public interest as well as profit."
12. Procurement and Management Assistance Program	". . . strengthen and foster the economic growth of small business concerns through the medium of additional Government prime and sub-contract opportunities; to stimulate greater competition through the introduction of more small firms to the national procurement system; to

Program	*Mission*
	assure that small firms receive an adequate share of Government surplus property and critical materials allocated from the national stockpile; and to strengthen the managerial skills of small business by providing face-to-face management counseling and group counseling and training.

This is to be accomplished through the following programs:

    a. Certificates of Competency, including technical assistance with production problems.

    b. Subcontracting.

    c. Prime Contract Assistance, including surveillance of the procurement actions carried out by other Government agencies.

    d. Facilities Inventory.

    e. Property Sales and Material Shortages.

    f. Research and Development, including New Product Assistance.

    g. Management Counseling.

    h. Management Training."

13. Government Liaison Staff — ". . . establish and maintain close relations and understanding at the policy level between SBA and the Federal military and civilian agencies in carrying out their procurement mission."

14. Size Standards — ". . . define small business for the purpose of identifying which concerns are eligible for SBA assistance. The Small Business Size Standards Program includes:

    a. Recommendation and development of size standards for promulgation by the Administrator. This includes study and analysis of all available data reflecting on market structure and market behavior of various industries.

    b. Implementation of SBA's size program

Program	*Mission*
	by the issuance of size standards regulations, size handbooks and directives."
15. Certificate of Competency and Technical Assistance Program	a. ". . . provide every responsible small business entering a low bid on a Government contract an opportunity to qualify for the contract. The Certificate of Competency program is, in effect, an appeals procedure whereby a small firm whose bid is rejected by a Government agency for lack of capacity or credit is allowed a second chance to prove its ability to perform the contract. b. Give assistance of an engineering nature to small business industrial concerns which are operating at less than their full economic potential, and help them work with procuring agencies."
16. Prime Contract Assistance	". . . enhance the participation of small business in Government procurement and increase the dollar value of contract awards to small concerns by means of resident procurement center representatives, the surveillance function, counseling, and procurement opportunity meetings."
17. Subcontracting	". . . give small firms added opportunities to expand sales, and use idle capacity through subcontracting; and particularly, to benefit from the rapid technological progress which is being generated by the Government's huge expenditures in the fields of defense, space, atomic energy, and civilian programs."
18. Facilities Inventory	". . . provide an added source of knowledge about small firms which will enable the Agency to better use its manpower in the accomplishment of procurement and other relevant programs."

Program	*Mission*
19. Research and Development and Products Assistance	". . . provide small business concerns with opportunities to undertake research and development and obtain its benefits in order to upgrade their technological positions."
20. Management Training	". . . The mission of this sub-program is to improve the management capabilities of the owner-managers of existing small businesses and of prospective small business managers through group-educational activities rather than person-to-person counseling. These activities consist of developing, or encouraging the development of, publications, courses, conferences, workshops, clinics, visual aids, audiovisual aids, and other materials for the purpose of small-business management training."
21. Management Counseling	". . . provide face-to-face management, procurement and technical counseling to prospective and operating small business owners. It encompasses administrative management principles, practices and techniques, how to share in government procurement and technical operating matters. It is accomplished by Agency employees and by volunteer advisors (SCORE)."
22. Property Sales and Material Shortage Program	". . . be a forceful advocate on behalf of small firms in the areas of (a) timber resulting primarily from the forestry management activities of the Forest Service, USDA, and the Bureau of Land Management, Interior Department; (b) surplus real and personal property resulting from military and civilian program actions and for disposal through the General Services Administration; and (c) critical materials resulting from the management of the national stockpile."

NOTES

Notes

CHAPTER 1

1. *New York Times,* May 25, 1966.
2. Robert A. East, "The Business Entrepreneur in a Colonial Economy," *The Tasks of Economic History,* Supplement VI (1946), 16.
3. 76th Congress, 3rd Session, *Problems of Small Business,* Monograph No. 17, Temporary National Economic Committee (Washington, 1941), 248–256.
4. Carl Bridenbaugh, *The Colonial Craftsman* (New York, 1950), 125–126.
5. James Truslow Adams, *Provincial Society, 1689–1763* (New York, 1927), 39.
6. Bridenbaugh, 128.
7. Malcolm Keir, *The Epic of Industry* (New Haven, 1926), 20.
8. *Ibid.,* 27.
9. Henry W. Farnam, *Chapters in the History of Social Legislation in The United States,* 90–91; Adams, 44–45.
10. E. A. J. Johnson, *American Economic Thought in the 17th Century* (New York, 1961), 16.
11. *Ibid.,* 119.
12. Carl Bridenbaugh, *Cities in the Wilderness,* 35.
13. Robert A. East, *Business Enterprise in the American Revolutionary Era* (New York, 1938), see Chapter 11, "The Revolutionary Economic Forces," 30–48;

Merrill Jensen, *The New Nation* (New York, 1950), 219–233; Frederick B. Tolles, "The American Revolution Considered as a Social Movement; A Reevaluation," *American Historical Review*, LX (October 1954), 9–10.

14. Curtis P. Nettels, *The Emergence of the American Economy* (New York, 1962), 289–290.

15. Saul K. Padover, *The Mind of Alexander Hamilton* (New York, 1958), 23–25, 197–414.

16. Harvey A. Wooster, "A Forgotten Factor in American Industrial History," *American Economic Review*, XVI (March 1926), 14–16.

17. Harvey A. Wooster, "Manufacturer and Artisan," *Journal of Political Economy*, XXXIV (February 1926), 65–66.

18. Lewis E. Atherton, "Itinerant Merchandising in the Ante-Bellum South," *Bulletin of the Business Historical Society*, XIX (April 1945), 36–37.

19. Lewis E. Atherton, *The Pioneer Merchant in Mid-America* (Columbia, Mo., 1939), 30–33.

20. Emerson D. Fite, *Social and Industrial Conditions in the North During the Civil War* (New York, 1910), 105–106, 108, 181.

21. Lewis H. Haney, *Business Organization and Combination* (New York, 1915), 17–18.

22. Merle Fainsod and Lincoln Gordon, *Government and the American Economy* (New York, 1941), 432–438.

23. William Z. Ripley, *Trusts, Pools and Corporations*, Rev. Ed. (Boston, 1916), xi–xii.

24. Clarence E. Bonnett, *History of Employers' Associations in the United States* (New York, 1956). A detailed study of the employers' associations of the late nineteenth and early twentieth centuries.

25. Allan Nevins, *The Emergence of Modern America* (New York, 1927), 37.

26. Eliot Jones, *The Trust Problem in the United States* (New York, 1928), 2–3.

27. 76th Cong. 3rd Sess., Temporary National Economic Committee, *Problems of Small Business*, Monograph N.17 (Washington, 1941), 25 and 66.

28. *Ibid.*, 82.

29. *Ibid.*, 329.

30. John D. Black, "Agriculture Now?" *Journal of Farm Economics*, IX (April, 1927), 151–152; United States Industrial Commission, *Report . . . on Agriculture and Agricultural Labor*, X (Washington, 1901), xi.

31. Harold U. Faulkner, *The Decline of Laissez Faire* (New York, 1951), 182.

32. Alfred R. Oxenfeldt, *New Firms and Free Enterprise* (Washington, 1943), 36–37.

33. Richard Owens, *Business Organizations and Combinations* (New York, 1946), 261–265.

34. Myron W. Watkins, "Trade Associations," *Encyclopedia of Social Sciences*, XIV (New York, 1937), 674–675.

35. Harmon Ziegler, *The Politics of Small Business* (Washington, 1961), 13–14; R. V. Rosa, "Small Business and Depression," *Harvard Business Review*, XXVI (January 1948), 58–62.

36. "Little Business Revolts," *The Nation*, 146 (February 12, 1938), 173; Joseph L. Nicholson, "Wanted: New Small Businesses," *Harper's Magazine*, CLXXX (April 1940), 547–548.

37. Ziegler, 13.

38. *Ibid.*, 14–15.

39. *Commercial and Financial Chronicle* (January 29, 1938), 691–692.

40. H. B. Eliston, "Little Businessman, What Now?" *Saturday Evening Post*, CCX (April 16, 1938), 36.

41. *Commercial and Financial Chronicle* (February 5, 1938), 844–845.

42. Ziegler, 15–18.

43. 79th Cong., 2d Session, U.S. Senate, No. 16, *Future of Small Business*, Progress Report of the Chairman to the Members of the Committee of the Special Committees to Study Problems of American Small Business (Washington, 1947), 6. Hereafter cited as *Future of Independent Business* (No. 16).

44. *Future of Independent Business* (No. 16), 7.

45. C. C. Abbott, "Small Business: A Community Problem," *Harvard Business Review*, XXIV (Winter 1946), 184.

46. U.S. Dept. of Commerce, Bureau of Foreign and Domestic Commerce, *Small Business—A National Asset*, Small Business Unit, Economic Series, No. 24 (Washington, July 1943), 1.

47. Kurt Mayer, "Small Business As A Social Institution," *Social Research*, XIV (September 1947), 342; for a discussion of "The Impact of War," see Rudolph L. Weissman, *Small Business and Venture Capital* (New York, 1945), 131–155.

48. A. D. H. Kaplan, *Small Business: Its Place and Problems* (New York, 1948), 19.

49. Ziegler, 100–101.

50. *Ibid.*, 116–120.

51. Small Business Administration, *SBA, What It Is—What It Does* (brochure) (Washington, 1964), 4.

52. John H. Bunzel, *The Small American Businessman* (New York, 1962), 273. See also 76th Congress, 3d Session, U.S. Senate Committee Print, *Investigation of Concentration of Economic Power, Problems of Small Business*, Monograph No. 17. (Washington, 1941), 66–67.

53. Mayer, 337–338.

54. *Ibid.*, XIV, 335.

CHAPTER 2

1. *Business Statistics, 1965 Biennial Edition*, "Explanatory Notes to Statistical Series, (Washington: U.S. Government Printing Office, 1966), 10–12. Also, letter from Lawrence Bridge, Chief, Business Structure Division, Office of Business Economics, U.S. Department of Commerce, August 12, 1966.

2. A more detailed analysis of these categories is found in Robert R. Nathan Associates, Inc., *The Outlook for Small Business* (New York, 1966).

CHAPTER 3

1. Ralph Epstein, *Industrial Profits in the United States*, National Bureau of Economic Research, 1934; William Crum, *Corporate Size and Earning Power*, Harvard University Press, 1939; H. O. Stekler, *Profitability and Size of Firm*, Institute of Business and Economic Research, University of California, Berkeley, 1963.

CHAPTER 4

1. Dun and Bradstreet, Inc., *The Failure Record Through 1965* (New York, 1966).

2. Kurt Mayer and Sidney Goldstein, *The First Two Years: Problems of Small*

Firm Growth and Survival (Brown University, Small Business Administration Report (1961), 57.

3. See Betty C. Churchill, "Age and Life Expectancy of Business Firms," *Survey of Current Business* (December 1955), 18.

4. Paul W. Paustian and John Lewis, *Small Business Instability and Failure in Alabama,* University of Alabama, Small Business Report (1963), 50.

5. Dun and Bradstreet, 2.

6. Irving Pfeffer and Seev Neumann, "The Survival Probability of a New Life Insurance Company," *Journal of Risk and Insurance,* Winter 1966.

7. William N. Kinnard and Zenow S. Malinowski, *The Turnover and Mortality of Manufacturing Firms in the Hartford Connecticut Economic Area, 1953–1958,* University of Connecticut, Small Business Administration Reports (1963), 50, 56.

8. William M. Hoad and Peter Rosko, *Management Factors Contributing to the Success or Failure of New Small Manufacturers,* The University of Michigan, Small Business Administration Report, 1964, 7.

9. Betty C. Churchill, "Size of Business Firms," *Survey of Current Business* (December 1959), 16; gives a size breakdown of all firms in the nation, which provides a valuable frame of reference.

10. Dun and Bradstreet, 7.

11. See Mayer and Goldstein, 111; and Kinnard and Malinowski, 44.

12. Elizabeth Y. Deran, *The Successful Shopkeeper,* University of Illinois, Small Business Administration Reports (1963), 52, 69, 77.

13. See Mayer and Goldstein, 102–105, 112–114; Hoad and Rosko, 10, 11, 90, 91; and Deran, 61, 62, 81.

CHAPTER 5

1. To avoid unnecessary complications, it is assumed throughout that r is constant over the life of the asset. For a discussion of the effects of allowing r to vary, see Robichek and Myers, *Optimal Financing Decisions* (Englewood Cliffs, N.J., 1965), Ch. 5.

2. Eugene F. Brigham and James L. Pappas, "Duration of Growth, Changes in Growth Rates, and Corporate Share Prices," *Financial Analysts Journal,* May–June 1966.

3. The sample of stocks used to obtain this figure was the 900 firms contained on Standard and Poor's Compustat Tape. These are all very large firms, most of which are listed on the New York Stock Exchange.

4. When firms with different tax rates are compared, it is necessary to examine before-tax capital costs.

5. Harold Bierman and Seymore Smidt, *The Capital Budgeting Decision* (New York, 1966), 146–147, provides a more detailed discussion of this procedure.

6. These objections would include the following: (1) The figures are based on book values, whereas market values should be used for required rate of return calculations; (2) the reported profits of smaller firms are understated because their owners take out excessive salaries and charge excessive personal expenses to the firms; (3) the large firms are profitable not because they are large per se but because their owners and managers are efficient and aggressive. Because of this efficiency the firms have grown and are now placed in the larger size categories—in other words, there is a continual movement of the most profitable small firms out of the small firm class; (4) small firms include both small firms and *new* firms undergoing heavy start-up costs that make the firms appear unprofitable.

If the effects of age of a firm could be removed, small firms might show up as being more profitable.

7. M. H. Miller and F. Modigliani, "Some Estimates of the Cost of Capital to the Electric Utility Industry, 1954–57," *American Economic Review*, LVI (June 1966), 333–391.

8. *Ibid.*, 373.

9. Eugene F. Brigham, "The Cost of Equity Capital to Electric Utilities, *"Public Utilities Fortnightly* (September 1964), 25–35.

10. Stephen H. Archer and Leroy G. Faerber, "Firm Size and the Cost of Externally Secured Equity Capital," *Journal of Finance*, XXI (March 1966), 69–83.

11. *Ibid.*, 82.

12. $K_e = K/(1 - F)$. If K is 8 per cent and F is 5 per cent for a large firm, then $K_e = 8.4\%$. Similarly, if K is 10 per cent and F is 25 per cent for a small firm, then $K_e = 13.5\%$.

13. Although the cost of capital discussed to this point has been the after-tax cost, it is useful when comparing firms with different corporate tax rates to use the before-tax cost.

14. The 9.5 per cent cost also applies to all rates of growth less than 8 per cent.

CHAPTER 6

1. For more complete exposition of graphic techniques, see W. J. Eiteman, *Graphic Budgets*, Ann Arbor, Mich.

2. Possible exceptions are found in William Beranek, *Analysis for Financial Decisions*, (Homewood, Ill., 1963).

CHAPTER 7

1. For a fuller definition of long-range planning, see George A. Steiner, "The Critical Role of Top Management in Long-Range Planning," *Arizona Review*, XV (April 1966), and George A. Steiner, "Long-Range Planning: Concept and Implementation," *Financial Executive*, XXXIV (July 1966), 54–61.

2. For a profile of successful small businessmen, see Orvis F. Collins, David G. Moore, and Darab B. Unwalla, *The Enterprising Man* (East Lansing, Mich.: Bureau of Business and Economic Research, Graduate School of Business Administration, Michigan State University, 1964).

3. Jack B. Weiner, "What Makes a Growth Company?", *Dun's Review and Modern Industry*, November 1964.

4. A. M. Woodruff and T. G. Alexander, *Success and Failure in Small Manufacturing* (Pittsburgh, Pa., 1958).

5. Charles G. Mortimer, "Motivating a Business Toward Profits and Growth," *The McKinsey Quarterly*, XI (Winter 1966), 33.

6. Delbert C. Hastings, *The Place of Forecasting in Basic Planning for Small Business* (Minneapolis, 1961), 23.

7. Roger A. Golde, "Practical Planning for Small Business," *Harvard Business Review*, XXIV (September–October 1964), 151–152.

8. See George A. Steiner, "Making Long-Range Company Planning Pay Off," *California Management Review*, IV, (Winter 1962), 28–41.

9. Joseph C. Schabacker, *Cash Planning in Small Manufacturing Companies*, Small Business Administration (Washington, D.C.: U.S. Government Printing Office, 1960).

CHAPTER 12

1. Corporate problems are emphasized because most frequently encountered. Most "blue-sky" laws, however, regulate the offering of interests in noncorporate as well as corporate businesses. For example, the federal Securities Act of 1933 defines *security* (the sale of which the Act regulates) to include the following:

> Any note, stock, treasury stock, bond, debenture, evidence of indebtedness, certificate of interest or participation in any profit-sharing agreement, collateral-trust certificate, preorganization certificate or subscription, transferable share, investment contract, voting-trust certificate, certificate of deposit for a security, fractional undivided interest in oil, gas, or other mineral rights, or, in general, any interest or instrument commonly known as a "security," or any certificate of interest or participation in, temporary or interim certificate for, receipt for, guarantee of, or warrant or right to subscribe to or purchase, any of the foregoing.

2. The Securities Act of 1933, the Securities Exchange Act of 1934, the Public Utility Holding Company Act of 1935, the Trust Indenture Act of 1939, the Investment Company Act of 1940, the Investment Advisers Act of 1940, and Chapter X of the Bankruptcy Act.

3. Under amendments enacted in 1964 a number of requirements of the Securities Exchange Act were extended for the first time to cover many companies that can reasonably be considered small business.

4. Six of the seven federal statutes listed in Note 2 (the Bankruptcy Act being the exception) contain express provisions preserving the states' power to regulate.

5. Article VI of the Constitution provides in part:

> This Constitution and the Laws of the United States which shall be made in Pursuance thereof; and all Treaties made, or which shall be made, under the Authority of the United States, shall be the supreme Law of the Land; and Judges in every State shall be bound thereby, any Thing in the Constitution or Laws of any State to the Contrary notwithstanding.

6. Notably Article I, Section 8 (the "commerce clause"); Article IV, Section 1 ("full faith and credit"), and Amendment XIV, Section 1 ("due process").

7. The foregoing discussion of usury is intended to be hypothetical; there may in fact be no conflict between the laws of Illinois and New York on this subject.

8. *Erie R. Co. vs. Tompkins,* 304 U.S. 64, 58 S.Ct. 817, 82 L.Ed. 1188, 114 A.L.R. 1487 (1938).

9. Examples of "procedural" rules that have frequently been the determining factor in cases include the statute of limitations, burden of proof, and the rules of evidence. Thus, a plaintiff may lose a case because the court of the state in which the action is pending will not permit him to introduce evidence that would have been admissible if the action were pending in a different state. Similarly, in a close case, the party having the burden of proof might lose; he might win the same case in a different state because the burden of proof might be on his adversary.

10. Only Delaware is without a blue-sky law among the fifty states. Nevada joined the fold in 1965.

11. United States Constitution, Article 1, Section 8:

[The Congress shall have Power] to regulate Commerce with foreign Nations, and among the several States, and with the Indian Tribes.

12. Securities Act of 1933, Section 2(3):

The term "sale" or "sell" shall include every contract of sale or disposition of a security or interest in a security for value. The term "offer to sell," "offer for sale," or "offer" shall include every attempt or offer to dispose of, or solicitation of an offer to buy, a security or interest in a security, for value.

13. The statutory waiting period is 20 days; in practice the waiting period is the full period of time required for processing the registration statement and may be several months.

14. Under Section 11(a) of the Act the defendants may include the following:

(1) Every person who signed the registration statement;

(2) Every person who was a director of (or person performing similar functions) or partner in, the issuer at the time of the filing of the part of the registration statement with respect to which his liability is asserted:

(3) Every person who, with his consent, is named in the registration statement as being or about to become a director, person performing similar functions, or partner;

(4) Every accountant, engineer, or appraiser, or any person whose profession gives authority to a statement made by him, who has with his consent been named as having prepared or certified any part of the registration statement, or as having prepared or certified any report or valuation which is used in connection with the registration statement, or as having prepared or certified any report or valuation which is used in connection with the registration statement, with respect to the statement in such registration statement, report or valuation, which purports to have been prepared or certified by him;

(5) Every underwriter with respect to such security.

15. The antifraud provisions of the Act may apply notwithstanding the exemptions.

16. *S.E.C. vs. Ralston Purina Co.*, 346 U.S. 119 (1953). The exemption has also been considered in detail by the S.E.C. in a number of releases, including a comprehensive discussion in Securities Act Release No. 4552, Nov. 6, 1962.

17. A "no-action" letter is an informal written opinion by the staff of the S.E.C. that it will not recommend that the Commission take adverse action with respect to a proposed transaction. It is *not* binding on the Commission.

18. The Act also applies to resales of securities, no matter how acquired, by controlling persons. They may decide to use this later registration statement to effect a distribution of some of their securities.

19. Securities Act Release No. 1459, May 29, 1937; also Securities Act. Release No. 4434, December 6, 1961.

20. 17 C.F.R. § 230.251–230.263.

21. The Rules contain a number of disqualifications and should be consulted in detail.

22. 17 C.F.R. § 230.133.

23. For analysis of *Perlman vs. Feldman,* see Hill, *The Sale of Controlling Shares,* 70 Harv. L. Rev. 986 (1957).
24. Berle, *"Control" in Corporate Law,* 58 Columb. L. Rev. 1212 (1958).
25. Regulation 14A; 17 C.F.R. 240, 14 a-1 et seq.
26. Section 14(c) and Regulation 14C; 17 C.F.R. 240. 14c-1 et seq.

CHAPTER 13

1. Section 1562 (b), IRC.
2. Section 482, IRC.
3. Section 61, IRC.
4. Sections 1371–1377 inclusive, IRC.
5. Section 1372 (c) (1), IRC.
6. Section 1371 (a), IRC.
7. See methods of termination of election under Section 1372 (e).
8. Catalina Homes, Inc. 23 TMC 1361, Dec. 26, 937 (M), TC Memo 1964–225.
9. Section 1374 (c) (2), IRC.
10. Section 704 (d), IRC.
11. Rev. Rul. 64–162, I.R.B. 1964–21, 24.
12. See Section 341, IRC for a discussion of Collapsible Corporations.
13. Income Tax Regulations Section 1.1244 (a)-1 (b).
14. Section 1244 (c) (2), IRC.
15. Section 1244 (b), IRC.
16. Section 706 (b) (1), IRC.
17. Income Tax Regulations Section 1.441-1 (b) (2). See exception under regulation section 1.441-2 for a 52–53 week taxable year.
18. Income Tax Regulations Section 1.446-1 (a) (2).
19. *Ibid.*
20. Income Tax Regulations Section 1.446-1 (a).
21. Income Tax Regulations Section 1.446-1 (a) (4) (i).
22. Income Tax Regulations Section 1.472-3.
23. Income Tax Regulations Section 1.472-2 (g) (2).
24. Section 167 (c), IRC.
25. Section 179 (b), IRC.
26. Section 179 (d) (1) (c), IRC.
27. Section 174 (b), IRC.
28. Income Tax Regulations Section 1.174-4 (a) (5).
29. Section 248 (a) IRC.
30. Sections 166 (a) and 166 (c), IRC.
31. Black Motor Company, Incorporated, 41 BTA 300.
32. Sections 531–537, IRC inclusive.
33. Section 531, IRC.
34. Section 6016 (a), IRC.
35. Section 48 (a), IRC.
36. Section 48 (c) (2) (A), IRC.
37. Section 46 (c) (2), IRC.
38. Section 46 (a) (2), IRC.
39. See note 37.
40. Section 47, IRC.
41. Section 46 (b), IRC.
42. Section 48 (d), IRC.

43. Section 48 (d) (1) and (2), IRC.

44. Income Tax Regulations Section 1.48-4 (j).

45. H.R. 17607.

46. Income Tax Regulations Section 1.105-5 (a).

47. Sherwood Swan & Co., Ltd. et. al., 42 TC 299, aff'd 65-2 USTC Para. 9742.

48. I.RB. 1966–25, 6

49. Internal Revenue Service Announcement 66-58, published Sept. 19, 1966.

50. Section 404 (a) IRC and Income Tax Regulations Section 1.451-1 (a).

51. Evelyn F. Gregory v. Helvering—Sup. Ct. (aff'g CA-2), 35-1 USTC Para. 9043, and so on.

52. Income Tax Regulations Section 1.451-1 (a).

53. Section 170 (a) (2), IRC.

54. *Ibid.*

55. Section 404 (a) (6), IRC.

56. Rev. Rul. 55-428, 1955-2 CB, 230.

57. Section 453 (b) (2), IRC.

58. Section 483, IRC.

59. Income Tax Regulations Section 1.453-2 (b) (1).

60. City Stores Co., 57-2 USTC Para. 9960.

61. Income Tax Regulations Section 1.453-2 (d).

62. Section 453 (a) (1), IRC.

63. Section 453 (c), IRC.

64. Section 453 (d), IRC.

INDEX

Index

Accounting system, 128t, 131–33
Accounts receivable, borrowing against, 217–22, 224–27, 244
Alabama Department of Industrial Relations, 88
American Bankers Association, 318
American Bar Association, 256
American Bar Foundation, 237
American Law Institute, 256
American Motors Corporation, 44
American Sugar Refining Company, 17
American Tobacco Company, 17
Amortization of loans, 201, 222, 226
Antitrust legislation, 17, 21, 22, 24, 25, 28
Archer, Stephen H., 112, 115
Arnold, Thurman, 28
Assets, 217
  borrowing against, 219, 220–28, 239–44
Association of Independent Bankers, 318

Atomic Energy Commission, 324

Bank of America, 318
Bank of North America, 8
Bank of the United States, 9
Bankruptcy, 87, 129, 238, 245
  government claim, 238
Banks, commercial
  loans to business, 199, 212, 217, 234–36
Banks, industrial loan, 212
Birth and mortality rates, 32, 40, 47–48, 82–94; *see also* Failure rates, Mortality rates
Book value, 221
Borrowing, 212, 213
  long-term, 229–49
  secured, 220–28
  unsecured, 217–20
Break-even points
  analysis, 164–67, 166t
  in cash budgeting, 138–40

Budget systems
  cash, 126–43
Bunzell, John H., 32
Business Economics, Office of, 37, 88
Business population, 14, 16–17, 37–38, 38t, 39t
  growth rates, 40–42, 40t, 41t, 42t

California Corporate Securities Law, 259
Capital, cost of, 97–125, 136
  effects of size on, 107–17, 124
  equity, 104
  expected rates of return, 99–102
  free capital, 105–06, 119
  marginal concept, 106
  stocks, 102–03
  tax adjustment, 103–04
  valuation, 98–102
  weighted average cost, 106–07, 107t
Capital, growth, 212–20
Capital, working, 129, 212–20
Capital gains, 104–05, 116, 206
Capital markets, 197–210
Capital structure, 107
  effect of size on, 117–25
  interest-bearing capital, 119
  total capital, 117
Cash budgeting, 126–43
  break-even points, 138–40, 139t
  cash flow model, 129, 130t, 131–32
  cost of capital, 136
  expenditures, 129–31
  financial forecasting, 133–38
  liquidity, 131–33
  self-liquidating bank loan, 129
  tradeoffs between flows and stocks, 136–38
  uncertainty, 140–42
  working capital, 129

Cash flow, 129–33, 130t, 218–20, 221–22, 230
Census of Manufactures and Business, 30
Civil War, impact of, 16–22
Clayton Anti-Trust Act, 22
Collateral, 222–26
Columella, Lucius, 157
Commerce, Department of, 24, 27, 30, 31, 37, 38, 50
Common stock, 102–03, 203, 240, 243
Community Development Loan Program, 328
Conference of American Small Business Organizations (CASBO), 30
Conflict of laws, 254–57
Consolidation, 265–66
Corporate powers, 267
Corporate-shareholder relationships, 266–74
Corporation, 266–74
  conduct of directors, 266–67
  shareholders actions, 273
  shareholders meeting and voting rights, 269–73
  transactions within, 268–69
Credit; *see* Loans, Financing
Crum, William, 70–74
Current ratio, 217–18

Data, limitations of, 68–69, 83, 86–87, 110
Debt capital, 102–103
  nontraditional sources of, 204–208
  traditional sources of, 198–204
Decision-making, case histories, 177–94
Defense, Department of, 31, 324
Depreciation, 285–86
  as source of capital, 208–209
Depression of 1929, 24–28, 74

Dun and Bradstreet, Inc., 18, 82, 84, 87–88, 90
Dupont de Nemours Powder Company, 17

Earnings, 216
Economic Opportunity Act of 1964, 321
Economic factors resulting in large-scale operations, 42–45
Economic factors resulting in small-scale operations, 45
Eddy, Arthur J., 23
Epstein, Ralph, 70–74
Equity base, 229–30
Equity capital
   definition, 213
   federally financed, 306–13
   as functional type of capital, 213–16
   as an investment, 215
Equity capital, cost of, 97–125
   effects of growth rates on, 121–24
   effects of size on, 110–13
   flotation costs, 112–13, 115–16
   privately owned firm, 114–16
   publicly owned firm, 110–13
   rate of return, 99–100

Factoring, 202–203
Failure rates, 82–94; see also Birth and mortality rates, Mortality rates
   by age, 87–90, 94
   causes, 92–94, 149
   cyclical pattern, 83–85, 93
   data on, 86–87
   historical, 18–24, 19t, 25t
   by line of business, 86–87, 93
   by region, 85–86, 86t, 93
   by size, 90–92, 94
   trends, 84t, 85t

Faerber, Leroy G., 112, 115
Federal Reserve Act, 25
Federal Reserve banks, 197
Federal Reserve Loan Surveys, 108, 304
Federal Trade Commission, 22, 30, 110
Finance companies, commercial loans to business, 202–203, 212, 231
Financing, 211–228
   accounts receivable, 224–26
   business combinations, 265–74
   deferred tax, 277, 294–98
   equity capital, 212–14
   government, 306–313
   growth capital, 212, 217–220
   institutional, 212
   inventory, 222–24
   legal aspects of, 253–74
   long-term, 229–49
   public, 212, 215–16
   secured, 220–26
   Small Business Investment Companies, 303–313
   subordinate debt, 240–241
   unsecured, 217–20
   working capital, 212, 217–20
Flotation costs, 112–13, 113t, 115–16
Flows and stocks, 132, 133, 136–38
Forecasting, 131–38, 149–50; see also Planning, long-range
   methodology, 65, 99
   tax expense, 275ff.
Funds, long-term; see also Long-term capital
   internal sources of, 208–10
   nontraditional external sources of, 204–208
   traditional external sources of, 198–204

GNP; *see* Gross National Product
General Foods Corporation, 153
George, Henry, 17
Glass, Carter, 27
Golde, Roger A., 161
Goldstein, Sidney, 90
Government regulation, 7, 8, 25–26
  business combinations, 265–66
  securities, 254–64, 268–69
  Small Business Investment Companies, 306–311
Gross National Product (GNP), 40, 45

Hamilton, Alexander, 9
Harvard Business Review, 303, 311
Heller, Walter, 202
Hoad, William M., 90
Hoover, Herbert C., 24, 25

Income, national, by industry, 35, 36t
Income tax, personal, 116
Industry classifications, 36t, 37t, 51–54, 54t
Insurance companies
  loans to business, 199–201, 212, 219, 233–36
Interest rates, 107–108, 108t, 109–110, 234–39, 310–311
Internal Revenue Code, 116, 266, 276, 277ff.
Internal Revenue Service, 37, 38, 276ff.
International Harvester Company, 17
International Paper Company, 17
Inventory, 134
  borrowing against, 221, 222–24, 244
Investment advisers, 204–207
Investment banking, 232, 234
  underwriting, 215–16

Jackson, Robert, 28
Johnson, Lyndon B., 3
Jones, Jesse, 29

Kinnard, William N., 90
Klaus, Gunther, 161
Korean War, 31, 75, 77

Leasing, 64, 109
  as financing device, 231, 241
Leasing companies, 201–202
Lenders, requirements for, 232–34
Lewis, John, 87, 88
Life Insurance Association of America, 200
Liquidity, 114, 131–33, 217
Lloyd, Henry Demarest, 17
Loan problems
  depth of management, 230
  earnings record, 230–231
  equity base, 229–230
  mortality rate, 231
  time and expense, 230–231
Loans
  against commodities, 223
  covenants and restrictions, 236–45
  Economic Opportunity Loans, 321–23
  equity capital, 214–15
  funded debt, 239–45
  government, 231, 277, 294–98, 314–33
  growth capital, 214
  interest rates on, 102t, 107–108, 108t, 234–36
  loan documents, 245–48
  long-term, 229–49
  secured, 108, 109t, 199, 220–228, 235–36
  security for, 108
  short-term, 220–221
  total, 108

unsecured, 108, 199, 217–20, 237

working capital, 214–15

Local Development Company program, 323–24

Long-term capital, sources

banks, 199

commercial finance companies, 202–203, 231

depreciation and retained earnings, 208–209, 209t

government, 303–313, 314–33

insurance companies, 199–201, 232, 246

leasing companies, 201–202, 231

mortgage, 200–202, 203

payables and salaries, 209–210

private, 203

public equity market, 207–208

savings and loan associations, 203

Small Business Administration, 204

venture capitalists and SBIC's, 204–207

Macmillan, Harold, 304

Magnetic Design Inc., 170, 175

Malinowski, Zenow S., 90

Martin, William McChesney, 304

Mayer, Kurt, 90

Mergers, 265–66, 311

Miller, M. H., 111

Miller-Tydings amendment, 25

Minimum wage, effect of, 25, 63

Modigliani, F., 111

Mortality rates, 32–33, 40, 47–48, 82–94, 231; *see also* Birth and mortality rates, Failure rates

Mortgages

arrangements for borrowing, 200, 221, 235

chattel, 221, 227

purchase money, 238

Mortimer, Charles G., 153

NARD; *see* National Association of Retail Druggists

NARG; *see* National Association of Retail Growers

NASA; *see* National Aeronautics and Space Administration

NFIB; *see* National Federation of Independent Business

NRA; *see* National Recovery Act

NSBMA; *see* National Small Business Men's Association

National Advisory Council of Independent Small Business, 27

National Aeronautics and Space Administration (NASA), 324

National Association of Retail Druggist (NARD), 26

National Association of Retail Growers (NARG), 26

National Biscuit Company, 17

National Federation of Independent Business (NFIB), 26

National Recovery Act (NRA), 25

National Small Business Men's Association (NSBMA), 26, 28, 30

Neumann, Seev, 88, 90

New York Insurance Law, 233–34

New York Stock Exchange, 110

PERT; *see* Program Evaluation Review Technique

Paustian, Paul W., 87, 88

Perlman vs. Feldman, 268

Pfeffer, Irving, 88, 90

Planning, long-range, 147–76

attitude toward, 153

barriers to, 148–49

break-even analysis, 164–67, 166t

cash flow forms, 167

comprehensive formal planning of centralized companies, 169–74

comprehensive planning in decentralized companies, 174–76

Planning *(cont'd)*
   definition of, 148
   forecasting, 149–150
   master planning forms, 160t, 161,
      162t, 163t
   operational approaches to, 157–
      69
   operational versus analytical
      steps, 155–57, 156t
   planning gap, 163–64, 164t
   return on investment, 163–64,
      165t
   revenue-expense forecast, 167–68,
      168t, 169t
   in small and large enterprises,
      151–52
   staff help, 174–76
   standard accounting statements,
      167–69
   strategic factors in, 158–59
   structure and process of, 154–55,
      156t
   value of, 149–151
Planning problems, case histories,
   174–194
Preferred stock, 103, 203, 241, 243
Profits
   as accounting concept, 131–32
   effect of size on, 67–81, 111t
   limitations of data on, 68–69
   measurement of, 69
   relationship to liquidity, 131–33
Program Evaluation Review Technique (PERT), 141–42, 143
Prozy system, 271
Public offering, as source of funds,
   207–208, 208t, 215–16

Rates of return, 99–102
   effect of officers' compensation on,
      72–74
   effect of size on, 70–74
   postwar data on, 74–79

Recession, effect of, 77
Reconstruction Corporation Act, 25
Reconstruction Finance Corporation,
   27
Rental; *see* Leasing
Revolutionary War, 10
Risk, 99–100, 114, 136–37, 137t,
   140–42, 152, 304–306, 310–
   312
Robinson-Patman Act, 25
Roosevelt, Franklin Delano, 25, 26,
   28
Roper, Daniel, 26, 27
Rosko, Peter, 90

SBA; *see* Small Business Administra-
   tion
SBIC; *see* Small Business Invest-
   ment Companies
SBIC Act; *see* Small Business In-
   vestment Companies Act
SCORE; *see* Service Corps of Re-
   tired Executives
SDPA; *see* Small Defense Plants
   Administration
SEC; *see* Securities and Exchange
   Commission
SWPC; *see* Small War Plants Corpo-
   ration
Savings and loan associations, loans
   to business, 203
Schaback, Joseph C., 167
Securities Act of 1933, 254, 259–64,
   266, 272
Securities Exchange Act of 1934,
   254, 268, 271, 272
Securities and Exchange Commis-
   sion (SEC), 25, 27, 110, 112–
   13, 212, 254, 260–261, 262,
   266
Securities laws, 254–64
   antifraud provisions, 258
   business combinations, 265–66

Securities Act of 1933, 259–64
securities registration provisions, 258
Service Corps of Retired Executives (SCORE), 324
Shareholders, 266–74
Sherman Anti-Trust Act, 22, 25
Small business
  definition of, 31–32, 44
  characteristics of, 46–50
  history of, 3–33
  position in individual industries, 50–60
Small Business, Office of, 30, 31
Small Business Administration (SBA), 44, 204, 206–207, 208, 212, 306ff., 314, 319–320
  bank participation, 317–18
  informations systems, 325–26
  origins, 31, 32
  programs, 321–33
  scope, 316–17, 328–33
Small Business Anti-Monopoly Conference, 31
Small Business Committees of Congress, 30, 31, 200, 303
Small Business Conference of 1938, 26–27
Small Business Investments Companies (SBIC), 204–207, 212
  controversy over, 318
  economic role, 303ff.
  leverage incentives, 306–310
Small Business Investments Companies Act (SBIC Act), 206–207, 304, 306, 310, 323
Small Defense Plants Administration (SDPA), 31
Small War Plants Corporation (SWPC), 29
Social Security Act, 25
State Insurance Commissioners, 197

Stekler, H. O., 70–74
Stocks; see Flows and stocks
Subsidiaries, 241–42
Supreme Court, 28, 261
Survival; see Birth and mortality rates, Failure rates, Mortality rates

TNEC; see Temporary National Economic Committee
Talcott, James C., 202
Tax incentives, 275–99
  charitable contributions, 291
  deferred tax, 277, 294–98
  investment credit, 288
  medical plans, 290–291
  pension, profit-sharing plans, 291–93
Tax structure, 276
  accounting, 283–85
  bad debts, 287
  corporate form, 278–82
  depreciation and amortization, 285–86
  fiscal year, 282–83
  inventory, 285
  research and development, 286–87
Taxation, 68, 102–105, 129, 131, 140
  differential corporate tax rates, 117, 121–23
  differential personal tax rates, 116, 121–23
  mergers, 266
  undistributed-profits tax, 25
Temporary National Economic Committee (TNEC), 25, 28–29
Trends, 60–66
  demographic, 63
  economic, 50, 57–58, 60, 81
  failure, 84t, 85t

franchising and leasing, 64
forecast, 65–66
industrial organization, 62
labor markets, 63
loans, 318
management, 64
political, 50
social, 50, 57–58, 61
technological, 50, 62

Uncertainty; *see* Risk
Underwriting; *see* Investment banking
United States Constitution, 254–55
United States Industrial Commission, 20

United States Shoe Machine Corporation, 17
United States Steel Corporation, 17

Valuation, of capital
capitalization of income method of, 98
historical rates of return, 100
marketability and rates of return, 100
risks and rates of return, 99–100
Venture capitalists, 204–207, 311

War of 1812, 8, 10
Wilson, Woodrow, 21–22
World War I, impact of, 22–24
World War II, impact of, 29–32

About The Editor

IRVING PFEFFER is Professor of Business Administration and Director of Masters Programs in the Graduate School of Business Administration, University of California, Los Angeles. Dr. Pfeffer has served as a consultant to many government agencies and private companies, and has written widely on insurance and finance. A director of several insurance and industrial corporations, Dr. Pfeffer has engaged in numerous financial analyses of small businesses. He is a contributor of articles to *The World Book Encyclopedia* and *The Encyclopedia Britannica Book of The Year.*

THIS PUBLICATION under the Arkville Press imprint was set on the Linotype in Caledonia, with display in Monotype Bulmer. It was printed letterpress and manufactured by The Book Press Incorporated, Brattleboro, Vermont, on paper supplied by S. D. Warren Company, Boston, Massachusetts. The colophon was created by Theodore Roszak.